RICHARD III *and the* MURDER *in the* TOWER

D1531390

RICHARD III *and the* MURDER *in the* TOWER

PETER A. HANCOCK

The History Press

This text presents an analysis of the events and circumstances which precipitated the execution of William, Lord Hastings at the Tower of London on Friday 13 June 1483. This investigation goes directly to the heart of the legitimacy of the assumption of the throne by Richard, Duke of Gloucester, who thus became the controversial monarch Richard III.

Cover illustrations: (front, upper) King Richard III, by an unknown artist © World History Archive; (front, lower) the Tower of London.

First published 2009
This edition published 2011

Reprinted 2011

The History Press
The Mill, Brimscombe Port
Stroud, Gloucestershire, GL5 2QG
www.thehistorypress.co.uk

© Peter A. Hancock, 2009, 2011

The right of Peter A. Hancock to be identified as the Author of this work has been asserted in accordance with the Copyrights, Designs and Patents Act 1988.

British Library Cataloguing in Publication Data.
A catalogue record for this book is available from the British Library.

ISBN 978 0 7524 5797 0

Typesetting and origination by The History Press
Printed in Great Britain

Contents

Acknowledgements

What I have presented is very much reliant upon the hard work and achievements of others, and thus my first duty is to acknowledge and recognise these individuals and their collective efforts and contributions. With respect to my initial account of the events of the summer of 1483, I am very much indebted to the work of the late Charles Wood, whose 1975 article has been of major importance. Unfortunately, Wood's account is built around the re-dating of the death of William, Lord Hastings that was proposed by Alison Hanham at the time he was writing his paper. As will be evident, I think this re-dating is in error and Wood's belief in this altered date led him to make a number of assumptions and interpretations which I have rejected here. Nevertheless, the evidentiary basis he gives for the events of that summer are, I believe, predominantly sound, and thus his factual information has been used extensively here. That the pre-contract is the pivotal issue in the way that the events of that summer played out is a prime motivator for the present text. This line of reasoning leads us directly to a consideration of Eleanor Talbot, Lady Butler. In examining the life and history of Lady Eleanor, the recent work of John Ashdown-Hill has proved critical. He has undoubtedly advanced our knowledge of this crucial individual by an order of magnitude and much of what I have to say here about Lady Eleanor comes from his series of outstanding papers. Any additional linkages that I have managed to find are directly contingent upon this base of knowledge which Ashdown-Hill has laid down.

Our knowledge of William Catesby depends in large part on the foundational articles by Roskell and Williams, and I have naturally relied on these important sources. However, the history of the Catesby family at this time has most recently been presented in illuminating detail by Payling and I am greatly indebted to his excellent chapter as a major basis of my observations on William here. Further, the recent text edited by Bertram, containing Payling's chapter, has provided many insights into the man which have been based upon emerging information about him and his immediate family. I am indebted to the various authors who contributed to this edited work for their observations and insights. The recently published monograph on Catesby by Judith Dickson has also proved critical for my evaluation of this fascinating character. In respect to William, Lord Hastings, Dunham's article has been helpful in deriving the final interpretation and account that I have offered, as Turner's text on the 'Hastings Hours'. The nineteenth-century transcript of Dugdales' manuscript on the Hastings family, held at the Huntington Library (MS HM, 52001), has also formed a part of the foundation on William, Lord Hastings, the victim of the present sequence of events. This latter is, of course, very much contingent upon the relationships between Richard, Hastings and Catesby.

The foregoing acknowledgements have largely been in relation to specific sources; however, my overall hypothesis is founded upon the whole pantheon of Ricardian scholarship. This must inevitably reflect the important works of Kendall and Ross, but especially a number of stalwarts of the Richard III Society who continue the battle for the truth of the man and monarch. I am always grateful to Geoffrey Wheeler, who continues to inform and inspire, as well as to luminaries of the Ricardian Society who, unfortunately, here remain to me just revered names. My very grateful thanks also go to Randy Williams for his untiring help with all of the illustrations in this book. On a more local level, I am always grateful to Carole Rike and Jo Anne Ricca, publishers and editors of respected journals, who are kind enough to feature my observations, but especially to Virginia Poch, (who kindly generated the index for the present text) Janice Wentworth and Richard Endress, who are my immediate fellow Ricardians who spread the message of calumny among the populous of central Florida. I am most grateful for their companionship and friendship – *loyalte me lie*.

P. A. Hancock
Orlando, Florida

Setting the Scene

'All the world's a stage …'[1]

How many of us have looked at the calendar and, with a mild to significant degree of trepidation, noted that the 13th of the coming month coincided with a Friday? Even in today's technological world, we still look on Friday 13th as potentially an unlucky occasion.[2] The precise origin of this superstition is uncertain; however, a strong candidate would be Friday 13 October 1307. For it was on this date that Phillippe IV, 'the Fair,' King of France, co-ordinated a state-wide attack on the Order of the Knights Templar. Arrests were made throughout the country and the Order's functional presence in France was effectively obliterated that day.[3] Subsequently, a number of its members were put to torture and eventual execution, while Templars throughout other parts of Europe were subject to state-sponsored oppression. The origin of the unlucky nature of Friday 13th may well have begun with this event. Whether Friday 13th was considered unlucky in 1483 is difficult to ascertain. However, a pivotal event took place that day which marked a turning point in the thread of English history.[4] This day proved the culmination of a sequence of events from the immediately preceding months and years, and its effects penetrated well into the future to change the balance of power and the path of the realm's progress. It is not an exaggeration to say that the fall of the Plantagenet dynasty and the rise of the House of Tudor was decided that day, although the actors then present on that stage could, of course, not have known this. To understand what went on that day and why, we have to probe into that past and the causes of what was, essentially, a family dispute which got out of hand.

The conundrum of presenting a larger context for any story was perhaps expressed most eloquently by P. G. Wodehouse. He observed that if the author spent too little time on the background to events, he or she would simply lose new readers who would have no idea of what was going on and abandon the text as incomprehensible. However, if the author spent too much time on the events preceding those of interest, one would bore the 'old crew' and thereby lose loyal readers. What is one to do? Here, I have decided to provide just a brief synopsis of such background events, since the involved reader can well go back and find several accomplished texts to fill any of the gaps I have left. Also, some of the individuals that I hope will read this work will have a much greater knowledge of this era than I, and a detailed account might well result in inadvertent errors which would perturb such scholars.

I think it is safe to say that Edward III reigned too long and had too many children.[5] His fifty years on the throne from 1327–1377 meant that, like Queen Victoria and the present queen, Elizabeth II, the immediately following generation did not get a real chance to rule. As should be immediately evident, this frustration breeds unhappiness and discontent, which itself has to find expression in later years. In 1328, Edward married Phillipa of Hainault and produced a total of twelve children.[6] Nine of them lived into adulthood, which was an exceptional survival rate even for royalty in those times. Of these nine survivors, five were male and essentially all that followed in the latterly named 'Wars of the Roses' was a glorified family argument between the descendants of these individuals, who each had some claim to the throne of England. Edward III's first son, Edward the Black Prince, was never to become king, dying a year before his father and, it is said, thereby contributing to his father's demise. However, the only surviving son of the Black Prince became Richard II, after Edward III's death in 1377. Richard II was himself a 'spare' and only assumed primacy when his older brother died in infancy. Like many 'spares,' he did not make a good or strong king and was deposed by his cousin, Henry Bolingbroke, the son of Edward III's third surviving son, John of Gaunt. Bolingbroke became Henry IV and took the throne, having his cousin Richard II executed early in 1400.[7] It was this form of 'might makes right' policy that set the stage for the later events of 1483.

Upon the death of Henry IV in 1413, his son Henry V became king, and one of his major claims to fame was his extensive pursuit by means of arms of the French throne. This he accomplished, and eventually married Katherine of Valois, the French king's daughter, thus uniting the thrones of France and England, if only for a little while. Unlike his great-grandfather, who lived too long and had too many children, Henry V made the opposite mistake: he had too few children and died too soon. Henry V expired very close to his thirty-fifth birthday and left his infant son Henry VI on the throne of both countries. Since baby Henry was at that time only 268 days old, the country was ruled by a regent and a council. What is important to note here is that regents generally did not do as well as might be expected in these circumstances. The example of the accusation and subsequent assassination of Humphrey, Duke of Gloucester for treason in 1447 was a salutary lesson that had to weigh significantly in the minds of those present in the Tower in 1483, some thirty-six years later. Being a medieval king was not for the faint-hearted, and by all accounts Henry VI would have been better suited to other more sedentary pursuits rather than being a monarch. Even after attaining his majority and having been crowned both King of England and of France, the relative power vacuum left by his own personality engendered dangerous times and conspiracy.

Due in part to Henry's indisposition and his frequent illness, the House of York, represented primarily by Richard, Duke of York, first secured the regency and then wrested from the king the right of succession. Henry essentially disenfranchised his own son, Edward, Prince of Wales in favour of Richard, Duke of York and his descendants. As one might well imagine, this action failed signally to please Henry's wife, Margaret of Anjou.[8] However, this was just the prelude to a much more elaborate degree of family strife. When Richard, Duke of York and his son Edmund, Earl of Rutland were killed at the Battle of Wakefield late in December 1460, the gloves came off. Particularly incensed by the treatment of his father's corpse and especially by the way in which his brother's pleas for mercy had been ignored, Edward, the eldest living son of Richard, Duke of York, conducted an active campaign against Henry VI and his Lancastrian following. Edward won several significant victories, including the battles of Mortimer's Cross and Towton, and was declared King Edward IV in London in 1461 with the strong support of Richard Neville, Earl of Warwick, latterly known as 'the Kingmaker.'

In the following eight years, the tumblers of fate turned again several times and Edward's army was defeated by the same Earl of Warwick at the

Battle of Edgecote Moor, by which time the Kingmaker had changed sides in the hope of exerting an ever-higher level of power. After a period when Edward IV was forced to leave the country and Henry VI was restored to his throne, Edward reappeared from the Continent and began again to fight his way back to the throne.[9] The Lancastrian forces were defeated first at the Battle of Barnet where Warwick the Kingmaker was killed and was followed by the decisive Battle of Tewkesbury on 4 May 1471, where Edward's victory put an end to all significant fighting for the duration of his remaining twelve-year reign. Either in the pursuit that followed the rout of the Lancastrians at Tewkesbury, or more spectacularly following the cessation of fighting, Edward, Prince of Wales, the son of Henry VI, was killed and the potential line of succession directly from Henry was broken.[10] Edward IV marched to London shortly after the battle and Henry VI himself met his fate, departing this world in the Tower of London shortly after Edward returned to the capital.[11] It is suggested that he died of melancholy, although the reality is most probably that it was a quite violent melancholy. In actuality, it is very likely that he was assassinated. For the time being, the House of York attained supremacy and, with no immediate claimant to champion, the House of Lancaster looked to be defeated. Of course, these were actually only family disagreements and the degree of consanguinity between the various combatants was always close. Edward IV resumed undisputed possession of the crown on Henry VI's demise and held it for some eleven and three-quarter more years until 9 April 1483. It was on this day that the king died quite suddenly, just short of his forty-first birthday. And it is here that our story begins.

I

The Path to the Throne

The King is Dead

Edward IV died on Wednesday 9 April 1483,[1] not yet forty-one years of age.[2] He was one of the youngest kings of England ever to die of natural causes.[3] While this might possibly suggest some form of foul play, there is existing evidence that Edward's health had perhaps been deteriorating for some time.[4] Indeed, it has even been speculated that he was suffering from the advanced stages of a sexually transmitted disease.[5] Regardless of the precise cause, the king's demise must have been a disconcerting event and the tension and uncertainty that it caused was felt around the realm. The primary issue to hand was, of course, the succession. Had Edward IV lasted only four or five more years, his eldest son, the youthful Prince Edward, would have been sixteen or seventeen years of age and in those times considered well able to rule in his own right. However, being aged twelve and a half, his father had appointed a protector for the young boy during his final years before maturity. The role of protector, and de facto ruler of the realm, fell naturally to Edward's younger brother.[6] This was natural, because Richard, Duke of Gloucester had been Edward's most staunch and loyal supporter throughout his brother's lifetime.[7] From this decision, expressed in Edward's last will and testament, we can assume that there was no one the dying king trusted more. Whether he was wise to do so has been a subject of contention almost ever since.[8]

Any judgment that is made upon the character of Richard, Duke of Gloucester, later Richard III, depends directly upon when one dates his conscious decision to take the throne.[9] The earlier one believes him to have made this decision, the more likely one is to render an adverse judgment on Richard and vice versa.[10] Although some individuals believe that the Duke of Gloucester schemed for the throne from his earliest childhood, most reasonable commentators would agree that up until the death of his elder brother he exhibited no direct ambition to rule the kingdom in his own right. Indeed, ensconced in his favorite castle of Middleham in Yorkshire,[11] (*see* Figure 1) Richard served one of the greatest possible supporting roles for his monarch in securing the northern counties and maintaining the strength of the border against the ever-troublesome Scots.[12]

Up until early 1483, Richard may well have expected to continue to fulfill this function as bulwark of the north throughout his brother's lifetime.[13] However, it would also be reasonable to suppose that even when his nephew did later ascend the throne, no matter how grasping the Woodville side of his family might be, it would still be a wise and prudent policy to keep Richard in this role he had assumed for ensuring the peace of the realm. Also, we have reason to believe that Richard himself was fairly content with his northern hegemony and, in the normal run of events, would most probably have proved as useful and loyal a servant to his nephew as he had previously for his brother.[14] Had this been the case, Richard would have proved to have been largely a footnote to history and not in the centre of the controversy that he currently occupies.[15]

The Duke of Gloucester Goes South

All changed on that day in early April 1483, as news of Edward's death spread across the country. The initial reaction of almost everyone, but especially Richard, Duke of Gloucester made it plain that the young prince would soon be crowned the next King of England.[16] However, the political realities of the situation mandated that Richard, now Lord Protector, travel as quickly as was practicably feasible to the capital, London. That it took him more than a week to prepare for this journey does not suggest a tremendous sense of urgency, but certainly information was beginning to accumulate with respect to the changing tide of events in London. The need for his personal presence in the capital was exacerbated by news that members of the queen's family were questioning the dead king's wishes and were arguing that a protectorate was simply unnecessary. Under the circumstances, it was very clear that there were the beginnings of a struggle for control of the heir to the throne and with it control of the realm itself. We have no evidence that Richard initiated this conflict. However, we do have a number of indications that the Woodville clan, many of whom were already resident in London, were the source of this emerging dispute.[17]

At the time of his father's death, the young prince, now nominally Edward V, was at his residence at Ludlow Castle on the borders of Wales. Arrangements were made for him to go to London as soon as possible. As the young Edward headed east, Richard headed south and was most probably kept in touch with the tenor of events in London by those still loyal to the old king's wishes. In this, his most reliable reported informant was William, Lord Hastings. As the contemporary commentator Mancini indicated:

> According to common report the chamberlain Hastings reported all these deliberations by letter and messengers to the duke of Gloucester, because he has a friendship of long standing with the duke ...[18]

At this stage of events, we can see that Richard had cause to be very grateful to Hastings, his old friend and comrade-in-arms, for keeping him apprised of developments. Indeed, he appeared not to be receiving information through more formal channels which, as Protector, he should have been. Thus, what was clearly coming, and what would have been evident to almost all, was nothing less than a struggle for the kingdom. Richard had to move quickly in order to neutralise the Woodville strategy of dominating events through the manipulation of the young king. In this, we have to be very sensitive to Richard's motivations, since his actions at this juncture were almost certainly self-protective in nature. There is little doubt that if the Woodvilles had succeeded in their immediate aspirations, Richard himself, along with others such as Hastings, would most probably have lost not only their position but probably their lives as well. The written evidence of the letter Richard sent to York from London indicates that he was certainly aware of this threat by 10 June. However, it is more than reasonable to suppose that he must have known of this danger even as he began his journey from the north down to the capital. If Edward IV's demise had been anticipated, it is likely that Richard cogitated upon such eventualities even before the death of his brother and, indeed, it is natural that he and those of his affiliation would have debated future possibilities anyway, even if Edward had not been in failing health.

The evidence which demonstrates Richard's unequivocal understanding of the situation comes from his actions as his party from the north and that of Edward V from the west met around Northampton and Stony Stratford in Buckinghamshire on 29 and 30 April respectively.[19] Richard moved with appropriate dispatch to secure the leaders of the Woodville faction that had accompanied the young Edward V from Ludlow. He had Anthony Woodville, Earl Rivers (the uncle of the new King), Sir Richard Grey (the new king's half brother), Thomas Vaughan (Edward's chamberlain) and Sir Richard Haute[20] all arrested and sent under guard to his strongholds in the north. Rivers, for example, was sent to Sheriff Hutton Castle in Yorkshire (*see* Figure 2). In adopting this course, Richard was evidently supported by a new ally, Henry Stafford, 2nd Duke of Buckingham. Buckingham perhaps resented the Woodvilles because by the age of eleven in 1466, he had been forced to marry the queen's sister, Catherine Woodville. Obviously, Buckingham had bided his time, and now saw the present situation as an opportunity to revenge himself upon his erstwhile oppressors. Together with the two dukes, Edward V now proceeded toward London and his expected coronation.

News of the events from Stony Stratford reached the queen and the rest of her party in London.[21] Realising their plans for near-term control were now defunct, they separated in order to find their respective places of safety. Elizabeth Woodville herself, now the queen dowager (*see* Figure 3), decamped with her youngest son and daughters to Westminster Abbey. She was certainly familiar with these surroundings, since she had previously availed herself of this sanctuary[22] and it was here that she subsequently stayed throughout the tumultuous summer to come.

The Entry into London

The king in waiting, Edward V, and his uncle, Richard, Duke of Gloucester, entered London on the auspicious twelfth anniversary of Edward IV's famous victory at Tewkesbury. It was 4 May 1483 and the old king had been dead less than a month. At this juncture, all appeared to have been proceeding as everyone would have expected and, despite the Woodville intrigues, the plan for the young boy's coronation progressed on schedule.[23]

Up to this point, we have no direct indication of any action by Richard that would show that he was seeking the throne. This is not necessarily to say that he was not. However, none of his actions to that time directly support such an interpretation and many of his actions, in contrast, show him discharging his duties as Protector appropriately.[24] Just over two months later, however, Richard was crowned king, and it is the events of this critical period of transition which form the present focus.

Preliminary preparations for Edward V's coronation, which was now scheduled for 24 June, appear to have been proceeding as planned. Letters were sent out summoning those who were to be honoured at the coming ceremony, which was indicated in some documents to occur on 22 June.[25] Those individuals so summoned seem to have begun preparations to attend on the young king in Westminster Abbey. A coronation of a new king was an involved business and from the records that we have, that business seems to have been proceeding apace. Letters also appear to have been sent out summoning individuals to a parliament to be held shortly after the coronation on 25 June.[26] What is vital here is to try to establish a specific window in time in order to identify when Richard takes the decision to deviate from this generally anticipated course of action. We can ascertain this date by working both forwards and backwards from events around this general interval to fix, with the greatest level of confidence that we can, when the fateful decision was made. De Blieck argues convincingly that a major dimension which would influence the timing of any such decision must have been the presence of troops in the capital available to Richard and by which he could enforce his decision. It is a dimension that certainly underlies the consideration of the account which follows.[27] Let us now see what we know of those events early in June 1483.[28]

The Events of June 1483

Thursday 5 June 1483

We know that Richard, Duke of Gloucester was at the Tower of London on Monday 2 June, as we have evidence of his presence there on that day.[29] Further, it is believed that Richard's wife, Anne Neville, arrived in London on Thursday 5 June, since on this same day it has been reported, perhaps incorrectly, that she sent wafers to John Howard's wife.[30] Richard wrote a letter to the city of York and gave it to John Brackenbury to deliver.[31] Richard moved from Baynard's Castle to Crosby Place, his London home, a move which may well have been associated with his wife's arrival in the capital. Letters were sent out in Edward V's name to individuals who would be honoured at the forthcoming ceremony.[32] The letter read:

> Trusty and well-beloved, we greet you well, and by the advise of our dearest uncle, the duc of Gloucester, protector of this, our royaume during our young age, and of the lords of our council, we write unto you at this time willingly, nathlelesse, charging you to prepare and furnish yourselves to receive the noble order of knighthood at our coronation, which by God's grace we intend shall be solemnized, the 22nd day of this present month, at our palace of Westminster, commanding you to be here at our Toure of London, four days afore our said coronation, to have communication with our commissioners concerning that matter, not failing hereof in any wise as ye intend to please us, and as ye will answer – Given the vth day of June.[33]

Much appears to depend upon how prepared some of these individuals were to receive the coming honours. The letter, dated 5 June, might have taken a number of days to reach some of the more distant points in the kingdom. Further, the individual who was, by this command, required to attend at the Tower was required to reach there by Wednesday 18 June. A journey of five days for the letter to reach the north country and five days for the individual in their turn to reach London would have left some honourees precious little time to prepare for such an important occasion.

Sunday 8 June 1483

It has been claimed that on this day Robert Stillington, the Bishop of Bath & Wells, provided evidence to the Council of the pre-contract between Edward IV and Eleanor Butler. The first individual to have identified Stillington as the source of this information was De Commines.[34] However, this specific date appears to originate with the early-twentieth-century speculation of Markham.[35] We shall return to this proposition later. However, in contrast to this later speculation, one contemporary observer, Simon Stallworth, who recorded the events of the Council that day, reported no such revelation.[36] It is highly probable that Stallworth would have made at least a note of such a significant happening had this actually occurred. The absence of any such observation in Stallworth's letter reflects unfavourably on the accuracy of Markham's interpretation of De Commines's report.[37]

Monday 9 June 1483

As we have seen, the letter that Simon Stallworth, the servant of John Russell, Bishop of Lincoln, wrote on this day, 9 June 1483, to Sir William Stonor is a vital clue in our search for the truth of the present matters.[38] He noted that, 'There is great business against the coronation which shall be this day fortnight as we say.' This we may take to mean that there was much business associated with the preparations which were going ahead for the crowning of Edward V. While plans for the coronation were quickly going forward, the negotiations between the Council and Elizabeth Woodville, the Queen Dowager, now in sanctuary in Westminster Abbey, had broken down. Council members refused to visit her any more, and Stallworth comments:

> My lord protector, my lord of Buckingham with all other lords, as well as temporal and spiritual, were at Westminster in the council chamber from 10 to 2, but there was none that spoke with the Queen.

Stallworth noted that a meeting of the Council had occurred, but had nothing to report except the plans for the coronation, now scheduled for 22 June. He said that the queen, her children, her brother Lionel Woodville and others remained in sanctuary. Stallworth also mentioned that the Prior of Westminster was in trouble because of certain goods that the queen's son, Thomas Grey of Dorset, had delivered to him (presumably in support of his mother). Stallworth's observations are critical here since they indicate that, although there were problems with the queen, the plans for Edward V's coronation were still progressing. In this light, we can see that Richard, Duke of Gloucester continued to fulfill his duties as Protector. Up to this point, then, there is no evidence that Richard had made any move which would indicate unequivocally that he intended to seek the throne.

Tuesday 10 June 1483

One day later, on Tuesday 10 June, Richard himself wrote to his supporters in the city of York. The letter, which eventually reached York five days later, on the 15 June (just one day after the letter sent on 5 June) specifically asked for help in relation to the actions of the queen, her blood adherents and affinities. He indicated that they were trying to destroy him, Buckingham and the old royal blood of the realm.[39] (Parenthetically, this letter cannot have left London until the day after, the 11th, since, as discussed below, it was carried by the same messenger as another letter dated on this subsequent day.). However, these appeals to his adherents in the city of York only reiterate what Richard had known since the events at Stony Stratford and most probably even before. Thus, the letter can hardly be described as recognition of any antipathy in respect to William, Lord Hastings who, after all, had himself warned Richard of the Woodville intentions in the first place. Again, from this evidence, we can look to place the window of Richard's decision in regard to the throne after the 10th and most probably after 11 June. The cessation of Privy Seal writs under Edward's name is, however, pertinent to the timing of this decision. Assuming Sunday 8th was exempt from business, this suspension of action would appear to have started on Monday 9 June. This observation is open to multiple interpretations, including the possibility that such issuances ceased because of other concerns or a natural lull in activity or a natural focus upon the more important business of the upcoming coronation. However, it is a point that should be borne in mind as we progress.

Wednesday 11 June 1483

As well as the letter cited above, Richard had written a further communication to his supporter, Ralph, Lord Neville of Raby, which Ratcliffe had carried to the North.[40] This letter, addressed 'To My Lord Nevill, in haste,' stated:

> My Lord Nevill, I recommend me to you as heartily as I can; and as ever ye love me and your own weal and security, and this realm, that ye come to me with that ye may make, defensibly arrayed, in all the haste that is possible; and that ye give credence to Richard Ratcliffe, this bearer, whom I now send to you, instructed with all my mind and intent.
>
> And, my Lord, do me now good service, as ye have always before done, and I trust now so to remember you as shall be the making of you and yours. And God send you good fortunes.

Written at London, 11th day of June, with the hand of your heartily loving
cousin and master,

R. Gloucester.[41]

At the same time, he may have been carrying the warrants for the executions
of Rivers, Grey and Vaughan. Although Richard's decision here might well
be considered to be one in defiance of the Council, it may well be an
act of self-defence against the queen, her family and her adherents. This
being so, it shows that Richard was certainly looking to counteract the
Woodville strategy in the strictest possible way. This possibility also accords
with Thomas More's observation about Hastings, knowing of the coming
execution of these individuals for whom he had little regard and indeed
much noted antipathy. Perhaps Hastings had actually seen Richard issue
these warrants of execution?

Thursday 12 June 1483

On this day, Richard sent out a summons to Buckingham, Hastings, Morton,
Rotherham, Stanley, John Howard and his son, Thomas, to attend a Council
meeting at the Tower the next day, while he scheduled another one for the
same day at Westminster, ostensibly for the finalisation of the coronation
plans, with John Russell presiding. The Croyland Chronicler noted that this
division of the Council represented a 'remarkable shrewdness' on the part of
the Protector,[42] but this is fundamentally a *post hoc* interpretation in which
the reporting individual already knew the outcome of the events of the
following day. It represents yet another case of hindsight bias.[43]

Friday 13 June 1483

It was on this tumultuous day that William, Lord Hastings was executed
(see Appendix II). How and why this happened is the central concern of
the present work.[44] A brief summary here is sufficient to introduce what
is considered the standard version of the events of that day. The most
detailed account we have provides extensive details of the meeting, but
these assertions, made by Sir Thomas More, have to be analysed carefully.[45]
The authorship of this extract has been the subject of extensive discussion,
particularly because there are several events which seem to have been
witnessed first hand, ostensibly by the author. The suggestion is that Thomas

More was either helped or highly influenced by John, Cardinal Morton who, as Bishop of Ely, was present that day at the Tower and in whose house More was brought up. Thus when we hear More's words we have to consider that they are, almost certainly, coloured by the opinion of one of Richard's most vehement enemies.[46]

More implies that William, Lord Hastings was 'escorted' to the Tower on this fateful morning. He further implies that Thomas Howard, son of John Howard, was the individual deputed to ensure Hastings' presence. This errand was apparently somewhat hampered by Hastings tarrying to talk with others along the way. The joke made about Hastings not needing to talk to a priest (who was one of the individuals he stopped to talk with) is certainly an effort to imply premeditation as to what was about to occur. However, this is fundamentally hearsay, being again a *post hoc* construction, and it is almost certain that More the lawyer would have seen through such a flimsy attempt at incrimination in his own practice. It is virtually certain that Hastings had no premonition as to what would happen later that morning (although again this is imputed by accounts of 'dreams and nightmares'). If he had any real suspicions, it is most probable that an old campaigner like Hastings would have provided himself with some form of protection. Indeed, as we shall see, Hastings was completely taken by surprise by the turn of events and this is an important dimension that any attempted explanation of what went on must tackle.

The vital question is whether Richard himself exhibited any evidence of premeditation in respect to what was to happen.[47] The production of a written document outlining Hastings' transgressions shortly after his execution does indeed argue for a degree of premeditation; especially if the document was as extensive and as carefully created as it has been represented to be. However, with respect to who might have possessed such knowledge, we shall need to explore further. The actual account of the meeting is relatively straightforward. Richard met with the assembled Council at around 9 o'clock in the morning. From More's account, he appeared to be in good spirits and even asked Morton, then Bishop of Ely, for 'a mess of strawberries' from his garden in Holborn. Happy to comply with this innocuous request, the bishop must presumably have sent a servant off to Holborn, a round trip of just over three miles and conservatively 30–40 minutes on horseback for the whole journey, including the picking of the strawberries[48].

Sometime around 9.30 a.m. or a little later, Richard appears to have excused himself from the Council, and then we have a vital hour in which a significant change clearly took place. Again, one's opinion of Richard is largely coloured by whether one chooses to believe that the whole of that morning's actions followed some specific, premeditated plan, or whether one views Richard's actions as a spontaneous response to vital information revealed to him during this critical hour. Irrespective of one's persuasion on this issue, Richard returned to the meeting with a 'wonderfully sour angry countenance, knitting the brows, frowning and fretting and gnawing on his lips …'[49] He was clearly deeply disturbed and asked the assembled members of the Council what would persons deserve who plotted his destruction, as the Protector of the realm and the brother of and uncle to kings? Obviously, his disposition seriously affected those present, but it was Hastings who answered that such individuals should be punished as traitors. It is Hastings' confidence in speaking out at this critical point that again confirms that Hastings himself has little to no inkling of what was to come. Richard then referred explicitly to the Woodville plot and the plan by the queen and her adherents to deprive him of his rightful place. More notes that some of the Council were 'abashed' at this observation, especially those who favoured the queen. However, Hastings, as an ardent opponent of the Woodville faction, was reportedly secretly pleased by this revelation, although a little disconcerted that he had not been taken into the Protector's confidence before the resumption of the meeting. But then things changed considerably for Hastings.[50]

It is Hastings himself who was immediately accused of betraying Richard and a melee occurred in the council chamber after the cry of 'Treason.' Some armed individuals, obviously prepared for a signal, entered the chamber. A scuffle ensued and a number of individuals were arrested, but it was Hastings who bore the brunt of Richard's anger. He was summarily executed on Tower Green, 'apone noon,' on a log that happened to be there but was not designed for the purpose.[51] The commentaries on Richard's actions and the execution of Hastings are direct and uniformly uncomplimentary to say the least. The *Great Chronicle* reported that Hastings was dispatched 'without any process of law or lawful examination,' while the continuator of the *Croyland Chronicle* was somewhat more oriented to the political nature of events. This individual reported that:

In the meanwhile, the lord Hastings, who seemed to wish in every way to serve the two dukes and to be desirous of earning their favour, was extremely elated at these changes to which the affairs of the world are so subject, and was in the habit of saying that hitherto nothing whatever had been done except the transferring of the government of the kingdom from two of the queen's blood to two more powerful persons of the king's; and this, too, effected without any slaughter, or indeed causing as much blood to be shed as would be produced by the cut of a finger. In the course, however, of a very few days after the utterance of these words, this extreme of joy of his supplanted with sorrow. For, the day previously, the Protector had, with singular adroitness, divided the council, so that one part met in the morning at Westminster, and the other at the Tower of London, where the king was. The lord Hastings, on the thirteenth day of the month of June, being the sixth day of the week, on coming to the Tower to join the council, was, by order of the Protector, beheaded. Two distinguished prelates, also, Thomas, archbishop of York, and John, bishop of Ely, being out of respect for their order, held exempt from capital punishment, were carried prisoners to different castles in Wales. The three strongest supporters of the new king being thus removed without judgment or justice, and all the rest of his faithful subjects fearing the like treatment, the two dukes did thenceforth just as they pleased.[52]

The Archbishop of York, Thomas Rotherham, was placed under the guardianship of James Tyrell and committed to the Tower. The Bishop of Ely, John Morton[53] (later cardinal and Henry VII's Lord Chancellor), was put in the custody of the Duke of Buckingham. Most Ricardians would, I think agree that Richard would have done rather better to have confined Hastings and executed Morton[54] rather than the other way around. The suggestion of contemporary commentators is that the latter two were saved by their status as clergymen and this is an issue to which we shall return later. In addition to these individuals, Lord Stanley, along with Oliver King[55] was also detained, and John Forster imprisoned. Again, these actions pertain to the central contention of the present work and will be discussed in further detail. Jane Shore, who presumably was not present at the events happening in the Tower that day, was rather harshly treated by Richard. Her possessions were confiscated, she was imprisoned and subsequently forced to do public penance two days later. The reason why Richard enforced this action is also a key question in any explanation of the events of that day. One key piece of information has been reported which appears to render support for the notion of the premeditation of the acts of this fateful morning. Apparently, some few hours after the execution of Hastings, a proclamation was sent out through heralds across the city to scotch rumours and gossip among the general public. It was said that this proclamation was so long and detailed and so readily available after the event that it must have been drawn up before. If true, this would show evidence of premeditation. But premeditation on behalf of whom? It has always naturally been assumed that Richard had this document drawn up earlier. However, I shall seek to challenge this interpretation, although not the notion of premeditation or the existence of the proclamation itself.

Hastings was remembered fondly by several of the contemporary and near-contemporary commentators. For example, Polydore Vergil's encomium says his 'bountifulness and liberality, much beloved of the common people, bearing great sway among all sorts of men and persons of great reputation.' More, never a lover of Richard and always wary with respect to Hastings himself, notes that he was 'a good knight and a gentle … a loving man and passing well-loved. Very faithful and trusty enough, trusting too much.' The *Great Chronicle* speculates on the reason for Hastings' demise and perhaps represents the source of the most traditional interpretation that Hastings stood between Richard and the throne. The relevant text notes that, 'And thus was this noble man murdered for his troth and fidelity which he bare until his master [Edward IV].' Here, we must respect the opinion of Wood, whose conclusion was that the execution of Hastings, far from being part of a carefully thought-out plot on the calculated path to the throne, was rather a political mistake and evidence of completely the opposite circumstance; that this act was done virtually on the spur of the moment.

Of course, Wood's overall interpretation is coloured by his acceptance of Hanham's re-dating of Hastings' death. If the execution did occur on the 13th, and the vast preponderance of evidence confirms that it did (*see* Appendix II), then the act is one of even more tactical and momentary reaction, rather than a measured, strategic response. Mancini concluded that 'the plot had been feigned by the duke so as to escape the odium of such a crime.' However, the Mayor of London had apparently received sufficient reassurance that the purported plot against the Protector was real and Hastings was in the center of it.[56] What form those reassurances took, and what form the Mayor might expect them to be in, we are not told, but presumably there was some form of documentary evidence?

Sunday 15 June 1483

On the day prior to this Sunday, Saturday 14 June, John Brackenbury had arrived in York with Richard's letter of 5 June. It expressed Richard's affection for the city and had taken nine days to traverse the distance between the first and second cities of the land. A day later, on Sunday 15 June, Jane Shore, who had been arrested on the Friday, was forced to do public penance outside St Paul's Cathedral, and, following her ordeal, which has become the stuff of legend, she was committed to prison. Thomas Lynom, Richard's Solicitor-General, later visited her and looked for permission to marry her, evidence surely of Jane's extraordinary power of attraction.[57] Following immediately upon the delivery of Brackenbury's earlier communication, Richard Ratcliffe arrived in York and gave Richard's message to John Newton, mayor of the city. Unlike Brackenbury, it had taken Ratcliffe only four days between setting out and subsequently delivering his letters from Richard to the city of York and to Lord Neville. As we have seen, the urgency was communicated in what the 'in haste' letter had to say[58].

Monday 16 June 1483

It has been indicated that it was on this day, after the critical interval of the weekend and following the fateful Friday 13th, that the coronation of Edward V was postponed from 22 June until the 9 November.[59] Although this interpretation treats the idea of a weekend rather anachronistically, the evidence seems to suggest that the decision by Richard about the course of future events had changed significantly between the previous Friday and this, the following Monday.

It was understandable that the following meeting of the Council on this Monday, 16 June, saw most individuals as 'wary and nervous.' Following upon the events of the previous meeting it would hardly be natural if they were anything else. The Cely letter (memorandum) of the period reflects the general uncertainty. Although there is no date, the internal evidence of this document suggests the relevant parts were written after the 13th but before the 26 June (*see* Figure 4).

Furthermore, although the fate of Hastings was known, it remained uncertain how the others arrested that day would be finally dealt with. The primary matter of interest was the young Duke of York, still in sanctuary in Westminster Abbey with his mother and sisters. It has been reported that the Duke of Norfolk, John Howard, had eight boats of soldiers escort Richard, the Duke of Buckingham, Thomas Bourchier (the Archbishop of Canterbury) and John Russell (Bishop of Lincoln), among others, to Westminster. They surrounded the Abbey. Mancini reports that:

> When the Queen saw herself besieged and preparation for violence, she surrendered her son, trusting in the word of the Archbishop of Canterbury that the boy should be restored after the coronation.

It is also of interest to understand how news of Hastings' execution must have played into this decision to surrender her son, a scene which has preoccupied historic artists ever since.[60] Why Elizabeth should worry now at this specific juncture about the violation of sanctuary after spending so many weeks in the Abbey is left largely unaddressed. However, it is clear that control of the young Duke of York was absolutely vital to Richard if he had now already made the decision to take the throne. The traditional accounts of this event suggest that Elizabeth Woodville, Edward IV's Dowager Queen, was persuaded by the prelates who went to her on that day.

Richard, Duke of York was taken to join his older brother Edward at the Tower. Largely because of the Tudor era, the Tower now possesses a rather dreadful reputation and people often read dark implications into this act. However, it would be a natural course of action to reunite the brothers as the Tower was a major London residence for royalty.[61] Mancini is largely responsible for our impression of the imprisonment of the boys. He noted that:

> after Hastings was removed, all the attendants who had waited upon the king were debarred access to him. He and his brother were withdrawn into the inner apartments of the Tower proper, and day by day began to be seen more rarely behind the bars the windows, till at length they ceased to appear altogether.

However, Mancini left England during July and never had any certain knowledge of their fate. He did note that they were seen shooting and playing in the Tower after this date and before the second week of July. Any subsequent pronouncements become pure speculation. As we shall see, the Stonor letter, written five days after the young Duke of York left the

Abbey on the 21st, shows that the immediate reaction of some individuals in London at that time was not so bleak.

Tuesday 17 June 1483

It was around this time that various writs were issued, which served to cancel the proposed meeting of Parliament which had been due to take place on 25 June. It is apparent that some of these cancellations failed to reach some of the recipients before they had begun their trip to the capital. What is clear is that progress on the preparations for the immediate coronation was now largely abandoned. This does not signify that Richard had determined to take the throne, but it is very persuasive evidence that some major re-thinking was now in process. A prime example of this comes from the letter to York, the relevant portion of which reads:

> ... And or thys, notwythstandyng bt at thys day [21 June] that a sups [supersedes] was direct to the Sheryffe for the plement, so bt it shallnot need to ony Citizin to go upp for the Cite to the plement ...[62]

We are fortunate in that we have a fairly good idea as to how long messages seem to have taken to travel between the two major cities of London and York. We know that with a more leisurely pace, Brackenbury[63] had taken nine days on this trip, while the more urgent journey of Ratcliffe was completed in about four days. This being so, and given the urgency of the present communication to halt the summons to what appears to have been a parliament of Edward V, it is reasonable to suggest that the present supersedes was sent out some time either late on Monday 16th or a little later on perhaps the morning of Tuesday 17th. If either of these eventualities is correct, and there is every reason to believe that they are,[64] then Richard appears to have altered his course of action by the start of the week, following on the events of Friday 13 June.

Saturday 21 June 1483

Our understanding of events of this day and those immediately preceding it are enlightened by another of the letters from Simon Stallworth to Sir William Stonor. Like the previous missive of 9 June, this critical communication is reproduced in full in the Appendix I of this work.

Stallworth indicated that he was unwell, which may account for the brevity of his letter, especially so in relation to the many critical events which had occurred since what we assume was his last letter. Stallworth then had much to report. First, he recorded the execution of Hastings. The hiatus in completing his letter (perhaps because of his illness) has helped cause the confusion over the date of the latter's execution (*see* Appendix II). What we do not know is the exact date on which Stallworth wrote (or had caused to be written) the first section of this present letter which was formally dated 21 June. However, we can infer that the first section was written almost certainly before Friday 20th, since it is his reference to Hastings' execution 'As on Fryday last was the lord Chamberleyn hedded sone upone noon' that caused much of the trouble about dates.

Stallworth further reported that the Duke of York had emerged from sanctuary, so we may also assume that the first part of the letter was written either late on or after Monday 16th. Of this event he reports that a 'gret plenty of harnest men' accompanied the cardinal, the Lord Chancellor and the Duke of Buckingham, who received the young prince and accompanied him to Westminster Hall, where Richard received him 'at the Starre Chamber Dore with many lovynge wordys.' Following the greetings, the young prince was accompanied by the Cardinal to the Tower of London, where Stallworth reported that he was 'blesid be Jhesus, mery.' It appeared to Stallworth that Lord Lisle, the queen's brother-in-law, 'is come to my lord protectour, and awaits upon him,' suggesting some degree of rapprochement on behalf of the former.[65] Stallworth then went on to speculate about the rumour that 20,000 of Gloucester's and Buckingham's men would soon be in the capital, presuming their role would be to keep peace and order. He noted that the allegiance of those formerly under the lordship of Hastings had now transferred to Buckingham. Stallworth reported on the fate of the Archbishop of York, the Bishop of Ely, Oliver King, John Forster and Jane Shore, speculating on their eventual fate and current circumstances. He excused himself at the end of the letter, noting that his illness was such that 'I may not wel holde my penne.'

This and other sources[66] suggest that from 16 June onward, after securing the young Richard, Duke of York, the behaviour of the Protector began to change. For example, Kendall suggested that Richard ceased to wear mourning clothes and started to wear purple, which is an evident sign of royalty. Also, he was seen riding through the city with a train of lords and attendants and dividing his time between Baynard's Castle and Crosby Place. Further, Kendall asserted that Richard now started to talk openly about Stillington's 'revelation' concerning Edward IV's alleged marriage pre-contract with Eleanor Butler before he married Elizabeth Woodville.[67] This change in behaviour is helpful in narrowing the window in which the actions of Richard, Duke of Gloucester seem to deviate from an expected course of events leading to Edward V's coronation and to his own eventual ascension as king. As we work toward a conclusion of the present sequence, it appears that the critical weekend period is from Friday 13 to Monday 16 June, and Stallworth's letter is a key piece of evidence for this proposition. As such, it is reproduced in full in the Appendix I. As Kendall concludes, 'When Stallworthe wrote his agitated letter on Saturday [21 June], Richard had come to his fateful decision.' In respect of Kendall's conclusion here, I thoroughly concur.

Sunday 22 June 1483

To the Ricardian scholar, the events which followed on from this crucial interval are vital in order to understand the way in which Richard claimed the throne.[68] However, for my present purposes, I shall only give a brief synopsis of these events,[69] since I believe that Richard's critical decision to assume the throne had been taken nine days earlier. What now plays out is the fulfillment of that fundamental decision. It was on this Sunday that the brother of the Mayor of London,[70] Ralph Shaa (Shaw) preached a sermon at St Paul's Cross on the theme that 'bastard slips shall not take root.'[71] It was clearly and explicitly directed at the sons of Edward IV, and would have certainly been appreciated by his audience as such. Mancini indicates that it was one of a number of such public announcements.[72] This being so, it must have been part of a concerted effort to lay the groundwork for Richard's taking of the throne. If Mancini is correct, then such a strategy would have required some form of planning and so fixes Richard's actions and thus his decision as occurring some time before this Sunday. Parenthetically, Shaa died in the following year and his death was attributed by More to shame and remorse.[73] Shame and remorse seem to have fallen out of favour as modern causes of death, and we can certainly see this as another attempt at *post hoc* condemnation on More's behalf.

From Conception to Completion

In the days that followed, the path that Richard had created to the throne must have followed to a reasonable degree upon his expectations. One of his primary concerns since Stony Stratford had been the fate of those of the Woodville clan that he had secured there and now his strategy here was completed. On 23 June, Anthony Woodville, Lord Rivers made his will while at the Castle of Sheriff Hutton.[74] Shortly after, he was moved from Sheriff Hutton to Pontefract (Pomfret) Castle. In his will, he named Russell and Catesby as executors. It is of more than passing interest that he named Catesby here, and it is a point to which I shall return. The campaign to push Richard's legitimate candidature as king persisted in the capital and was met with some degree of doubt and reticence. However, since the power resided with Richard this was largely a public relations exercise rather than a potential plebiscite. On 24 June, in the north of England, Ratcliffe arrived at Pontefract with the execution orders for Rivers, who had come from Sheriff Hutton, as well as Grey, who was brought from Middleham Castle, and Vaughan, who was at Pontefract already.[75] A day later they were executed, and, like Hastings, they received no trial.[76] It is just conceivable and barely logistically possible that Ratcliffe could have returned to London after delivering Richard's letter of 10 June to York and 11 June to Lord Neville. This would, presumably, have involved some very hard riding from the 16th onward to London in a four-day journey and then another four days to return to Pontefract. It appears much more likely that Ratcliffe had the orders of execution with him when he first left London on, presumably, 11 June. This being so, it is certainly possible that Hastings saw the execution warrants as More speculated. As such, Hastings would surely have had occasion to be even more grateful and loyal to Richard, who had now dispatched some of his principal enemies. Of course, we cannot rule out the possibility that the orders were carried to Ratcliffe by a subsequent messenger,[77] but this seems an unlikely task to have entrusted to anyone but a very close and influential associate.

In the days which followed, it appears to have been Buckingham's role to act as the 'front-man' to convince a sufficient number of people to accept Richard's claim. At a meeting in Westminster, Mancini noted that Buckingham was to present these respective grounds, which later appeared in the *Titulus Regius* of 1484. Among these claims, the issue of the pre-contract stands out. Although not the only objection, it must have been the one with the greatest probability of material provenance. The accusation of the use of witchcraft, especially in relation to Jacquetta, Duchess of Bedford, might well have been an expected and even required smear. The problem concerning the secrecy of Edward IV's marriage to Elizabeth Woodville, the lack of approval by the lords and the absence of the publication of the banns are hardly crucial reasons, since the alleged marriage with Eleanor Butler was of exactly the same form. Thus we are left with Stillington's confirmation of the pre-contract.

On 26 June, just one day after the Pontefract executions, the lords gathered at Baynard's Castle in order to petition Richard to take the throne.[78] As the front-man for this enterprise, Buckingham's activities were nearing fruition. After an evident show of humility, Richard accepted the throne and began to put his own administration in place.[79] Of particular interest for the present work, William Catesby was made Chancellor of the Exchequer. Later he would be Speaker of the House in the only Parliament held during Richard's reign. The final outcome of this train of events was that on the 6 July 1483, Richard, Duke of Gloucester was crowned Richard III in Westminster Abbey.[80] It was but two years and two months to the Battle of Bosworth Field.

I started this chapter with the central question which acts to bias any assessment of Richard III and his ambitions. If one sees Richard looking for the crown on or before his brother Edward's death then one is likely to adopt a position reflective of Richard as a long-term, scheming usurper.[81] The later one places Richard's decision to assume the throne, the more lenient one is liable to be in one's viewpoint. In what I have tried to set forth here, I have suggested that the interval around the critical Council meeting on Friday 13 June was the juncture at which Richard made this fateful decision. In fact, although not indispensable to my present argument, I would like to suggest that it was the events of that very morning that proved the pivotal turning point which changed Richard from fairly assiduous Protector to aspiring monarch. Thus, to understand the story of Richard III, we have to understand the events of that critical day: Friday 13th June 1483. It is to the examination of this fateful day that I now turn.

Eleanor Talbot,
Lady Butler

The holiest harlot in his realm.

The Uncrowned Queen?

Any explanation of the events which took place on 13 June 1483 at the Tower of London has to begin some decades earlier and some distance away from London. John Ashdown-Hill, whose recent work has been most informative and influential,[1] has asserted that the events of that summer have to be viewed in light of the question of the so-called 'pre-contract,' since, as he points out, 'Richard III's claim to the throne was based chiefly on the presumption that Lady Eleanor Talbot was the legitimate wife of Edward IV.'[2] It is this relationship between Edward IV and his nominal 'uncrowned queen'[3] which proves to be crucial in respect of the explanation of events that I propose.

Eleanor's Early Life

Since this issue of the pre-contract is so important, it is fundamental to begin with some of the facts of Eleanor Talbot's life (c. 1436–1468) and her actions and activities before and after the so-called 'pre-contract' occurred. Eleanor was the tenth of the eleven children of John Talbot (*c.* 1387–1453), the 1st Earl of Shrewsbury, whose spectacular demise is recorded to have occurred in battle with the French at Castillon on 17 July 1453. The earl himself was the first child of Richard Talbot (4th Baron Talbot of Goodrich) and his wife, Ankaret (Le)Strange. This couple was also blessed with a large family and had nine children, the last of whom, Alice, we shall hear more of presently. John Talbot married twice. The first time was around 1405 to Maud Neville (*c.* 1390–1424), with whom he had five children, two of whom died in early childhood. Talbot's second marriage occurred sometime around 1424[4] to Margaret Beauchamp (1404–1467), by whom he had a further five children, the penultimate child of that marriage being Eleanor herself. We can see painted representations of John Talbot and his second wife in Figures 5 and 6.[5]

To the best of our knowledge, Eleanor was born probably in either February or March 1436, possibly at the manor house of Blakemere, near Whitchurch in Shropshire.[6] Ashdown-Hill argued for this location, as it was a house that her father John had inherited from his mother and was apparently a favourite residence. However, as he also notes, it could equally well have been Goodrich Castle in Herefordshire.[7] As will become evident, the latter location is one of potentially great importance and can perhaps serve to render some insight into Eleanor's subsequent relationships and actions. It is probable that Eleanor would have been brought up in one main location but would almost certainly have visited a number of the family residences, including the likes of Sheffield Castle. Although John Talbot's favouritism toward Blakemere is suggested by his eventual nearby burial under the porch of St Alkmund's church in Whitchurch, Shropshire,[8] Eleanor may have been bought up in Goodrich Castle, since on the monument which commemorated his first burial at Rouen in Normandy, her father is titled 'Lord of Goodrich and Orchenfield'.[9]

The Butler Marriage

If we have the date of her birth correct, and we can be reasonably certain of the general period, then Eleanor's subsequent marriage to Sir Thomas Butler (the son of Ralph Butler, Lord Sudeley), which occurred around late 1449 or early 1450,[10] would have seen Eleanor as a bride at the age of just thirteen or fourteen years of age. It has been speculated that Eleanor would have then lived in the house of her in-laws until the age of sixteen, when the marriage would have been consummated sometime in 1452, or possibly early 1453.[11] Indeed, in early May of 1453, Eleanor is mentioned in a document in which Ralph, Lord Sudeley presented a deed of gift to his son (Thomas) and his wife (referred to as Eleanor, daughter of the Earl of Shrewsbury) and their legitimate heirs with the manors of Griff, Fenny Compton and Burton Dassett (sometimes noted as Great Dorsett or Chipping Dorsett after the market held there). All of these were in the county of Warwickshire, although Eleanor apparently held some other lands in Wiltshire also.[12] As we shall see, geographical issues play almost as crucial a role in the present proposition as those of history itself and so it is important to confirm here that the manors of Fenny Compton and Burton Dassett (or Great Dorsett) adjoin each other in south-west Warwickshire. While it has been a somewhat difficult search, the latter manor of Griff (or Grieve), lies approximately twenty miles north of Great Dorset in the vicinity of the suburbs of modern day Coventry, just south of Nuneaton. The map of the two adjacent properties of Fenny Compton and Burton Dassett is shown in Figure 8.

Perhaps this gift followed on the consummation of the marriage? Although we do not know this for certain, it may very well have been around this time in 1453 that Eleanor and Thomas[13] set up their own household, most probably on the manor lands which they had been granted. At this time, Great Dorsett was a much more substantive gift than it might appear today. Earlier, Henry III had granted permission to hold a market there every Friday and an annual fair of three days from the eve of St James. Such was the prosperity of the town that in 1332 Great Dorsett had paid taxes to the king's treasury of almost one-quarter of those paid by the whole of the city of Coventry.[14] We do not know what the equivalent revenues were at the time of Eleanor's possession. However, it would appear that this was still a major centre and the manor of Great Dorsett most probably included all of the present-day settlements of Burton Dassett, Avon Dassett, Little Dassett, Temple Herdewyke and Northend. This being so, the gift of Lord Sudelely to his son and daughter-in-law certainly appears to have been an appropriately generous one. Parenthetically, this property was later broken up by the actions of Sir Edward Belknap who, at the very end of the fifteenth century, evicted sixty people in his conversion to pasture. Sir Edward's actions, although purportedly logical at the time, seem to have spelled the end of Great Dorsett's fame. The actual village of Burton Dassett is now only a few farms and farm buildings around All Saints' church, and the most evident landmark of the settlement is the tower on the Dassett Hills (now a country park), which can be seen from the nearby motorway, the M40 (*see* Figure 31).

Around the time that Eleanor and her husband were gifted the property, she would have been approximately seventeen years of age. Thomas Butler, her husband, as best we know was in his early thirties. Let us accept then, as a reasonable possibility, that Eleanor Butler (née Talbot) was now the young and inexperienced lady of the manor. It seems reasonable to assume that they would have taken up their respective roles as the lord and lady of this demesne, which would certainly appear to have been their largest and most profitable property (*see* Appendix III notes on the Manor of Great Dorsett). Indeed, there is an intriguing possibility that one of the major charities of the area could have been associated with Eleanor.[15] It is important here to consider for a moment what Eleanor's social life would have been like at this time. To help understand a critical social connection with an extended part of her family, I again have to delve further back in time and explore her relations within the Talbot family and especially the youngest sister of Eleanor's father, Alice Talbot.

Joan Barre, Eleanor's First Cousin

Earlier, I noted that Richard Talbot (4th Baron Talbot of Goodrich) had a total of nine children with his wife Ankaret (Le)Strange. The first of these was Eleanor's father, John Talbot (1st Earl of Shrewsbury). However, the last of the nine, and thus Talbot's youngest sister, was Alice Talbot, who married Sir Thomas Barre. Their only child, a daughter, was Joan (or Jane) Barre. In terms of familial relationship, Joan was Eleanor's first cousin with the common grandfather and grandmother in Richard Talbot and Ankaret Strange. However, in terms of age, the two women were separated by a number of years. To the best of present knowledge, Joan was born about 1422, with her first marriage, to Sir Kynard de la Bere, taking place some time around late 1430s, since their son Richard was recorded as being born in 1440 (*see* Figure 9), by which time Joan would have been perhaps eighteen. However, following the death of her first husband, Joan re-married, this time to Sir William Catesby of

Ashby St Ledgers (*see* Figure 7), to the best of our knowledge sometime around 10 June 1453.[16] It was a second marriage for both of them, she being approximately thirty years of age and he somewhat older at approximately thirty-three years old. Sir William had been previously married to Phillippa Bishopston, the daughter of William Bishopston and Phillippa Willcott, and by her he had already three children, two girls and one boy. Phillippa was recorded as dying on 7 December 1446,[17] when the young boy, also William, was only six or seven years old. He would have been born around 1440, and was the oldest of Phillippa's children. He was, of course, 'the Cat' of Colyngbourne doggerel, and represents the key figure in the present work. Following his 1453 marriage to Joan Barre, William's father, Sir William, had three more children, two boys and a girl, the latter of whom died as a child.[18]

Given the dates involved, it appears that the young William Catesby was still a child and just about into his teen years when he gained his new stepmother. In contrast, Eleanor was about seventeen years old and, by the standards of the day, almost a full adult when her first cousin married Sir William Catesby. As we shall surmise, the link between Eleanor and Joan now becomes critical to the question of the legitimacy of Edward IV's subsequent marriage to Elizabeth Woodville, in light of the revealed pre-contract with Eleanor (Talbot) Butler.

Now we must step from the realms of reasonably well-documented information and proceed rather carefully into the world of speculation. The first such speculation is one that might not be too difficult to sustain. Joan was born into the extensive Talbot family around 1422. As noted, she was the niece of the famous John Talbot, who was by now the head of the whole family. John Talbot himself married twice, and his second marriage occurred on 26 September 1425 to Margaret Beauchamp. He was then forty-one and she twenty-one years old. I think it must be a supportable proposition that Joan Barre, the niece of the bridegroom, was at the wedding. Indeed, I suspect Joan's mother, Alice, and the new bride, Margaret, were friends. We know that some years later Joan married Sir Kynard de la Bere and was known by the appellation 'Joan of Clehonger.' Clehonger itself is a small village right outside Hereford, and is just under thirteen miles from Goodrich Castle. Both Goodrich and Clehonger are directly adjacent to the River Wye and, in fact, Goodrich Castle itself dominates its banks. It might be objected, however, that Joan was married to Sir Kynard de la Bere, who was the lord of Kinnersley Castle. However,

Kinnersley is itself only nine miles further on from Clehonger, and is again very near to the Wye. I think, therefore, there is some justification for believing that Margaret acted as a form of older advisor or older sister to Joan, especially perhaps in the first years of Joan's marriage. This, I must especially note, is pure speculation; I cannot substantiate this relationship at the present time. However, as we shall see, this early association, while strengthening my argument, was not absolutely essential to the overall proposition that I set forth here.

Given these family connections and the close proximity of where Joan was presumably living (at either Clehonger or Kinnersely) to one of the major residences of the senior Talbot family (at Goodrich), it is perhaps no great stretch from this premise to speculate that Joan Barre knew Margret Beauchamp's daughter Eleanor from the moment of her birth. If, as is possible, Eleanor was actually born at Goodrich, and I suspect she was, Joan may well have attended the confinement, being a young lady of approximately fourteen years of age at the time. By that juncture, some time early in 1436, Margaret had already given John Talbot three children. I have no date for the death of Sir Kynard de la Bere, but it is probable that Joan saw Eleanor grow up, at least to her late childhood and early teen years, and strong attachments are made during such formative years. It was in 1449–1450 that Eleanor, at the age of thirteen or fourteen, was married to Sir Thomas Butler, and must have moved from her familiar surroundings to her new domicile, perhaps in the home of the father of her husband-to-be in Gloucestershire. It was only three or four years later, in 1453, that Joan herself married her second husband, Sir William Catesby.

Now, this brings us to the time when the new married couple of Eleanor and her husband Thomas Butler set up home in the manors of Great Dorsett and Fenny Compton. At this time and in this place, Eleanor's mother would have been somewhat remote from her, perhaps back in Herefordshire and a fair distance to travel in such times. However, not so very far away, in fact only just over ten miles distant, along a pleasant river valley, in Ashby St Ledgers, resided her first cousin, Joan Barre. It may even be possible that the association between the two women actually began at this time (thus obviating the necessity for an earlier association), when Eleanor and Joan each moved to what for them were relatively unfamiliar surroundings. Regardless of exactly when the two first began their association, it is my contention that there would have been significant social intercourse between the two families, the Catesbys and the Butlers. Of course, we cannot know the frequency of their interaction, but we can confirm that there was certainly more than passing contact, since Sir William Catesby (the father of 'the Cat') acted as a witness to several documents pertaining to Eleanor, including deeds of gift,[19] and had previously acted extensively on behalf of John Talbot, Eleanor's father.[20] In reality, I suspect there was a great closeness between the families both before and after the death of Eleanor's first husband.

There was one further, but frankly tenuous, connection between Burton Dassett and Ashby St Ledgers. At the present it is one that must remain an intriguing speculation which awaits future resolution. However, in All Saints' Church at Burton Dassett, as shown in Figure 10, there is a series of wall paintings (*see* Figure 33). These are composed of a sequence of illustrations which for a long time have been covered over by whitewash. Over an original Passion series appears a representation of the Virgin, St John and two censing angels. The date of these paintings is though to be mid-fifteenth century. The most intriguing aspect of them is as follows:

> This series is unusual in that a Doom which symbolises the gates of Heaven and that one must be judged before one can enter Heaven. However, there is a painting of similar subject and style in Ashby St Ledgers (near Daventry in Northants.) Ashby has three Passion series, all by different painters, the centrally placed painting is very similar in style to the painting here and could be the work of the same painter.[21]

If we speculate that such work occurred during the time that Thomas Conway was vicar of All Saints' church at Burton Dassett, then is it possible that each of these pictures was commissioned by Eleanor Butler?[22] This is indeed a stretch of probability, but if the paintings at Great Dorsett and the paintings at Ashby St Ledgers[23] (*see* Figure 32) were by the same artist then it might be possible that, in representing the Virgin, the painter astutely commingled some of Eleanor's features with those of the Mother of God. The upshot of this is that the representation in Figure 11 might just possibly contain something of the facial features of Eleanor Butler. It would be of great interest to integrate the features of her father and mother, shown in Figures 5 and 6, to see any possible resemblance. This would also address the speculation as to the image of Eleanor suggested by Ashdown-Hill.[24] However, to be useful, speculation should not be unbounded.[25]

The Pre-Contract

Much has been written about the pre-contract, and much of this concerns the nature of the relevant statutes and jurisdiction at the time that the pre-contract supposedly occurred. As the pivotal factor in the present theory it is important to describe the major facts as we know them. However, I do not intend here to go into the nuances of the law as it applied at that time, which is a topic that I leave for others.[27] Sufficient to say that the present consensus appears to be that had the pre-contract occurred at the time it is speculated to have done, then Edward IV's subsequent marriage with Elizabeth Woodville would have been invalid and the children of that marriage barred from succeeding to the throne.

We do not have explicit information as to when Sir Thomas Butler died. We know that his death appears to have occurred before 15 January 1460 and it has been suggested that he died sometime in the latter part of 1459, perhaps in December, as a result of injuries sustained at the Battle of Blore Heath,[28] which had taken place on 23 September of that year . His death left Eleanor a widow at the age of twenty-three. At around this same time, the manor of Grieve seems to have been returned to her father-in-law, and to have been directly exchanged for the controlling interest in Fenny Compton.[29] Where would a young woman in the unenviable position that Eleanor now found herself turn but to her friends and relatives? We must examine the events of that fateful winter in order to understand what happened next and how it may have had a critical influence on the events of the summer twenty-three years later. Following the death of her husband, Eleanor had to appeal to the young king, Edward IV, then coming up to his nineteenth birthday on 28 April 1461, for the return of her various properties. Edward had confiscated them on the grounds that Lord Sudeley had given them to his son and daughter-in-law without the sanction of a royal licence. It is thus asserted that Eleanor had to seek an audience with the King to secure her lands.[30]

We do not know exactly where and when this fateful meeting between Eleanor Butler and King Edward IV took place. A survey of Edward's itinerary for that period provides a number of candidate locations, ranging from London to East Anglia or perhaps the Warwickshire or Gloucestershire areas.[31] Again, we are here into the realms of speculation as to location, but the fact that they actually did meet seems to be supported by the subsequent documented retention of the respective lands by Eleanor.[32] One reasonable possibility that must be considered is the royal residence at Woodstock in Oxfordshire. The proximity between Woodstock and Great Dorsett is perhaps the most persuasive factor in favouring this location. There are only twenty-two miles between the two, and winter travel at the time cannot have been easy. However, the journey between Woodstock and Great Dorsett would have been along major thoroughfares, going through or close by large towns such as Banbury and Oxford and perhaps therefore a little less daunting. One fascinating alternative possibility is Grafton Regis. It is very tempting to speculate that Edward IV engaged in the same activity (marriage of a beautiful young widow) in the same place, but this symmetrical interpretation is belied by the fact that Grafton Regis (*see* Figure 12) was a home of the Woodvilles and this particular site of Edward's later marriage to Elizabeth Woodville is most probably related to their occupancy there rather than any sentimental attachment on behalf of Edward himself. Wherever we seek to place the location of the pre-contract with Eleanor, we have to remember that the itineraries of the king, Eleanor and Robert Stillington, later Bishop of Bath & Wells, have to overlap spatially as well as temporally. That Stillington may have been attending on the king is a possibility, if not a probability, but again empirical efforts may help us to determine this site at some time in the future, and it is possible that advanced simulation and modelling can help decide these propositions.[33] Of course, at present we cannot even rule out the possibility that the site of the pre-contract was Great Dorsett itself. Again, this is simply speculation at this stage. What seems quite well established was that only the king, Eleanor and Stillington were present at this ceremony.[34]

The most direct evidence of the pre-contract that we have is derived from the commentary in the *Titulus Regius* which reads:

And howe alfo, that at the tyme of contract of the fame pretenfed Mariage, and bifore and longe tyme after, the feid King Edward was and ftode maryed and trouth plight to oone Dame Elianor Butteler, Doughter of the old Earl of Shrewefbury, with whom the fame King Edward had made a precontracte of Matrimonie, longe tyyme bifore he made the faid pretenfed Mariage with the faid Elizabeth Grey, in maner and fourme abovefaid. Which premiffes being true, as in veray trouth they been true, it appearreth and foloweth evidently, that the faid King Edward duryng his lif, and the feid Elizabeth, lived together finfully and dampnably in adultery, againft the Lawe of God and of his Church;

We can confirm that this pattern of behaviour fits in with what we do know about Edward IV, especially during his younger years. We have evidence that Edward took such advantage on at least four occasions. Of course, the primary case in point is Edward's subsequent liaison with Elizabeth Woodville (Lady Grey) herself at Grafton Regis, which is discussed in a later chapter.

In respect of this pre-contract it appears that, as far as canon law was concerned, the promise in exchange for sexual favours was sufficient to cement the contract. As we shall see, the French diplomat de Commines[35] named Stillington as the source of the knowledge of this pre-contract. However, there is little corroborating evidence,[36] and some have suggested that Stillington was not actually the source that revealed the pre-contract to Richard.[37] This proposition will also be examined in further detail. The fact that Eleanor died in 1468, before the birth of Edward's two sons by Elizabeth Woodville, raises some interesting points that would have had to be considered in the ecclesiastical courts (where the case for legitimacy would presumably have been heard). However, events of the summer of 1483 seem to have overtaken this issue.

We have relatively little information about Eleanor's activities between the pre-contract and 1464, after the announcement of Edward's marriage to Elizabeth Woodville,[38] and so the next steps that I wish to take must also be labelled largely as speculation.[39] Since she died possessed of her lands, we can assume that Eleanor was successful in her petition. But what was her state of mind, and what was the state of her body? Presumably, contraception would have been fairly rudimentary in such times. Again, we do not know how long the liaison between Edward and Eleanor persisted. Was it simply a 'one-night stand,' or was there more extensive activity? Presuming either of these conditions, could Eleanor have become pregnant, and given the death of her husband could such a pregnancy have been passed off as a legitimate birth? These are questions that arise but cannot at present be answered.[40] One speculation does seem reasonable. As a young widow in such difficult circumstances, it does seem likely that she would have turned to her family for help, and most probably to an older female relative. Of course, my postulation is that Joan (Barre/de la Bere) Catesby fulfilled that role. There is circumstantial support that this might also be so because of the legal help rendered by Sir William to both her and her father, and perhaps also by the budding young lawyer in the family, Sir William's son – William Catesby 'the Cat.' Where else would one take such a thorny question other than to a lawyer?[41]

What I am suggesting here is that the familial and dependent relationship between Eleanor (Talbot) Butler and the Catesby family meant that the young, twenty-one-year-old William Catesby learned around this time of the pre-contract from his second cousin Eleanor at a family meeting to decide what best to do under the circumstances. We must remember that Eleanor had no witness other than Robert Stillington and certainly no pushing mother such as Jacquetta, Duchess of Bedford[42] to advance her case. It appears that the decision was taken not to press the young king on this issue.[43] I have little doubt that an able lawyer of Catesby's acumen would have put this information aside for use at a later and more advantageous time. I am suggesting that he used this information to advance himself somewhat with William, Lord Hastings, and later in that fateful summer of 1483 in his critical switch of masters to Richard III. Thus it is to an assessment of Catesby and his actions before, during and after the 'long weekend' in June 1483 that I now turn.

William Catesby,
Esquire of the Body

a man well learned in the laws of this land

William or Sir William?

William 'the Cat' Catesby was the first-born child of Sir William Catesby, a well-to-do member of the Northamptonshire gentry.[1] Although we do not have his precise date of birth, it appears from evidence in respect of his father's first marriage that William was born sometime around 1440.[2] This would have made him about forty-five at the time of his execution in Leicester immediately following the fateful Battle of Bosworth Field.[3] It has been a point of dispute as to whether William himself was a knight, as was his father. Indeed, in the *Testamenta Vetusta*[4] we read the entry 'Sir William Catesby, Knt', followed by 'William Catesby, Knight, 1485. My body to be buried at Ashby Ledgers; Margaret, my wife.' However, a more detailed source, the *Dictionary of National Biography*[5] is emphatic that, although he was an esquire of the royal body, William, unlike his father, was not a knight.[6] As a result of this established difference in status, in what follows I shall refer to the father as Sir William, while I shall call his son 'the Cat'[7] just William.

Our knowledge about the latter part of William's life is much more extensive than that of his earliest years. It will help set the context for his childhood and early youth by understanding the career of his father, Sir William, and the strides that he had made in his own life by the time William was born. Sir William's grandfather, John Catesby, had acquired what was to become the family home at Ashby St Ledgers through marriage to Emma Cranford. It was at this time that the Catesbys moved the short distance from their former home of Ladbroke[8] in Warwickshire and took up residence in their new home (*see* Figure 13).[9] Much of our contemporary information about the family comes from their actions in and around the village of Ashby St Ledgers and their memorial brasses in the local church[10] (*see* Figure 15).

The Father of 'the Cat'

The legal profession certainly appears to have run in the Catesby family. Emma Cranford's husband, John Catesby, was apparently a lawyer, as was his son (also John). Sir William himself, the latter's son, was also a lawyer, and we know from Thomas More's essay on Richard III that William 'the Cat' Catesby also followed this family tradition.[11] Sir William's own father died in 1437 when, according to a family tradition, Sir William himself was just short of the age of majority. Like the lawyer that he was, Sir William's father John had, just before his death, placed a portion of his lands in feoffment in order to avoid Sir William being adjudged a royal ward and having the spoilage of his inheritance that often accompanied this latter status. In this, he was not successful. However, for Sir William, the status of ward turned out to be a very profitable turn of events. He was committed to the keeping of a relative by marriage, a courtier named John Norris, who Payling[12] speculates helped find the young Sir William a very advantageous marriage. If he was yet to reach his majority in 1437 and we know that he was married by May of 1442 and, further, we know that his first wife died in 1446, having already produced three children,[13] then some time around 1440 seems a reasonable estimate for the birth date of his son, William 'the Cat' (*see* Figure 14).

John Norris seems to have been a good mentor to his young ward. Sir William followed the family tradition and spent time at the Inner Temple, but also established a link with the royal court and was given an annuity of ten pounds in 1442. Around this same time he and his new wife received a papal indult for a portable altar.[14] This was clearly a young man now making his way in the world. From a series of records we know that

Sir William began to assume a significant position in his now-home county of Northamptonshire. However, there also exist records to show that he was active on the wider stage of events and it is here that a number of the crucial linkages in respect of the present story begin to become evident. As well as giving gifts to leading local personages, in 1447–1448 Sir William is recorded as having sent gifts of fish from his fishpond at Ashby to Humphrey Stafford, Duke of Buckingham, and, even more importantly, John Talbot, Earl of Shrewsbury.[15] In respect of our present search for the truth of Richard III, we should be aware that Humphrey Stafford was succeeded as Duke of Buckingham by his grandson Henry Stafford, and, critically, Eleanor Butler (née Talbot) was the daughter of John Talbot, Earl of Shrewsbury. Thus, we have direct evidence that these respective families were in some degree of contact. At this time, Eleanor herself would have been about ten years of age and presumably, still living at home with her family. We should not be overly surprised, however, by such linkages. As an active lawyer and aspiring member of the land-owning gentry, it is unsurprising that Sir William would have made efforts to ingratiate himself with the rich and powerful. The gift of fish may well have been by the way of some form of introduction. Regardless of whether this was an introduction or something less formal, the interaction with John Talbot was to prove rather important to Sir William's future and, as I propose here, that of his son.

Sir William's Second Marriage

We know relatively little about William's mother, and Sir William's first wife, Phillippa Bishopston. We do know that she helped her husband by bringing him a considerable income. Further, we know that she fulfilled what would then be seen as her principal duty by providing children to carry on the family line. She had, of course, in her first child, produced a male heir. What is most evident is that she died young, almost certainly less than ten years after her marriage and perhaps as little as five. I have suggested that she may have died as a result of complications in childbirth; however, at the present this is simply a speculation which, although apparently reasonable, awaits further clarification.[16] What the death of poor Phillippa meant was that Sir William was a widower at a relatively young age and that William had lost his mother at the most impressionable age of between five and eight.

Sir William's association with the Talbot family seems to have flourished in the years following his first wife's death. Perhaps the fish worked, because just as John Talbot (*see* Figure 5) was preparing for what would turn out to be his final military campaign in France in autumn of 1452, he named Sir William as one of his executors.[17] At this juncture then, when Eleanor was presumably just taking her first steps into the full marriage state, Sir William Catesby was one of the main advisors to her father. This Talbot connection, which would also assumedly have included some form of social interaction, was perhaps the basis for Sir William himself finding his second wife. As we have seen previously, this second wife was Joan Barre, widow of Sir Kynard de la Bere of Kinnersley in Herefordshire. More directly, she was the daughter of Alice, the youngest sister of the Earl of Shrewsbury and was thus John Talbot's niece. The best estimate is that Sir William was about thirty-three while Joan was about thirty-one. Obviously, both had been married before and both had living children. It appears that the brother of Joan, Sir John de la Barre, had suggested some form of legal contract and, although Sir William Catesby was willing to provide this, he sought to emphasise that no such formality was really necessary.[18] Perhaps it was, in part, a love match second time around? Regardless, it appears that the two were married, most probably on 10 June 1453. It is, of course, pure coincidence that it was almost exactly thirty years to the day before the fateful events which were to take place at the Tower of London.

Like his son who was to follow him, Sir William was an Esquire of the Royal Body and now, in later 1453, he was knighted. Like many in those times, Sir William had to navigate carefully amongst the politics of the respective ascendancy of first, the Lancastrian and then the Yorkist cause. In this, Sir William seems to have been modestly successful, relying largely on his various relations and relationships, and like many others, never investing too deeply or heavily in any one cause such that the other could not see his value when the tide of affairs turned. It must have been a very important phase in the development of his son William who, now in his middle and later teens, must have been a keen observer of such events and strategies. It was perhaps these early experiences that schooled William in the notion of the expediency of switching allegiances as the times and the conditions changed? We have some very tentative evidence that the son, William Catesby, attended the University of Oxford as a student at what would then have been recognised as Gloucester College. This college was founded in

1283 and later in 1560 became Gloucester Hall, which was administered through St John's College. Eventually, the institution became Worcester College after benefiting from the will of Sir Thomas Cookes.[19] At exactly what age William would have been a student at Oxford we do not know but perhaps this was part of his preparation as a lawyer in looking to continue the family tradition?

The swaying vicissitudes of the times eventually seem to have caught up with Sir William, especially around the time of Henry VI's readeption, which should have been of advantage to him as a previous Lancastrian supporter. However, although well treated, Sir William's mind seems then to have been more on things spiritual than events temporal. In early January 1471 he was involved with the arrangements for a ceremonial at Ashby St Ledgers to take place on 26 July, which may well have been his birthday. The record of the respective arrangements noted his service to the Talbot family in the late 1440s and early 1450s and especially notes his link to the now deceased John Talbot, Earl of Shrewsbury. Significantly, it also notes Sir William's link to Talbot's second wife, Countess Margaret, and most intriguingly two of their children, John, Viscount Lisle and, most especially, Eleanor Butler,[20] the so-called 'uncrowned queen' of Edward IV.[21]

William and his Father

It was at about this time, when William[22] was around twenty-one years of age that, probably with the guidance of Sir William, he made a strong marriage in the sense of its important familial linkages. The young lady was Margaret Zouch and she was the daughter of William, Lord Zouche of Harringworth and his second wife, Elizabeth St John. Elizabeth herself was the maternal half-sister of Margaret Beaufort and this may help account for a later conundrum associated with William and his appeal to Margaret Beaufort's son, Henry VII, in the city of Leicester in late August 1485. Elizabeth, it seems, went on to marry her second husband, Lord Scrope of Bolton, and it was through this association that William received her life interest in some of the Zouche lands in Leicestershire. At the same time (most probably associated with the marriage also), William was the recipient from his father of the Bishopston lands that had come as part of his own mother's inheritance. It is very possible that this was the essential beginnings of William's search to build up a territorial hegemony of his own.

It might also have been this acquisitiveness that was one of his fundamental motivations for his later recorded actions.

Despite the continuing disputation between the Houses of York and Lancaster, this seems to have been a good time for the Catesbys, *pere et fils*. Sir William, it seems, had a connection with George, Duke of Clarence, and it was also around this time that the Catesby connection to William, Lord Hastings grew in magnitude and importance. It was perhaps this latter association that saw Sir William again avoid the fall-out from Clarence's demise and he returned for a final time as the Sheriff of the County of Northamptonshire. Indeed, Sir William died in office in the autumn of 1479 and despite his adaptation to the Yorkist administration, his memorial brass reads, '*quondam unus trencheatorum Regis Henrici sexti.*' Apparently, his persuasion was Lancastrian to the end.[23] (*See* Figure 15)[24]

The Rise of 'the Cat'

To understand the events of the summer of 1483, we need to delve further into the career and aspirations of young William Catesby. While we are still uncertain about his attendance at Oxford, we do know with a degree of certainty that William followed in his father's footsteps and pursued the family vocation of law at the Inner Temple. We first hear of him as 'W. Catysby, lectorem,' discoursing on the nature of the Magna Carta[25] and there are some formal records that show his progress in the profession.[26] Payling noted that Catesby was most probably unlike the general run of students of the Inner Temple at the time. He had already made a very advantageous marriage and had a considerable income from this source, as well as from the lands his father had given him. Indeed, it is in regard to his wife's family, the Zouches of Harringworth, and their extended relations, now including Lord Scope of Bolton, that we see William's penetration into the world of influence.[27] It appears as though he could have settled into a life of quiet, country gentility, and yet the impression we get from the legal records of the time is one of his evident ambition.

In the present thesis, it is very important to note that the first ever royal appointment of which we have a record for William Catesby was to a commission of inquiry on 18 May 1473.[28] It is not the date *per se*, but rather the subject of this commission which is particularly important. With others, he was commissioned to make inquiries as to the Warwickshire lands and estates of the late Ralph, Lord Sudeley.[29] As we know from the previous chapter, Ralph, Lord Sudeley was Ralph Butler, the father-in-law to Eleanor Butler (née Talbot). We should also recall that his son and Eleanor's husband Thomas had died earlier, perhaps from wounds received at the Battle of Blore Heath, fought on 23 September 1459. His daughter-in-law, Eleanor, had herself died on 30 June 1468, so Ralph Butler was in the sad situation of seeing at least one branch of his direct family die out completely.[30] It was perhaps this lack of a direct heir that indeed led to the commission to which William Catesby was appointed. Given the death of his son and daughter-in-law, it is more than likely that some of the lands around Great Dorsett and Fenny Compton reverted to his control. From investigation of the pattern of land acquisition of William Catesby, we can see that these particular properties lay squarely in the path of the quickly expanding Catesby holdings (*see* Appendix VI, The Offices and Lands of William Catesby). Thus, the commission represented a pivotal opportunity for William to influence the destiny of some properties that he and his family may well have coveted, perhaps even for decades. For, as we know, the original Catesby family holdings were in Ladbroke, less than five miles from Great Dorsett, and it is likely that their original lands bordered on these manors. The implication is that William must have worked hard to get himself appointed to this commission, potentially with the help of some of his influential relatives.[31] Of course, as a local landowner, it may be that this was seen as 'natural' appointment. The property eventually found its way by means of the marriage of Lord Sudeley's sister into the eventual possession of Sir Edward Belknap, whose draconian action, added to the decimation wreaked by an earlier bout of the Black Death, eventually dispelled the glory of Great Dorsett, which continues only as shadow of its past self today.

After the death of his father in 1479, William would have been a very rich man indeed, and had more than enough wealth for the rest of his life. Yet there appears to have been continual and unstinted effort. This acquisitiveness and ambition are reflected in his purchases in the later 1470s and early 1480s of various properties. We have information as to his acquisition of the manors of Oxhill, just a short distance from Ashby St Ledgers, and Tilbrook, just across the county border in Bedfordshire. Indeed, the pattern and development of the acquisition of Catesby's lands may well give us direct insight into his political motivations.[32]

Like everyone else's, Catesby's world was changed with the death of Edward IV. In his early forties, Catesby saw the main chance for advancement and took it. He was well acquainted with many of the individuals whose influence now came to the fore. Not only was he a trusted advisor to Lord Hastings, he had dealings with Henry Stafford, the Duke of Buckingham, who was taking the emerging opportunity to flex his political muscle. It is most probable that Catesby also knew and interacted with Francis, Lord Lovell, who was arguably the closest friend and advisor of Richard, Duke of Gloucester, having known the duke since childhood.

It was such connections that now brought Catesby to the fore in the tumultuous times of that summer. Ten days after Richard had accompanied his nephew Edward V into London, Catesby was appointed Chancellor of the Earldom of March on 14 May 1483 with an annual fee of forty pounds. This may have been the result of his association with Buckingham, since the earldom was put under the latter's control the next day, although Roskell attributes this appointment as Richard continuing to curry favour with Hastings by appointing one of his affinity to this advanced office.[33] The next day Catesby was made a Justice of the Peace for the first time in his home county of Northamptonshire. One gets the sense of the Protector dispensing offices and asking individuals who they would like their administrators to be. Clearly, an able individual and lawyer such as Catesby rose to the forefront here. In respect of the specific events of Friday 13 June 1483, again our most detailed account comes from More, and it is worth examining his observations on Catesby's actions around that time. They form the basis for what I shall refer to as the 'traditional' account of motivations and events and Catesby's role in them.

Catesby and the Tradition of Friday 13th

Sir Thomas More, from whom we derive our most detailed account of the critical meeting of the Council on Friday 13 June 1483, is rather complimentary in his initial observations on William Catesby. Whether this is in the nature of a professional courtesy of one lawyer to another or whether More's opinion is framed rather by the impressions of Morton we shall have to leave largely in abeyance at this point. What we can evaluate are More's specific words and phrases. With respect to Catesby he notes that:

> besides his excellent knowledge of the law (of this land) he was a man of
> dignified bearing, handsomely featured, and of excellent appearance, not only

suitable for carrying out assignments, but capable also of handling matters of grave consequence."[35]

In general, this would seem to be approval for Catesby's skills, capabilities and actions prior to the critical events of that Friday. I think it is fair to take this initial assessment as the general persuasion at that time of a talented, useful but also self-serving administrator. Catesby's record of appointments by various influential individuals very much seems to confirm that this was the collective opinion.

However, now we come to the events of that fateful Friday and Catesby's pivotal role in Hastings's demise. The traditional story has it that Catesby was considered to be almost exclusively of Hastings's affinity. However, as Roskell pointed out, Catebsy should not be considered solely as Hastings's servant, given his associations with other highly placed persons. The traditional version relies extensively on More's account, so let us first proceed on that basis. The circumstance of the split Council does not seem to have worried Hastings especially, because of his reported confidence in Catesby:

> Thus many things coming together, partly by chance, partly of purpose, caused at length not common people only, that wave with the wind, but wise men also, and some lords eke, to mark the matter and muse thereon; so far forth that the lord Stanley, that was after earl of Derby, wisely mistrusted it, and said unto the lord Hastings, that he much misliked these two several councils. 'For while we (quod he) talk of one matter in the tone place, little wot we whereof they talk in the tother place.' 'My lord, (quod the lord Hastings) on my life never doubt you. For while one man is there which is never thence, never can there be thing once minded that should sound amiss toward me, but it should be in mine ears ere it were well out of their mouths.' This meant he by Catesby, which was of his near secret counsel, and whom he very familiarly used, and in his most weighty matters put no man in so special trust, reckoning himself to no man so lief, sith he well wist there was no man to him so much beholden as was this Catesby; which was a man well-learned in the laws of this land, and by the special favor of the lord chamberlain, in good authority; and much rule bare in all the county of Leicester, where the lord chamberlain's power chiefly lay.

Having reported this, we now turn to More's surmise about the reasons for Catesby's actions. In respect of his approach to Hastings concerning his position on Richard's aspiration for the throne, More is characteristically ambiguous.[36] He reported that:

So surely thought he (Hastings) that there could be none harm toward him in that council intended where Catesby was. And of truth the protector and the duke of Buckingham made vert good semblance unto the lord Hastings, and kept him much in company. And undoubtedly the protector loved him well, and loath was to have lost him, saving for fear lest his life should have quailed their purpose. For which cause he moved Catesby to prove with some words cast out afar off, whether he could think it possible to win the lord Hastings into their party. But Catesby, whether he assayed him or assayed him not, reported unto them that he found him so fast, and heard him speak so terrible words, that he durst no further break. And of truth the lord chamberlain, of very trust, showed unto Catesby the mistrust that other began to have in the matter. And therefore he, fearing lest their motions might with the lord Hastings minish his credence, whereunto only all the matter leaned, procured the protector hastily to rid him. And much the rather, for that he trusted by his death to obtain much of the rule that the lord Hastings bare in his county; the only desire whereof was the allective that induced him to be partner and one special contriver of all this horrible treason.

Note that the way More approaches this issue is exactly the same way in which he later does in respect of the burial place of the princes. In this way, More describes a situation and its natural alternative, thus allowing him to cover the whole field of possibilities.[37] In the present case it is found in the phrase, 'But Catesby, whether he assayed him or assayed him not, reported unto them that he found him so fast, and heard him speak so terrible words, that he durst no further break.' The overall tenor of the comment is that Catesby did approach Hastings and that he received a negative response, which subsequently sealed Hastings' fate. What is not explained is: who identified and approached Catesby as the go-between if he did actually act as the conduit between Richard and Hastings in this case? Who was it who thought that Catesby would be the right individual, and what gave them the belief that he would carry this through in adherence to their own strategy and not continue to support the person who was supposedly his major patron? On this issue, More is silent. Further, when did this purported approach take place? If Hastings was happy to reassure Lord Stanley about Catesby's fidelity, he surely cannot have made this statement after Catesby's approach. However, where is the time for Catesby to approach Hastings privately if the timeline More identifies is correct? It suggests the morning of the 13th at the very latest, but there is precious little time to achieve this at all in any practical manner. It is one of the many problems of taking More at face value.

However, if we do take More at his word, in a strict sense Catesby acted only as a messenger in this matter.[38] Thus it is important to understand why some writers interpret his actions as 'betraying' Hastings. Roskell is in no doubt when he observes that 'Catesby climbed over the body of his patron [Hastings] into possession of certain of his posts.[39] It is, indeed, undeniable, as we shall see, that Catesby did accrue great benefit from the fall of Hastings. However, from this traditional account it is hard to see why. Were all of the rewards he received just for simply conveying a message? And, importantly, we must remember that if Richard charged him with trying to persuade Hastings to join with himself and others, Catesby's mission was essentially a failure. Given this 'failure,' it is more than puzzling then that the level of remuneration he was given for his 'service' was so great. Indeed, the vast rewards he did receive argue for a much greater level of service that he rendered to the then-Protector (*and see* Appendix VI).

Thus Hastings fell. More thought Catesby was motivated to assist with his execution, implying that Catesby believed he had lost Hastings' trust and favour. Of course, if 'he assayed him not', this whole motive is obviated. While it might be true that Catesby lost something of Hastings' confidence, it is hard to see this as the sole reason why Catesby should seek the complete removal of his patron. For surely Hastings would most probably have been replaced with another potential overlord, who might not have treated him with the same level of consideration. Thus, as will become evident, I believe there is something much more involved here than Catesby being just a mere messenger who had been chosen for the role of a conduit from Richard of Gloucester, with whom Catesby seems to have little to do, to Edward IV's boon companion William, Lord Hastings, his previous, strong sponsor.

'The Cat' and the Cream

The vast preponderance of evidence shows that William, Lord Hastings was executed on 13 June 1483.[40] I think therefore, the primary question which follows is – *cui bono?* In simple terms, who benefited most from Hastings' removal? More argued that Richard benefited most of all because the events of that day helped remove some of the primary supporters of Edward V who were not directly from the Woodville extended family. These individuals included Morton, Rotherham and Stanley. The three named were major players, it is true, but other individuals, whose story will also be considered in more detail later, were immediately affected by these actions and events at the Tower. Thus More interpreted Hastings' demise as a pivotal opportunity for, and therefore as representative of, Richard's manifest bid for the throne. This interpretation is, I believe, largely incorrect. However, as we are presently focusing on William Catesby, let us see what the immediate effect was on his personal circumstances.[41] In respect to the fall of Hastings, William Catesby did very well indeed. Shortly following Hastings' execution, he was made Chancellor of the Exchequer, Chamberlain of the Receipts and Constable of the Castle and Master Forester of Rockingham, as well as being named steward of certain Crown lands in Northamptonshire. Each of these were offices formerly held solely or primarily by Lord Hastings. As Roskell chose to put it, 'Catesby climbed over the body of his patron into possession of certain of his posts.' In addition to these vestiges of Hastings' preferments, Richard made Catesby Esquire of the Body and a full member of Council. It is thus very evident that Catesby benefited enormously, and, for a mere messenger, disproportionately from the death of his previous mentor,[42] especially when compared to almost anyone else involved in the actions which occurred on the morning of Friday 13 June. An important accounting of Catesby's various gains has recently been given in some detail.[43] In consequence, only brief synopses of those gains that he made during Richard's formal reign are given here (a fuller listing appears in Appendix VI).

As well as all the offices and preferments noted above, Catesby began to reap the benefits of his new-found authority virtually from the moment of his appointments by Richard and the recognition of his new authority by others. For example, one week following Hastings' execution, Catesby, along with others, was appointed as an overseer of the wardship and marriage of Edward, son and heir of John Stafford, late Earl of Wiltshire. As we have heard earlier concerning the wardship of William's own father, such a position could well prove very profitable to those so appointed.

My central thesis is that Catesby clearly profited the most from Hastings' removal. However, there are some indications that people had begun to recognise Catesby's ascending star even before the events of the 13th. For example, when Earl Rivers drew up his final will and testament at

Pontefract Castle in Yorkshire on the 24 June, he named Catesby as one of his five executors. As we have previously seen, it took approximately four days for messages to travel from London to York, and if the warrants for the executions of Rivers, Vaughan and Grey had come north with Ratcliffe, who left on the 11th, it is uncertain whether the news of Hastings' execution could have reached Rivers before his own demise.[44]

Catesby seemed also to profit from the immediate aftermath of the events at the Tower in other ways. A companion, and perhaps rival lawyer, under the patronage of Hastings was John Forster. I contend that he was a rival because I think Catesby manoeuvered to have him arrested in the general fall-out after the fateful Council meeting. Forster was apparently held in the Tower without food or water and was, under this compulsion, forced to sign over to Catesby his appointment as steward to the estates and manors of the Benedictine Abbey of St Albans, a post which he had held since June 1471, and apparently a position that Catesby coveted. If Forster thought such acquiescence was going to provide him with an overall amnesty he was wrong. In fact, he was detained at the Tower from 13 June 1483 until 10 March 1484. However, we can infer that by complying with Catesby's demand he was at least then provided food and water.

Forster was not the only individual in desperate straights with whom Catesby now exerted leverage. Sir Richard Haute, who was purportedly also executed alongside Rivers,[45] also drew up his will with Catesby as an executor. Catesby used his skills to bargain and cajole some of Sir Richard's lands in exchange for the manor of Welton in Northamptonshire, which is what he clearly wanted in the first place.[46] Catesby had to engage in some legal legerdemain in order to secure what he wanted, but it is evident that he succeeded.[47]

At the time of Richard's coronation in July 1483, the promise of a renewed stability and a more certain future must have seemed reasonably reassuring after the tumult of the early summer. The new king was relatively young, but already well tested in battle. Married with a young son, Richard's only viable rival was an ill-supported exile whose prospects for success were, at this juncture, considered remote at best. Although there were stirrings of discontent, Buckingham's revolt had yet to materialise and Richard began his formal progress around his new realm. Catesby had a formal role in the coronation itself, where he reportedly bore the mantle and cap of estate in the vigil procession.[48] The late summer of 1483 was a busy time for Catesby. He must have been working rather hard to come to terms with the responsibilities of the new offices he had secured. We might also reasonably assume that later in 1483 he would have also been working to prepare for the upcoming Parliament, which was scheduled to begin on 6 November of that year, only to be disrupted by Buckingham's rebellion and the associated unrest. He was, of course, subsequently the Speaker of Richard's only Parliament when it did convene from 23 January until 22 February 1484.[49] He was elected by the Members as the collective choice for Speaker and presented to the king on 26 January, with whom Richard 'was well content.' His appointment may well have been a done deal before Parliament even convened.

As well as his official duties, Catesby did not neglect to ensure the advancement of his own interests. Presumably, and wherever possible, he would have seen to it that the two coincided as much as was feasible. Indeed, as we know from his prior behaviour, he was an ambitious and acquisitive individual and his new appointments must have provided an expanded vista for realising his greater ambitions. For example, by early August he was serving as a Justice of the Peace for the contiguous counties of Gloucestershire, Warwickshire, Worcestershire, Northamptonshire and Leicestershire. It was, of course, no coincidence that his major land holdings were to be found in these respective counties. In late September and early October, Catesby was involved in further accumulations, as documented in the Harleian Manuscript 433,[50] and it was at this time that he gained part-control over the manor of Stanford in Northamptonshire as well as properties in nearby Oxfordshire. As I have tried to demonstrate, these acquisitions were not necessarily the random accumulations of a grasping member of the *nouveau riche*. Rather, they formed part of a systematic programme of acquisitions that looked to build a strong and contiguous region of influence. One could potentially make the argument that the holdings of both Hastings and subsequently Buckingham served to thwart this effort, at least until the time that they were each respectively executed. It is not beyond the realms of possibility that Catesby looked to engineer the downfall of both of these individuals in order to facilitate his longer-term plans. However, this speculation is based almost completely upon the spatial distribution of lands and, at present, I can find no original documentary evidence to support this proposition.

As a result of his role in various proceedings, we actually know quite a lot about Catesby's actions during Richard's reign. For example, we know that despite his earlier association with Buckingham, Catesby was very much a supporter of King Richard during the unrest of October and November 1483. As such, he reaped significant rewards which were derived from those found to be in rebellion. The lands that he obtained following the rebellion from Buckingham alone amounted to almost £300 in value, an enormous sum in those days.[51] He was also named to a number of commissions to look at the actions of various traitors which met at Exeter on 13 November 1483. Significant in light of later events, Catesby was granted an annuity of five marks for 'goodwill and counsel' on 17 December, given by none other than Thomas, Lord Stanley. This was the same man who less than two years later stood by and watched Catesby be executed, despite pleading for his life.

By this time, it must have been clear that Catesby was a major power in the land, and this elevation would have been even further reinforced by Catesby's pivotal role as the elected Speaker in the January Parliament.[52] For it was during this Parliament that a number of critical resolutions were enacted. The first was the resolution of the question of Richard's legitimacy. It was here that the reasons for Richard being rightful king were explicated. Following this a number of attainders were promulgated against those who had participated in Buckingham's rebellion. Further, Richard was granted the tonnage and poundage of the wool subsidies for life. This generous arrangement ensured the king an ample and continuing source of income. Although, unusually, Catesby did not himself benefit in a direct financial manner, his various accumulations continued. His in-laws granted him further manors in Northamptonshire, as did his control of the son of John Acton. However, it was the statements concerning Richard's claim to the throne in the *Titulus Regius* which are of particular interest.

It has been implied by a number of commentators that Robert Stillington must have had a large hand in the formulation of the legislation and writing of and declarations in the *Titulus Regius*. However, I think it is much more plausible and convincing that Catesby was the primary architect of this document. This proposition is based on two fundamental points. First, Catesby was a lawyer and the *Titulus Regius* was essentially a legal document. Second, as Speaker, Catesby would have had a direct hand in the processes and procedures of Parliament, not just its content. That is, he would have had a major role in passing any legislation as opposed to just framing it. Even if Stillington did participate in the document's creation, someone must have had a significant role in passing it through Parliament. Although I suspect there would not have been much in the way of direct objection, a Speaker who was also a lawyer must have had a critical say in what transpired. I am unaware of any evidence that Stillington himself attended this Parliament, but I think it is more than reasonable to assume that, as Speaker, Catesby must have certainly been present in person. It is in the *Titulus Regius* that we find the primary source of evidence that names Eleanor Butler, née Talbot, as the lady to whom Edward IV had pre-contracted himself. It is to this issue that I shall necessarily return at the end of this work.

The remainder of Richard's short reign is dotted with references to Catesby's prospering career and advancement. He was a member of numerous commissions and one of the four principal negotiators with respect to a peace treaty with Scotland, which also considered the potential marriage of the son of Scotland's James III with Richard's niece, Anne de la Pole. Written evidence of Richard's partiality to Catesby still exists and Figure 16 is an example illustration of that fact. Thus, it is clear that Catesby remained high in the esteem of his monarch, but the evidence which has cemented Catesby's reputation for favour by the king and, indeed, the one that has principally served to establish his name in history, derives from just one piece of doggerel, which was most certainly meant as a direct insult. It is the rhyme attributed to William Colyngbourne and it is to this evidence I now turn.

'The Cat, the Rat, and Lovell our dog'

Some time around 18 July 1484,[53] a rhyme attributed to William Colyngbourne[54] was pinned to the door of St Paul's Cathedral. It read:

> The Cat, the Rat, and Lovell our dog
> Rule all England under an Hog.[55]

The implication was direct and unequivocal. In simple terms it stated that Catesby, Ratcliffe and Lovell had the management of England under Richard, whose badge was the White Boar. I should like to treat this remarkable couplet in a little more than ordinary detail, since I think such a perusal will repay the effort. First, one must know that Colyngbourne was accused and convicted of being an agent of Henry Tudor and his subsequent execution was for this betrayal and not for supposedly authoring this couplet.[56] We are not dealing here with suppression of free speech. The primary accusation was that Colyngbourne had tried to second and bribe one Thomas Yate into taking a message to Henry Tudor, urging the latter to land and invade, as well as telling the exile that Richard was dealing in false faith with the authorities in France, where it was claimed Richard meant to invade himself. It was some months later at the Guildhall in early December that Colyngbourne's case was heard and here he was condemned to death.

Colyngbourne met the gruesome fate reserved for traitors in the late Middle Ages: he was hanged, drawn and quartered. Executed on Tower Hill, Fabyan reports that he was 'cut down, being alive and his bowels ripped out of his belly and cast into the fire there by him, and lived till the butcher put his hand into the bulk of his body, insomuch that he said at the same instant, "O Lord Jesus, yet more trouble," and so died.'[57] And although it seems fairly clear that Colyngbourne was finally condemned for his more serious seditious actions, it is his rhyme that lives in the historical memory. So let us look at this rhyme in a little more detail.

On the face of it, the rhyme was insulting, but it was more than that. Referring to the king as 'an hog' was certainly an injudicious thing to do in those times, but the attribution in relation to Richard's emblem is essentially correct. What I find of particular interest is the first line. If we take Colyngbourne's rhyme at face value and, in light also of observations made by Thomas More, we can argue that Catesby was the *primus inter pares* of the triumvirate of himself, Lovell and Ratcliffe.[58] It might not be overstating the case to suggest that he actually exerted the greatest level of day-to-day influence under the then-Protector and subsequently crowned monarch. Such a conclusion is buttressed by the bitter observation of the Croyland Chronicler who, concerning Catesby's own execution, stated:

> there was also taken prisoner William Catesby, who was preeminent along all the counselors of the late king, and whose head was cut off at Leicester, as a last reward for his excellent service.[59]

The conclusion that we seem justified in drawing is that Catesby had reached the position of first minister. Again, we have to recall that Catesby had been at best a minor figure upon the death of Edward IV some two-and-a-half years earlier, and in the interim he had risen to become arguably the second most important political figure in the realm, after the king. This can only have been under the direct sponsorship of Richard and, as Catesby was not one of his northern affiliation and most probably not a long-time friend or colleague, it argues strongly that he had performed a signal and perhaps unprecedented service to his king. As I have suggested, I think this concerned his revelation of the pre-contract and Hastings' prior knowledge of it through Catesby, and perhaps, of course through, Edward IV himself.

As we have here strayed quite far into the realm of speculation, perhaps one last observation can be forgiven. I think the first line is in some way also descriptive. As Reynard is the term often associated with a fox, so Lovell was a term so associated with a dog. It seems to imply that Lovell was in some ways Richard's 'lap dog.' Perhaps a similar relation was argued for Ratcliffe as having the attributes of a 'rat.' This would leave the first mentioned, Catesby, as possessing the character of a cat. Perhaps in these terms Catesby was seen as cunning and occasionally playing with people as cats are wont to play with mice. If these interpretations hold any degree of validity, the rhyme is not merely insulting on its surface, it is cunningly seditious against the leading cadre of the day, as indeed it would appear it was meant to be.[60] But Catesby's pre-eminence, even in this brief piece of doggerel, is suggestive of just how high he had climbed. If we have asked the question *cui bono*, who benefited most from the fall of Hastings, the name William Catesby must come out on the very top of that list. When looking for motivations for actions, the subsequent degree of advantage gained is a most telling clue.

Bosworth and Beyond

Throughout the short reign of Richard III, William Catesby did very well. Indeed, the epitome of his power was, if we are to believe the Croyland Chronicler, expressed most clearly in the matter of Richard's potential wedding with his niece, Elizabeth of York. Sadly, Richard had lost his son and legitimate heir, Edward Plantagenet, who died on 9 April 1484. To pile further tragedy on an already crippling loss, Richard's wife, Anne Neville, died on 16 March 1485. Despite Richard's personal grief, such circumstances must have inevitably brought into question the issue of succession. Croyland suggests that Richard considered marrying his own niece. It is worth reading this allegation in his own words:

Eventually the king's plan and his intention to marry Elizabeth, his close blood-relation, was related to some who were opposed to it and, after the council had been summoned, the king was compelled to make his excuses at length saying that such a thing had never entered his mind. There were some at that council who knew well enough that the contrary was true. Those who were most strongly against this marriage and whose wills the king scarcely ever dared to oppose were in fact Sir Richard Ratcliffe and William Catesby, squire of the body. These men told the king, to his face, that if he did not deny any such purpose and did not counter it by public declaration before the mayor and commonalty of the city of London, the northerners, in whom he placed the greatest trust, would all rise against him, charging him with causing the death of the queen, the daughter and one of the heirs of the earl of Warwick and through whom he had obtained his first honour, in order to complete his incestuous association with his near kinswoman, to the offence of God. In addition they brought in over a dozen doctors of theology who asserted that the Pope had no power of dispensation over that degree of consanguinity. It was thought by many that these men and others like them put so many obstacles in the way through fear that if the said Elizabeth attained the rank and dignity of queen it might be in her power, sometime, to avenge the death of her uncle, Earl Anthony and of her brother, Richard, upon those who had been the principal counselors in the affair. Shortly before Easter, therefore, the king took his stand in the great hall at St John's [The Hospital of St John of Jerusalem] in the presence of the mayor and the citizens of London and in a clear, loud voice carried out fully the advice to make a denial of this kind – as many people believed, more by the will of these counselors than by his own.[61]

This story is interesting for a number of reasons. For us here, it argues that Catesby had grown powerful indeed. If he and Ratcliffe were such that they were individuals 'whose wills the king scarcely ever dared to oppose' then the Northamptonshire lawyer had risen high indeed. The second dimension of this commentary implies that Ratcliffe and Catesby (among others) opposed the match because they feared that as queen, Elizabeth of York might seek revenge on them for the death of her relations. However, for Catesby, such a fear would surely have been largely groundless because at the time Elizabeth of York's uncle and step-brother were condemned, Catesby was yet to join the affinity of Richard III. It is true that Ratcliffe may have been concerned, and, as his relation, Catesby may have feared for him, but what I see here is something more like rumour elevated beyond its actuality. It seems somewhat unlikely that Richard would have sought to marry his niece and the rumour may have arisen as a result of the actions of Henry Tudor, who, in promising to marry Elizabeth himself, was trying to garner support within the realm. The political view would have had Richard's marriage to Elizabeth 'block' this manoeuvre by Tudor. However, it seems more probable that Richard never had such an intention and his eventual agreement to issue a public statement of denial to that effect may well have been urged by his advisors who saw him in jeopardy of losing vital popular support because of this gossip. It is apparent that the political rumour mill is not an invention of the modern media but rather an age-old human institution in which gossip is often purported to be fact; that Catesby and others advised Richard to deny this in public is not at all unlikely. Modern poitical campaign managers direct their candidates in a similar manner even today. If he did so, it does reinforce Catesby's power and position. However, we must be careful in giving credence to stories that so clearly are meant to disparage.

Several commentators have suggested that Catesby must have engendered a degree of envy and even hatred as he went on this meteoric rise to the very pinnacle of society, and indeed this jealousy might well have occurred independently of Catesby's apparently avaricious actions. The end for William Catesby came quickly and tragically, immediately following Richard's own fall on the battlefield at Bosworth. It is one of Shakespeare's most quoted lines, and is often incorrectly articulated as, 'The first thing we should do is kill all lawyers.'[62] Although Shakespeare used the line in a different context, we cannot help but think of the lawyer Catesby and his immediate dispatch upon the ascendancy of the throne by Henry VII as perhaps the original stimulus for this thought. What we know about the battle traditionally referred to as Bosworth Field is lamentably little,[63] although recent archeological efforts promise to provide us with greater insight. Apparently, the battle itself was of a relatively short, two-hour duration, especially in comparison with some of its peers like Towton. During this interval, the Duke of Norfolk lost his life, a number of other notables were killed and King Richard himself 'died manfully in the press of his enemies.' The preponderance of evidence places Catesby alongside Richard at Bosworth and we have a similar degree of certainty as to Catesby's capture following cessation of hostilities. We know that Catesby was a lawyer and, given his early training, it seems unlikely that he would have taken a significant part in the fighting itself. This begs the question of Catesby's role on the battlefield. To my knowledge, there is no specific evidence at all as to Catesby's activities on the 22 August 1485. We know that there were relatively few executions following the period of conflict.

The great exception was William Catesby. We know of his execution, which took place in Leicester three days following the battle on 25 August 1485.[64] We do possess his last will and testament which, because of its importance, I have reproduced here in full:

Thy sys the Wille of William Catesby esquyer made the XXV day of August the first yere of King Henry the VIIth tobo executed by my dere and Welbelovid wiff to whom I have ever be trewe of my body putting my sole trust in herr for the executione thereof for the welthe of my soule the which I am undowted she will execute: as for my body, whan she may, [it is] tobe buried in the churche of Saynt legger in Aisby [Ashby St Ledgers, Northamptonshire] and to do suche memorialles for me as I have appoynted by for. And to restore all londes that I have wrongfully purchasid and to pay the residue of suche lond as I have boughte truly and to deviene yt among herr childrene and myne as she thinkithe good after herr discrecione. I doute not the King wilbe good and gracious Lord to them, for he is callid a full gracious prince. And I never offended hym by my good and Free Will; for god I take my juge I have ever lovid hym. Item: that the executours of Nicholas Cowley have the lond agayn in Evertoft withoute they have their C.li. Iterm: in like wise Revellhis lond in Bukby. Item: in like wise that the coopartioners have their part in Rodynhalle in Suff. [sic] in we have right thereto or els tobe restored to themthat had yt befor. Item: in like wise the londes in Brownstone if the parte have right that hadd yt befor. And the londes besides Kembalone bye disposid for my soule and Evertons and so of all other londes that the parte hathe right Iue. Item: that all my Fader dettes and bequestes be executed and paid as to the hous of Catesby and other. Item: that my lady of Bukingham have C.li. to halp herr children and that she will se my lordes dettes paid and his will executed. And In especialle in suche lond as shold be amortesid to the hous of Plasshe. Item: my Lady of Shaftisbury XL marke. Item: that John Spenser have his LX li withe the olde money that I owe. Item: that Thomas Andrews have his XX Li. And that all other bequestes in my other will be executed as my especialle trust is in you masteres Magarete And I hertly cry you mercy if I have delid uncurtesly withe you. And ever prey you leve sole and all the dayes of your liff to do for my soule. And ther as I have, be executour I besech you se the Willes executed. And pray lorde [bishop of] Wynchester [Winchester] my lord [bishop] of Worcetour [Woucester] my lord [bishop] of London' to help you to execute this my will and they will do sume what for me. And that Richard Frebody may have his XX li. agayne and Badby X li. or the londes at Evertons and ye the X li. And I pray you in every place se cleiernese in my soule and pray fast and I shall for you and Ihu [Jesus] have mercy uponne my soule Amen.

My lordis Stanley, Strange and all that blod help and pray for my soule for ye have not for my body as I trusted in you. And if my issue reioyce [sic] my londes I pray you lete maister Johne Elton have the best benefice. And my lord lovell come to grace than that ye shew to hym that he pray for me. And uncle Johanne remembrer my soule as ye have done my body; and better. And I pray you se the Sadeler Hartlyngtone be paid in all other places.

There are numerous important points which arise from Catesby's last words. Some of these have been raised by Richardson,[65] who, in a similar vein to many commentators, writes:

The chief interest for this historian in Catesby's brief, last document lies first, in an apparently pointless plea to Henry Tudor ... And the opening sentence of in the ... final paragraph which reads 'My Lords, Stanley, Strange ... help and pray for my soul for ye have not for my body as I trusted in you.' Why did he trust in the Stanleys? ... And what possible reason could Catesby have had to expect decent treatment ... from a man as mean and vengeful as Henry Tudor?

We can, potentially, address these and other issues that arise from this fascinating document. For example, one of the lines that especially stands out in discussions concerns Catesby's 'abject' appeal to Henry VII, presumably to save his life. As with Richardson's perplexity, it has often been seen to reflect the grovelling of a very desperate man. Indeed, this is certainly a reasonable interpretation for, as we now know, Catesby was *in extremis*. However, there is another aspect to this appeal beyond the clear grovelling. As noted earlier, the mother of William's wife was the half-sister of Henry's mother. Thus, in this way, they might be considered fairly close family. It is doubtful that Catesby had ever met with Tudor, although it is reported that Catesby had been sent to Brittany in September 1484, possibly to secure Tudor as a captive. Thus the appeal was unlikely to be on a personal basis. However, it is most probably through his family connections that Catesby talks of having 'ever loved him' and by his good and free will having 'never offended him.' If we take this as more than the pleadings of a condemned man, then perhaps William's assertions are not quite as grovelling as they are often construed. In fact, they may represent indications that William Catesby was quite ready to transfer his adherence to Henry Tudor from Richard III as he had been from William, Lord Hastings to Richard in the first place. The appeal here may be more subtle than a number of commentators suspect. Perhaps this is in part the answer to Richardson's explicit question as to why Catesby hoped he might be treated by Henry Tudor with some leniency. As we know, he was wrong.

Richardson goes on to ask why Catesby expected help at the hands of the Stanleys, *pere et fils*, and why he should trust them. To this I think there are also substantive answers. Let us deal firstly with the trust placed in Lord Strange, the son of Lord Stanley. Three days before Catesby penned his last will and testament, he had stood with Richard facing the armies of Tudor and the Stanley forces. When Richard called upon Lord Stanley to join with him he received no positive response. Upon threatening to execute Lord Strange who was held by him as hostage, Stanley is supposed to have returned the ominous reply that he 'had more sons.' At this juncture, this would seem to state a definite intent and things must have looked very black for Lord Strange. Yet we know he survived the battle and perhaps we can now speculate as to why. It is my suggestion that Catesby, being a lawyer and probably no fighter, was put in charge of Strange. My expectation is that his orders were to execute Strange the moment that Stanley joined in the battle on Tudor's side. However, being in a prudent and legal way of thinking Catesby hedged his bets. I suspect that he held off this task and waited for the outcome of the battle. If Stanley did prove a traitor and Richard won, it would be short work to remove Strange's head as Richard returned to his camp. If however, Richard lost, the promise of leniency to Strange may have been seen by Catesby as a possible bargaining chip. Thus, he placed his trust in Lord Strange to the benefit of both father and son, but as we know this trust was misplaced, as Catesby bitterly lamented in the last paragraph of his will.

However, I think there is more. Not only was Catesby a benefactor to the Stanleys on that fateful day of 22 August 1485, I believe he was also instrumental in preserving Lord Stanley on 13 June 1483. From the accounts of the Council meeting, blows were apparently aimed at Stanley by those rushing into the council chamber and he sustained some hurt while sheltering under the table. I believe the preservation of his life was facilitated by Catesby in the immediate aftermath of the in-flow of guards into the chamber. I suspect that Catesby had some words with Richard to the effect that the primary concern was Hastings and that Stanley, although the possessor of suspicious motives, was not the principal target of concern that day. Indeed, we know that Stanley later made Catesby an annuity of five marks for 'goodwill and counsel' and granted him the manor of Kimbolton in Huntingdonshire on 17 December 1483. It was not the greatest of gifts possible but it seems to suggest some degree of concordance between these two individuals. I suspect that Catesby viewed Stanley to be in his debt for his action in 'saving' Lord Strange, but also for his previous actions some two years and two months before. I suspect this, but I cannot show it, that the reference to the unpaid gratitude due Catesby from Stanley then refers to his act of dissuading Richard from more severe action against Stanley that day in the Tower. Although I cannot prove it, the suspicion is there. The fact that later Henry VII had the brother of Lord Stanley, Sir William Stanley executed is of small consolation, and none for the scared and quickly beheaded Catesby.

So, as with the son, Catesby was also badly mistaken about the father, for the Stanleys were ever the ultimate betrayers. William Catesby was facing immediate execution but I think in his last hours he could not help but record his anger and bitterness against the Stanleys, a bitterness that still echoes across the centuries.

However, the central question still remains: why did Catesby have to die and why was he executed with such dispatch? As Payling cogently noted, Catesby was 'the only man of importance to suffer death among those captured in the battle.'[66] We must here understand why. After all, many individuals more directly involved with the actual fighting seemed to have incurred only minimal penalties. It has been argued that Catesby's acquisitiveness, which was evidently exhibited throughout the reign of Richard III, had made him many enemies who, in the aftermath of Bosworth, took their chance to get revenge. There may be an element of truth in this assertion. Catesby's relatively humble origins and his ascendency to great power must have caused considerably jealousy. However, was this sufficient to single him out? After all, he would be personally unknown to the likes of the Earl of Oxford, but especially Henry Tudor, who now held the reins of power. His demise suggests there was something more than just personal antipathy or individual jealousy involved here. His execution, conducted so quickly after the cessation of hostilities, is suggestive of a more important political expediency. In general, as Henry Tudor sought to establish his authority in his new realm, it would appear sensible to found his reign on the rule of law, especially as his hold on the throne was so tenuous. His action in declaring his reign as dating from the day before Bosworth was indeed a more than ambivalent one, setting a precedent Henry might well have regretted. However, in general his actions following the battle are those one might expect of a new king. There is perhaps a danger here of attributing to Henry Tudor those very characteristics that have been attributed to Richard and against which so many have argued. Given this, perhaps we might seek another reason for the untoward haste of William Catesby's death.

I believe the primary reason that he lost his head is because of what he knew. And what could he have known that would have threatened the new regime? It could only be something relevant to the succession and thus the hopes and stability of Henry VII, now only three shaky days into his reign. I believe it was Catesby's knowledge of the certainty of the pre-contract and thus the illegitimate status of Elizabeth of York that threatened so much. After all, Henry had promised to marry her in the hope of legitimising his own very tenuous claim to the throne. If she was illegitimate, even after the marriage there would be large numbers of individuals with better claim to the throne than Henry and his new wife. Later in this work, I shall look into what this might have meant to her brothers also. However, I think it was this certain knowledge and potentially some written proof of it that proved the death of William Catesby.

The Catesby Memorial

Following his execution in Leicester, the body of William Catesby was returned to Ashby St Ledgers and assumedly interred in a grave site, presumably somewhere adjacent to the high altar. Yet his memorial brass was not laid at that time.[67] Nine years later saw the death of his wife Margaret, but even then the memorial does not appear to have been finished. What we have today as the final version of this completed memorial brass is shown in Figure 17. The particular element showing William Catesby in detail is given in Figure 18.

Figure 18 shows a close-up of Catesby's head and in large part it is a stylised representation, but if we have to interpret, as presumably the artist did, then it looks like a rather sad and worn visage. Whether or not this representation looked anything like Catesby is now almost impossible to discern. What is much more interesting is the mutilation that has occurred and, as can be seen from the illustration, this takes the form of a posthumous 'beheading.' It remains a small source of contention as the actual process by which Catesby was executed. The traditional notion has it that he went under the axe or the sword. However, Kendall contends that he would have been hanged.[68] I think, however, it is best to rely more on Croyland who, as noted in a quotation previously given in this chapter, asserted that Catesby had his head cut off. And the vandalism to the brass image seems to confirm this in some small way.[69] It is suspected that the brass was laid after 1507 and presumably the damage was done some time after. There may be, of course, a much more prosaic explanation of this defacement, in that it simply represents the actions of some potential thief who, attracted by this wonderful memorial, sought to steal away a valuable piece of history. This may well be possible since the adjacent brass of William's father, Sir William is now sadly damaged and almost completely gone (*see* Figure 15).[70]

The full brass of William Catesby and his wife has been suggested to be a mixture of styles (*see* Figure 17). The main body seems to have been produced in a workshop known as London 'G.' However, the plate at the base of the memorial appears to have come from a much less accomplished set of artisans (*see* Figure 19).[71] The plate itself reads:

> Here lies William Catesby, Esquire, and his wife Margaret, the which William died 20th August, 1485, and the aforesaid Margaret died 8th October, 1494, on whose souls many God have mercy.

The two most interesting things about this plate are: first, the incorrect dating of William's death, and second, the shoddy nature of this plate compared with the rest of the memorial. Concerning the first issue, it has been suggested that the incorrect date is representative of the efforts of some later descendants of William and Margaret to hide the disgrace that came to their forebear following the Battle of Bosworth. This sort of effort was apparently not unprecedented.[72] The mutilation of Catesby's head was perhaps an intentional political statement, with the action itself taken some time during the Tudor period, perhaps during the process of the dissolution of the monasteries. That this may have been no random act of vandalism is founded on the fact that there are precedents for this posthumous disgrace of the individual in a process referred to as *damanatio memoriae*.[73] It is thus possible that this process of defacing the tombs of so-called traitors may have also included removal of the original name plate. If this were the case, the remaining family might have sought to replace the offending plate with something less provocative and more mundane in nature (*see* Figure 20). Perhaps this was undertaken by Sir Richard Catesby, William's grandson, or perhaps even a later generation of the family. It is likely that the plate was produced relatively locally since the fabrication is clearly inferior to the rest of the original (*see* Figure 19). Badham and Saul noted that:

> ... the inscription as a whole is a poor thing. It is set at an angle to the canopy, the lines are not square to the plate and the lettering is inconsistently formed. Moreover, the two references to William's wife Margaret have been added later where blanks were originally left; not the sort of omission likely to have been made while she lived.

It seems likely that the Tudor dynasty continued to treat William Catesby as shabbily after his execution, as the founder of that house, Henry Tudor, had in the first place. It is evident from his treatment of the body of Richard III that Henry Tudor had few qualms in this direction. It remains at present unknown whether Catesby ever did possess direct evidence of the pre-contract and whether the subsequent mutilation of his and his wife's memorial had anything to do with that possibility or whether the defacement was part of a more general expression of disapprobation. Regardless, the brass can be found today alongside the high altar in the church of Ashby St Ledgers, a mute witness to the earthly presence of William 'the Cat' Catesby.

A Concluding Summary

William Catesby's rise to power was nothing short of meteoric. From a solid foundation in the established gentry of middle England, he followed in the family tradition of law and, despite his father's Lancastrian affiliation and affection, the son had done reasonably well within his own sphere, but primarily advanced though an advantageous marriage. All this changed radically in early June 1483. In the immediate aftermath of the execution of William, Lord Hastings he rose to be among the highest in the land and, arguably, the first counsellor of Richard III. This was a staggering ascendancy to the very pinnacle of power, when such power was most jealously guarded by the nobility who possessed it. Indeed, Catesby remained high in Richard's favour throughout his reign. Why? What did Richard have to be grateful for? While it is true that someone of Catesby's capacities might have done well under Richard, he was not one of Richard's friends, nor one of Richard's northern followers or of their favoured affiliation. No, what Catesby did for Richard must have been unprecedented. My postulation is that his unprecedented act was to reveal the pre-contract and thus provide Richard with the legitimate path to the throne.[74] In the process, I think he manoeuvered to have Hastings eliminated because of Hastings' sin of omission. Thus Hastings knew of the impediment to the boys but did not reveal it. So Catesby was able to deflect criticism of himself while simultaneously removing the primary barrier to the increase of his conjoined land holdings in the Midlands of England. His plan seems to have worked brilliantly and his star rose accordingly. Indeed, on the day of his execution, Catesby was one of the largest landholders in the Midlands and arguably the whole country.

Catesby's unprecedented rise was matched by his equally dramatic fall. When the last King of England personally to fight in battle died that day in August 1485, Catesby did not have long to live. He played the meagre cards that remained to him, but neither affection nor affiliation was strong enough to save him. And no-one who put their trust in the Stanleys for too long ever prospered. But for him there was to be no disgrace and imprisonment with the hope for subsequent redemption. No, for Catesby it was the axe. And I think it had to be because he had knowledge and, indeed, perhaps even written documentation, that was just too dangerous to the new administration to be allowed to live. I think he could prove that Richard was legitimate and thus Elizabeth of York and her brothers were illegitimate. I think he had the pre-contract itself, or something representative of it. Henry Tudor was always sensitive to the issue and repressed the *Titulus Regius* after executing Catesby, its author. I think Henry Tudor feared what documents might appear and it took over a decade for Catesby's son George to convince the authorities that they now had nothing to fear from the remaining family members. George's mother, Margaret Zouch, died on 8 October 1494 and was laid alongside her husband near the high altar in Ashby St Ledgers. The reversal of the attainder was achieved in the next Parliament one year later, in October 1495.

I think this sequence is significant. Catesby himself was silenced in 1485, but there was still the fear of documentation (since lawyers through the ages have loved documents). The greatest fear was from the individual closest to Catesby, which was his wife, described by him as 'my dear and well beloved wife to whom I have ever been true ...' If anyone had access to such knowledge or such papers, surely it would be her. Yet after a decade, death silenced Margaret Catesby and the tension eased to the extent that her son could begin the formal process of rehabilitation, which occurred at the next feasible opportunity of the next Parliament. This is an hypothesis. I cannot prove it. However, it is a reasonable account that emerges from the facts as we presently know them. Catesby was indeed a lynchpin in the fall of William, Lord Hastings and may have sought to repeat the strategy in relation to Buckingham. However, he was a much more involved character than just the 'cat' of Colyngbourne's rhyme or the background, bit-part player of Shakespeare's fictional frippery.

4

William, Lord Hastings

killed not by those enemies he had always feared,
but by a friend whom he had never doubted.

The Life of Lord Hastings

In any situation in which we have someone subjected to a violent death,
we can learn something of the reasons for their demise from the character
of the individual themselves. In what follows, I do not try to provide an
exhaustive account of the life of William, Lord Hastings, much as a full
biography is still greatly needed. Rather, I shall try to provide information
that is most relevant to his death, since that is the issue that concerns us
most here.[1] However, we must frame Hastings within his times, and so a
brief account of his life is important to serve as a backdrop to the discussion
of the execution itself.

In many ways, the life story of William, Lord Hastings is not dissimilar to
that of William Catesby. Born around 1430, he was also the son of a Midlands
landowner, Sir Leonard Hastings, whose own forebear had been one-time
steward of Henry II.[2] William's father was of the affinity of Richard, Duke
of York,[3] and it would be this same family that William would serve all his
life. Indeed, William swore that he would serve the duke 'before all others,

and at all times, his allegiance to the King excepted.'[4] On his mother's side, William, Lord Hastings was the great-grandson of Edmund Mortimer, who was himself one of the sons of Edward III, whose longevity was identified earlier as one of the precursory factors to these later events. Thus Hastings was actually a second cousin to the sons of the Duke of York, the eldest of whom, Edward, he would serve as both friend and advisor during the latter's rise to power as Edward IV. Hastings himself had been attainted after his efforts on behalf of the losing Yorkist cause at the Battle of Ludford Bridge in 1459. However, he was with the son, Edward, and not the father, Richard, Duke of York, on the fateful December day in 1460 when both the duke and one of his younger sons (Edmund) lost their lives at the Battle of Wakefield. Hastings was subsequently very much part of Edward's drive for retribution for the killing of his father and brother, and served his younger companion loyally as the tides of fortune swayed between the two primary parties of the day.

When Edward came to the throne, it was for his loyalty and friendship that Hastings was rewarded with the post of Chamberlain of the Royal Household, a position he would hold throughout his lifetime. Also, in 1461 he was created Baron Hastings, and greatly benefitted from the lands forfeited by the losing Lancastrians.[5] Sometime before 6 February 1462[6] he had made a very advantageous marriage when he became the second husband of Katherine Neville, the sister of Richard Neville, more famous as 'Warwick the Kingmaker.' It was, if nothing else, a productive marriage, as they had four children and it appears that in the course of his life Hastings had something like eleven children in total.[7] Hastings was present when Edward IV was crowned on 4 March 1461[8] and again stood alongside his king at the influential Battle of Towton later in that same month, on Palm Sunday, the 29th. Such was Edward's recognition of his service in helping win this pivotal conflict and in other ways, that he knighted him on the field of battle. Over the years Hastings would become Edward's closest associate. The honours that followed in trail of the monarch began readily to accrue to Hastings. On 21 March 1462 he was made a Knight of the Garter and his stall plate can still be seen in St George's Chapel today (*see* Figure 21).

In the years between 1461 and 1469, Hastings acted on Edward's behalf in any number of official capacities and his role in negotiating both marriages and truces is well documented.[9] Indeed, it was over the question of marriage and marriage negotiations that the seeds of the later 1469 rebellion were sewn. One of Edward's great attributes, in addition to his prowess in battle and undoubted physical capabilities and charms, was his status as one of

Europe's most eligible bachelors. This card was a very potent political one and could be played to great advantage if managed appropriately. The man in the centre of this management process was Warwick the Kingmaker. He had been engaged in these respective manoeuvres and was in the process of preparing a suitable alliance when Edward casually announced at a 28 September Council meeting at Reading that he had secretly married Elizabeth Woodville some time earlier, actually on 1 May 1464.[10] Clearly this news dumbfounded many of his listeners and must have angered Warwick greatly. Not only was the secret nature of the marriage galling, but the lady herself clearly did not even come from the first rank of nobility in England. It must have been pivotal moment indeed when Warwick first heard this news, although he reconciled himself to it well enough to escort the new queen into the chapel of Reading Abbey for her first formal appearance at court. What perhaps angered Warwick even more, however, was that Elizabeth Woodville almost immediately set out to promote her own family. She looked to establish links with the upper nobility of the realm by marriage of her closest relations to the most eligible and advantageous matches. On occasion, these efforts produced highly mismatched individuals, which in the case of the heir to the Duke of Buckingham resulted in an enmity that festered over the coming years. Warwick began to harness this resentment and particularly the disaffectation of the king's own brother, George, Duke of Clarence, and eventually achieved the overthrow of the king by force of arms at the Battle of Edgecote Moor on 26 July 1469. Edward himself was not at the battle, but following the cessation of hostilities he was captured at Olney in Northamptonshire, parenthetically just six miles from Grafton Regis, the site of his wife's family home. He became a prisoner in his own kingdom. Eventually, after failing to rule in Edward's name, Warwick was forced to release the king, but the situation failed to improve and, eventually, warned by Hastings, Edward was obliged to flee to the Continent.[11]

Throughout all of this, Hastings remained ardently and unswervingly loyal to his friend and king. He had hitched his wagon to Edward's star and there was never any disloyalty. It was apparently Hastings who largely created the platform for Edward's return from exile and Hastings who worked to achieve a reconciliation between Edward and his brother, George.[12] Now began a sequence of sharp and decisive engagements in which Hastings played his part, although not always with distinction. On 14 April 1471 he commanded one wing of the king's army at the Battle of Barnet. It was here that Hastings' own brother-in-law, Warwick the

Kingmaker, was killed, most probably in error during the melée following the rout of the Lancastrian forces. Shortly after this, Hastings received from Edward licenses to crenellate a number of his houses, among which were Ashby[13] and Kirby Muxloe. This was evidently a mark of trust on behalf of his monarch, but also perhaps a reward for his efforts in the field at Barnet.[14] Hastings again stood alongside his king and his younger brother Richard, Duke of Gloucester at the decisive Battle of Tewkesbury, fought on 4 May 1471. It was the last full-scale battle in which Hastings would be involved.

In 1471 Hastings was made Governor of Calais, and in the immediate following years he treated with Louis XI and Charles VIII, to whom de Commines claimed to introduce him.[15] His governorship of Calais was a source of contention with the queen, who had looked to have the appointment for her brother, Earl Rivers. It was part of an ongoing dispute between Hastings and Rivers that would represent a potentially influential factor in the events of summer 1483.[16] Despite the antipathy of Queen Elizabeth Woodville, Hastings remained high in the king's favour.[17] Indeed, the queen had more than one reason to be unhappy with Hastings, because, as More reported, he was 'secretly familiar with the King in wanton company.' The later historian John Stow made this just a little more explicit when he observed this was 'wanton doings with light women.' As we shall see when we subsequently explore the character of Jane Shore, the sexual politics of Edward IV's reign seem especially prominent and influential.

The Master of the Mint

One of the more interesting appointments that came the way of William, Lord Hastings was the position of Master of the Mint.[18] This was one of his gains derived from the fall of the Lancastrian party; in this case Hastings replaced Sir Richard Tunstall in 1461. In 1464 he appears also as Engraver of the Mint and Keeper of the Exchanges of England, Calais and Ireland, the indenture being dated 13 August 1464.[19] Despite the titular appearance, the Mint and Exchanges were effectively managed by the deputy master, in this case Sir Hugh Brice,[20] Sheriff of London in 1475. It was a natural appointment since Brice had been the Prime Warden of the Worshipful Company of Goldsmiths on multiple occasions and Lord Mayor later in

1485. It was around the middle of the 1460s that a degree of devaluation occurred, as the Mint had trouble attracting gold in order to produce sufficient coinage. As he had a deputy master, so Hastings had a deputy engraver. In this case it was Sir Edmund Shaa, himself an alderman and goldsmith, who himself was Mayor of London in 1482.[21] Shaa held the post of deputy engraver for twenty-one years and was the brother of Friar Ralph Shaa, who preached at St Paul's Cross on 22 June 1483 using the theme of his address 'bastard slips shall not take root.' The sermon was one of the turning points in Richard's ascendency to the throne.[22]

Upon Edward's successful restitution in May 1471, his original Mint officials were also restored. We have two indentures, the first dated 23 February 1472 and the second dated 3 February 1477, setting out Hastings' conditions of mastership and remuneration. It looked very much like a position for life. But now we come to a small and presently unexplained incident. On 12 February 1483 Hastings was replaced as Master of the Mint by Bartholomew Reed. This indenture, for the first time in the fifteenth century, omits any reference to the Calais Mint. Why Hastings was deprived of this office is still difficult to ascertain. What we do know is that two months later he was fully restored to the mastership. Two months later was almost exactly the time when Edward IV died.[23] Whoever Reed was, perhaps a protégé of Hastings, he resurfaced later as a master-worker in the reign of Henry VII. It is certain that control and creation of the coin of the realm conferred great power and, although Hastings probably took little part in the actual manufacture, the fact that he was deprived of this control shortly before Edward's demise is a small mystery that may well lead to further insight into Hastings and his actions, if we can resolve it.

Edward's Last Days

In his last days, Edward seems to have been anxious to mediate between these contentious parties and sought to achieve some degree of reconciliation between Hastings and prominent members of the Woodville faction, particularly Earl Rivers. In this, Edward was at best only partially successful, as subsequent events show. On the death of his friend and mentor, Hastings was left in a very precarious position. Despite the naming of his old comrade in arms, Richard, Duke of Gloucester, as Protector, the early manoeuvres of the Woodvilles to cement their power began almost immediately after the king's death. In particular, Hastings expressed special concern over the size of the escort that Edward V proposed to bring with him from Ludlow. He was quoted as objecting in a 'passionate demand' whether the proposed army was intended to be used 'against the people of England, or against the *good* Duke of Gloucester' (emphasis mine). A compromise was reached only after Hastings threatened to decamp to Calais, an eventuality that it seemed the Woodville faction was anxious to avoid. An alternative hypothesis concerning his motivations and actions will be presented in the final chapters of this work. For now, let us briefly evaluate the existing accounts of Hastings' death.

The Death of Lord Hastings

So much depends upon the date of the execution of Lord Hastings that I have sought to make that issue a special Appendix (Appendix II), dealing with the evidence and the more recent controversy.[24] However, there is much less contention over the fact itself or the manner in which the execution occurred. Here I want to look at some of the contemporary and near-contemporary accounts, so let us start with Croyland and Mancini, whose respective accounts were written around this very time.

Most of the following accounts were as antagonistic to Richard as they were laudatory to Hastings. In particular, they praised his loyalty and fidelity to his former master, Edward IV, and his continuing allegiance to his son, Edward V. I think these observations were, at their heart, correct. For, if my hypothesis concerning the veridical nature of the pre-contract is true, then the act of preventing Richard from knowing of it was indeed one of loyalty to Edward IV and his son. Hastings, if he was actively and knowingly pursuing this course of hiding information, might well have understood it as one of continuing loyalty. However, as we shall see, what was loyalty to the father and son could certainly also be interpreted as betrayal of the brother and uncle in the person of Richard, Duke of Gloucester.

In terms of contemporary commentators, Croyland is characteristically succinct. He noted that, 'On 13 June, the sixth day of the week, when he came to the Council in the Tower, on the authority of the protector, Lord Hastings was beheaded.'[25] Mancini, by contrast, was much more discursive, but, again, as an outsider to events, he got several things wrong and for some others he provided only limited information or half-truths. Let us hear from him in his own words:

One day these three and several others came to the Tower about ten o'clock to salute the protector, as was their custom. When they had been admitted to the innermost quarters, the protector, as prearranged, cried out that an ambush had been prepared for him, and they had come with hidden arms, that they might be first to open the attack. Thereupon the soldiers who had been stationed their by their lord, rushed in with the duke of Buckingham, and cut down Hastings on the false pretext of treason; they arrested the others whose life, it was presumed, was spared out of respect for religion and holy orders. Thus fell Hastings, killed not by those enemies he had always feared, but by a friend whom he had never doubted.

Here, Mancini failed to mention the Council meeting, perhaps being confused by the occurrence of the other, separate meeting that day at Westminster under John Russell. He also seems similarly vague as to the issue of time, and this suggests that he was not in the local environs when these events took place. Similarly, his comments on the actual action appear to be vague and ill-informed compared to More, whom, we presume, had details of this meeting from an eye-witness. Perhaps the most telling line of Mancini's account is the last one. It is admittedly, just an opinion, and one most probably based largely on hearsay. But it is important again to note that, had Hastings been in fact plotting against Richard with Elizabeth Woodville, the Queen Dowager, why would he have been so surprised? Indeed, why, if Hastings had adopted this role traditionally attributed to him as a conspirator, why would Richard have been a friend that he would 'never doubt.' If a person is in a conspiracy against someone, he doubts them continually. Clearly here Mancini's observations do not accord with the received account of Hastings and his supposed motivations at this time.

The Great Chronicle of London provides an account that is a compromise between those given by More and Mancini. This account reads:

Upon the thirteenth day of June, he [Richard] appointed a Council to be held within the Tower to which he desired to attend, the Earl of Derby, the Lord Hastings with many others but most of such as he knew would favor his cause, and upon the same day dined the said Lord Hastings with him and after dinner rode behind him or behind the Duke of Buckingham unto the Tower, where when they with the other Lords were entered [in] to the Council chamber, and the season had come in such a matter as he had before purposed. Suddenly one made an outcry at the said Council chamber door

– Treason, Treason, and forthwith the usher opened the door and then pressed in such as before were appointed and straightway laid hand upon the Earl of derby and the Lord Hastings and incontinently without the process of any law or lawful examination, led the said Lord Hastings out onto the Green beside the Chapel, and there upon an end of a squared piece of timber without any long confession or other space of remembrance struck off his head. And thus was this noble man murdered for his trust and fidelity which he firmly bare unto his master, upon whose soul and all Christ Jesus have mercy, Amen.

This account provides us with some additional detail: the usher waiting to admit the strong-arm supporters is an interesting addition, as it gives us a little more insight into the whole process. Overall, there is nothing here that contradicts Croyland, and indeed it argues greater access to those with direct knowledge of the event compared to Mancini and his account. The event itself is also described by Fabyan, who reported:

And so daily keeping and holding the Lords in Council and feeling their minds, suddenly upon the 13th day of June, being within the Tower in the Council chamber, with diverse Lords with him, as the Duke of Buckingham, earl of derby, the Lord Hastings the Lord Chamberlain, with diverse others, an outcry by his assent of Treason was made in himself to the chamber door and there rushed in such persons as he before had appointed to execute his malicious purpose, the which incontinently set hand upon the forenamed Lord Chamberlain [Hastings] and other, in which stirring the Earl of Derby was hurt in the face and kept awhile under hold. Then by commandment of the said protector, the said Lord Chamberlain in all haste was led in the court or plain where the Chapel of the Tower stands, and there without judgment or long time of confession or repentance, upon an end of a long and great timber log, which there lay with others for the repeating of the aid Tower, caused his head to be smitten off, and for all he knew well that he would not assent to his wicked intent, whose body with the head was after carried unto Windsor and there buried by the tomb of King Edward.

Fabyan's account is probably derivative, but it again emphasises the main points of the sequence of events and provides us, along, with More, with the basic facts and actions which must be explained.

The Council Chamber

Up to the present point, I have tried to provide a summary of the various accounts of what happened at the Council meeting of 13 June. In the earlier chapter on Catesby we encountered More's extensive account of this event and here I have also summarised accounts from other 'contemporary' commentators. These can be used to distill a common consensus account of how Hastings lost his head. In general, the contemporary accounts do not differ in any greatly significant way. Rather, they show similar stories with the degree of detail reflecting the status of each commentator as either an eyewitness, an insider or an outsider to events. But now it is time to turn from what is recorded in written accounts to a more detailed consideration of exactly how this event happened in its geographical and spatial context. Our information here is less certain and, to a degree, we must look to constructive speculation.

We do not have detailed plans of the Tower of London in 1483. The earliest survey that we have is that by Haiward and Gascoyne in 1597.[26] However, the overwhelming likelihood is that the fateful Council meeting took place within the White Tower, which is the central Norman keep and is the most recognisable building within the Tower of London today (*see* front cover).

This was one of the first structures to be built by William the Conqueror and was erected on the site of some earlier Roman fortifications. As can be seen from the front cover of this book, the White Tower is not completely symmetrical in shape and also has a clear variation in the morphology of the individual towers at each corner, although three of the corner towers are basically similar. It is an extremely solid structure, having walls some 15ft at the base and 11ft wide at its upper levels. The critical point to note here is that the original wall configuration has varied little since it was first built and must have been substantively the same in 1483.

Even though the walls of the White Tower may have changed little, the flooring within it has most certainly been altered over the ages. It has been asserted that, in its original configuration, the White Tower had two main floors, together with the lower levels for storage and a dungeon. This number of floors has been increased to three. Fortunately, for our present purposes, these internal changes do not seem to have affected the location and configuration of what is purported to be the council chamber (*see also* Figures 22 and 23). This is because the council chamber is represented by authorities at the Tower as being the chamber immediately connected to the chapel of St John, which was built into the original configuration and has not changed across the intervening millennium in any meaningful manner (*see* curved extension of the White Tower on the front cover). The chapel itself stands on the nominal 'upper' floor of the White Tower in the south-east corner and is characterised by its curvilinear apse. By tradition, the council chamber was the large chamber that led off to the north of the chapel. I cannot show that this identification is true with anything like conclusive proof. However, this does appear to be the consensus identification of those who presently guard the Tower. Of course, even if this was established as an unequivocal identification of the chamber itself it does not necessarily mean that the 13 June meeting took place here. However, it is upon the basis of these two recognised assumptions that I wish to proceed.

There are multiple entrances to this larger chamber, which itself has recessed windows on its eastern side. There is also a garderobe within the east wall of the chamber, but the account we have is of the entry of many men into the chamber and this location is neither sufficient nor convenient for this purpose. In the north-east corner of the chamber is access to the main spiral staircase of the White Tower, and this is a possible location for the invading group, but it is rather an unlikely one if Richard had time to prepare, as the missing half-hour in the Council meeting suggests that he had. A more likely candidate is the chapel of St John itself (*see* door at far end of Figure 22). As can be see from Figure 22, there is a doorway between the chapel and the council chamber and the chapel is certainly capable of holding many individuals. However, entry from this end might have permitted some degree of escape down the staircase at the other end of the chamber and the single narrow door inhibits the passage of several armed men at one time. What I take to be the most likely course of events would use the doorways from the adjacent large chamber (*see* Figure 24).[27] These latter two chambers are connected by two doors, one to the north and one to the south (although only the south entrance is shown on Figure 24). In my view, it was through one or both of these doors that the armed men entered upon the given signal, with the cry of 'Treason.' The signal, as indicated in More, was probably some fist crashing on the table and even the usher, as the *Great Chronicle* tells us, appears to have been ready to facilitate entry.

The hastily made plan worked. The people inside the chamber were taken by relative surprise, and those coming in had very little doubt as to who were the intended targets. It seems possible that the armed party entering the chamber were of Buckingham's affiliation. Although Mancini suggests that Buckingham himself was leading them, this seems unlikely. The consensus is that Lord Stanley (the Earl of Derby) suffered some injury to the face and that a number of blows were aimed at him. One account has it that he dived under the table to avoid attack.[28] The two churchmen, Rotherham and Morton, were also taken, but the blow itself fell on Hastings. The origin of the idea of a conspiracy against Edward V's putative supporters may have come from the constitution of the group of individuals who were taken that day. Indeed, it is a reasonable inference. But if this is so, why was Hastings alone executed, while the others were imprisoned and shortly after largely excused for their actions?[29] One can argue that Hastings was the ringleader, but such a conspiracy between so powerful a group of individuals (and the traditional account also implicates the queen dowager), should surely have argued for much more even-handed and stiffer punishment, certainly for the likes of Stanley, who had neither the cloth nor his sex to protect him? In contrast to Hastings's quick execution, we find Stanley positively rising in Richard's young administration. Two weeks after the 13th he appeared as a 'trusted counselor' and with Buckingham witnessed Richard's delivery of the Great Seal to now-Chancellor John Russell, Bishop of Lincoln. At Richard's coronation on 6 July he carried the mace before the king and queen and was soon after appointed Constable of England for life. Does this sound like the treatment of a traitor involved in a conspiracy with the now-dispatched Hastings? Surely not. Indeed, it may have been sparing Stanley on 13 June that resulted in Richard's eventual demise. He had to have known that Stanley was the father-in-law of his only rival claimant after the princes had been barred by the pre-contract? In this sparing of Stanley, I see the hand of Catesby also. But I rather suspect that the so-called conspiracy is more in the minds of the subsequent commentators than in the minds of those present that day.

Given the Protector's state of mind, it would appear that Hastings was given little if any time for reconciliation or contemplation. Perhaps Hastings was taken to the chapel of St John? However, I think it is more likely he was escorted down the main stairs and out on to the green alongside St Peter ad Vincula. He may well have emerged from the north door of the White Tower adjacent to this area, which today contains a monument to Hastings and several others who lost their heads on Tower Green. The accounts virtually all agree as to immediacy and the extemporaneous nature of his actual beheading, each mentioning the use of convenient materials, especially the piece of timber designed for the repairs of the Tower. None of these observations foreshadow either long or extensive planning. Further, the treatment not only of Hastings's bodily remains but also that of his immediate family further provide insight into Richard's mind and his decision that day. It was the nicely written condemnation of Hastings that gave many their suspicion of prolonged planning, but I suggest that Catesby had a hand in this also.

The Hastings Chantry, St George's Chapel

We may be able to gauge Richard's subsequent response to his own precipitate action if we examine how he treated Hastings in death. Unlike the later, very shoddy treatment of his own body and his own estate by Henry Tudor, Richard treated Hastings and his family in a most generous manner. But why? Why, if the cry of 'treason' had been so vehement, was Hastings, now an evidently dispatched traitor, treated so well? We can see the remains of this generosity today in St George's chapel, Windsor Castle, where the Hastings Chantry stands next to the tomb of William's old friend and monarch, Edward IV.

Hastings' chantry chapel appears to have been in the process of construction during his lifetime and perhaps had been planned to be located in close proximity to where Edward expected to lie. Some building accounts appear to indicate that the final completion of some of its very fine decoration, were still being made in the 1490s. These decorations show a series of fifteenth-century panels depicting the scenes of the first Christian martyr, St Stephen. As is evident from its wonderful ceiling, the chapel is designed as 'an ornate cage of stone.'

A Summary and a Speculation

In the final analysis, as we look to understand Lord Hastings, we must here examine his relationship with the man who ordered his execution: Richard, Duke of Gloucester. The first thing to emphasise is that Hastings had served Richard's family virtually all his life and was evidently devoted to Edward

IV. This was a loyalty Richard and William both shared and neither broke faith with Edward at any time during his lifetime. They each shared exile with their monarch and similarly they shared his field of battle, and indeed Hastings and Richard fought alongside each other on multiple occasions and at particularly pivotal encounters. The two men must have known each other well and shared many hardships. Although they were colleagues in this sense, they were not of an age. At this time, Richard was thirty-one, while it is estimated that Hastings, at approximately fifty-three years old, was some twenty-two years his senior.

On Edward's death, we have some evidence that Hastings was actively seeking to help Richard. He acted to limit the size of Edward's retinue and apparently kept Richard apprised of developments as he prepared to come south. These do not sound like the actions of an antagonist. Indeed, these cordial conditions continued when Richard reached London. Largely, the talk of Hastings being part of a conspiracy of any sort is directly derived from *post hoc* interpretations of the events of the morning of Friday 13 June. Thus we need to expose these interpretations and their origins. As we have seen, virtually all the inside, contemporary chroniclers elaborated upon what happened and each appear to provide a fairly reasonable degree of concordance as to actual events. It is Mancini and later More who tried to address why this event happened. However, the prior chronicles each seem to agree that the consensus was that Hastings fell because of his loyalty to Edward IV and thereafter his son Edward V. But surely in this, his loyalty to Edward IV would have been applauded by Richard, who shared such loyalty, not represent a source of dispute?

What, then, we must ask, can be the possible circumstances in which Richard would fail to honour this loyalty? Perhaps the only situation we can envisage is that such loyalty coincided with a betrayal of Richard himself. The pre-contract bastardisation of Edward V and his brother and other siblings fulfills these conditions exactly. The traditional *post hoc* interpretation of why Hastings was executed then become complex. Mancini renders some general account but he provides no direct accusation of conspiracy. What he does confirm is that Richard and Hastings were actually friends. The specification of conspiracy comes from More, and More, as we understand, was heavily influenced by Morton, who had a strong vested interest in smearing Richard's reputation. I strongly suspect that the purported plot in association with the queen was an indirect result of the way More reported Morton's verbatim account of the conversation within the council chamber. The implication of the presence of a plot was then derived from an interpretation in respect of who was arrested and detained that day. The particular issue of Jane Shore will be examined in the following chapter.

The various strands can thus be disentangled to a degree. On the one hand, there is the issue of Hastings' loyalty to the Edwards, father and son. On the other hand, there are the supposed conspirators who range from the Queen Dowager to the former king's favourite mistress, to the accused clerics and the opportunistic Lord Stanley, later Earl of Derby. Why the latter (Lord Stanley) should be so loyal to Edward V when his loyalty throughout life seems to centre almost completely on himself, and on at least one recorded occasion excluded his own son, is rather difficult to comprehend. If we take Morton as his own man, and subsequent events seem very much to show this, then the supposed alliance being 'loyal' to Edward V begins to disintegrate. It is very possible there never was such a conspiratorial alliance in the first place but rather a group who erred on the side of conservatism as the dynamic events played out. Regardless, in the end we find in the words of More that even after the execution 'the Protector loved him (Hastings) well and was loath to lose him.'[31] Loath indeed, for Hastings' presence may well have tilted the balance at the Battle of Bosworth some two years later. My conclusion must be that the supposed conspiracy is actually an 'after the fact' proposition, created to account for the beheading and the detentions that followed this very dramatic meeting. That various strands of the Woodville effort to snatch power mixed with the sudden demise of Hastings is eminently understandable as both insiders and outsiders struggled to make sense of the day's events. However, I believe these accounts are largely wrong and lead us away from the main issue of why Richard of all people should put Hastings to death at that critical juncture.

5

Jane Shore,
Mistress of the King

For many he had, but her he loved.

Too Slight a Thing

Of all the individuals who played a part, either directly or indirectly, on that fateful day of 13 June 1483, perhaps none is harder to evaluate than Jane Shore.[1] Although she is known to the world through Shakespeare's plays and Thomas More's words, we know frustratingly little about her.[2] This confusion encompasses her name, and the historical personage we have come to know as Jane almost certainly began her life as Elizabeth Lambert, the daughter of a relatively wealthy London merchant.[3] The forename 'Jane' appears to have been given to her by a later playwright, Thomas Heywood, who, like Shakespeare, never let facts get in the way of a good story. Contemporary records refer to her only as Mistress Shore or Shore's wife.[4] Perhaps one major reason for this lack of information and confusion is precisely because she was a woman, and in More's words was, at that time, considered 'to[o] sleight a thing, to be written of and set among the remembraunces of great matters.' Although times have indeed changed, some commentators[5] have argued that Jane is one of the quintessential expressions of how women are represented as symbols rather than true characters in the melée of sex and politics in any age. As we shall see, Jane's continuing fame is founded largely upon this symbolism, and it is very hard to disengage Jane the historic individual from the Jane of poetry and tragic theatre, as well as more recently of feminist scholarship. Although the latter perspectives are certainly worthy studies, the purpose here is to find the Jane of history,[6] and to seek to understand her actions, motivations and effects in the month of June in the year of three kings.[7]

The Historical Jane

Any attempt to try to understand the historical figure of Jane Shore must centre on Thomas More's history of King Richard III. For it was here that Jane featured quite prominently in a story that Helgerson[8] opined was, 'a polemical history, a book intended to blacken the reputation of its principal subject.' As with the account of the Council meeting in the Tower, we must again look through the lens of More's text, always remembering that the shadow of Cardinal Morton ever hovers in the background. However, More's commentary on Jane may be a little more veridical because it seems that she was alive at the time More was writing. He may have even known her.[9] More painted a most interesting portrait and I have here quoted from him extensively, since he provides the major source of our knowledge:

Now then by & bi, as it wer for anger not for couetise, the p[ro]tector sent into the house of shores wife (for her husband dwelled not with her) & spoiled her of al that euer she had, aboue the value of .ii. or .iii. M. marks, & sent her body to prison. And when he had a while laide vnto her for the maner sake, that she went about to bewitch him, & that she was of counsel with the lord chamberlein to destroy him: in conclusion, when that no colour could fasten vpon these matters, then he layd heinously to her charge, & the thing that she her self could not deny, that al the world wist was true, & that natheles euery man laughed at to here it then so sodainly so highly taken, that she was nought of her body. And for thys cause (as a goodly continent prince clene & fautles of himself, sent oute of heauen into this vicious world for the amendment of mens maners) he caused the bishop of London to put her to open penance, going before the crosse in processionvpon a sonday with a taper in her hand. In which she went in countenance & pace demure so womanly, & albe it she were out of al array saue her kyrtle only: yet went

she so fair & louely, namelye while the wondering of the people caste acomly
rud in her chekes (of whiche she before had most misse) that her great shame
wan her much praise, among those that were more amourous of her body
then curious of her soule. And many good folke also that hated her liuing, &
glad wer to se sin corrected: yet pitied thei more her penance, then reioyced
therin, when thei considred that the protector p[ro]cured it, more of a corrupt
intent then ani vertuous affeccion.

This woman was born in Lodon, worshipfully frended, honestly brought
vp, & very wel maryed, sauing somewhat to sone, her husbande an honest
citezen, yonge & goodly & of good substance. But forasmuche as they were
coupled ere she wer wel ripe, she not very feruently loued, for whom she
neuer longed. Which was happely the thinge, that the more easily made her
encline vnto the kings appetite when he required her. Howbeit the respect
of his royaltie, the hope of gay apparel, ease, plesure & other wanton welth,
was hable soone to perse a softe tender hearte. But when the king had abused
her, anon her husband (as he was an honest man & one that could his good,
not presuming to touch a kinges concubine) left her vp to him al togither.
When the king died, the lord Chamberlen toke her. Which in the kinges
daise, albeit he was was sore ennamored vpon her, yet he forbare her, either
for reuerence, or for a certain frendly faithfulnes. Proper she was & faire:
nothing in her body that you would haue changed, but if you would haue
wished her somewhat higher. Thus say thei that knew her in her youthe.
Albeit some that now se her (for yet she liueth) deme her neuer to haue
ben wel visaged. Whose iugement semeth me somwhat like, as though men
should gesse the bewty of one longe before departed, by her scalpe taken out
of the charnel house: for now is she old lene, withered & dried vp, nothing
left but ryuilde skin & hard bone. An yet being euen such: whoso wel aduise
her visage, might gesse & deuise which partes how filled, wold make it a
faire face. Yet she delited not men so much in her bewty, as in her plesant
behauiour. For a proper wit had she, & could both rede wel & write, mery in
company, redy & quick of aunswer, neither mute nor ful of bable, sometime
taunting without displeasure not without disport.

The king would say that he had .iii. concubines, which in three diuers
properties diuersly exceled. One the meriest, an other the wiliest, the thirde
the holiest harlot in his realme, as one whom no man could get out of the
church lightly to any place, but it wer to his bed. The other two were somwhat
greter parsonages, & Natheles of their humilitie content to be nameles, & to
forbere the praise of those properties. But the meriest was this Shoris wife, in

whom the king therfore toke speciall pleasure. For many he had, but her he loued, whose fauour to saithe trouth (for sinne it wer to belie the deuil) she neuer abused to any mans hurt, but to many a mans comfort & relief: where the king toke displeasure, she wolud mitigate & appease his mind: where men were out of fauour, she wold bring them in his grace. For many that had highly offended, shee obtained pardon. Of great forfetures she gate men remission. And finally in many weighty sutes, she stode many men in gret stede, either for none, or very smal rewardes, & those rather gay then rich: either for that she was content with the dede selfe well done, or for that she delited to be suid vnto, & to show what she was able to do wyth the king, or for that wanton women and welthy be not alway couetouse. I doubt not some shal think this woman to sleight a thing, to be written of & set amonge the remembraunces of great matters: which thei shal specially think, that happely shal esteme her only by that thei now see her. But me semeth the chaunce so much the more worthy to be remembred, in how much she is now in the more beggerly condicion, vnfrended & worne out of acquantance, after good substance, after as gret fauour with the prince, after as gret sute & seking to with al those that those days had busynes to spede, as many other men were in their times, which be now famouse, only by the infamy of their il dedes. Her doinges were not much lesse, albeit thei be muche lesse remembered, because thei were not so euil. For men vse if they haue an euil turne, to write it in marble: & whoso doth vs a good tourne, we write it in duste which is not worst proued by her: for at this daye shee beggeth of many at this daye liuing, that at this day had begged if she had not bene.

In respect of his three concubines, it may well be merry Jane, wily Elizabeth and holy Eleanor. It is primarily on this story, but also the rare contemporary sources that mention Jane, that the present analysis is founded.

The Behaviour of Edward IV

One of the critical issues in the present thesis concerns the consistency and motivations of the individuals involved, and we must consider in detail the actions of one of the prime movers of events: Edward IV. In particular, we need here to examine Edward IV's behaviour in relation to women,[10] and one of the first we know about is Eleanor Butler. The pre-contract between Edward and Eleanor seems to have been almost completely driven by Edward's sexual desire.[11] This form of motivation again appears directly to underlie a subsequent major event upon which, of course, we have much more information. That is, we know that in September 1464 Edward IV announced he had married Elizabeth Grey in a secret ceremony.[12] At this secret ceremony had been a priest, Elizabeth's mother Jacquetta, Duchess of Bedford and two gentlewomen.[13] There may also have been a boy member of the choir to help the priest with the ceremony. A sign formerly outside the church in Grafton Regis (*see* Figure 12) implied that the marriage had occurred within the confines of the parish, but not necessarily within the church itself (although this sign has itself now been removed). It is not the fact of this marriage itself which is under immediate discussion, since detailed records are to hand.[14] Rather, it is the nature and character of the marriage and the way in which Edward IV approached and used women that is of present concern. One suspects that Edward's apparently lusty appetites would have certainly been expressed among the less gentle females of the day, and this characteristic is observed by a number of contemporary or near-contemporary commentators, including de Commines, More and Croyland. For example, in Mancini we read: 'He was licentious in the extreme: moreover it was said that he had been most insolent to numerous women after he had seduced them, for, as soon as he grew weary of dalliance, he gave up the ladies much against their will to other courtiers …' In respect of these liaisons with ladies from the upper classes, Edward seems to have had a penchant for married women, especially those in a degree of distress. Of those that we know he seduced and bedded, all were either married or recently widowed. The list includes Eleanor (Talbot) Butler, Elizabeth (Woodville) Grey, Elizabeth (Wayte) Lucy[15] and Elizabeth 'Jane' (Lambert) Shore. We have some evidence, for example, that Edward had numerous children out of wedlock, including some attributed to Elizabeth Lucy.[16]

His preference for married women of the upper classes may have been based upon a natural reticence to seduce unmarried females and be thus involved with the attendant complications. However, this is speculation based upon our state of understanding, not necessarily on Edward's actual propensity. The primary concern here surrounds Jane. All of the others I have noted were of high or noble birth, and it says much for Edward's attachment that Jane is arguably the most persistent[17] and perhaps the most loved of the women in his life, for, as More noted, '… the merriest was this Shore's wife, in whom the king therefore took special pleasure. For many he had, but her he loved.' More was also complimentary about Jane in general, noting her kindness and her influence over the king when he was out of temper. We get the impression of a companionable and calming presence; in fact, More leaves us with a very positive picture of the woman who was the mistress of the king. Despite his philandering and his high living, it must have been a tremendous blow to Jane when Edward died. It was then that she was caught up in the turmoil of the summer of 1483.

The Pertinence of Penance

Much as Jane is an interesting character in and of her own right, and much as she is worthy of study in the context of her life and times,[18] there is only one focal issue with which I am concerned here, and it centres around her role and influence in respect of the Council meeting of 13 June. In this respect, we can say that Jane suffered in the fall-out of the events of that day. Popular legend has it that Jane was originally 'spotted' by William, Lord Hastings, and came to the attention of the king through him. Assumedly, Jane was a beautiful woman, although her charms encompassed more than her physical appearance (*see* Figure 26). To what degree Hastings was initially attached to and involved with her we cannot at present say with any certainty. However, after Edward's death it does appear that he assumed the protection, and presumably the favours, of 'Shore's wife.'[19] It was her association and involvement with Hastings that appeared to have fired Richard's wrath, and she was accused of plotting with the Lord Chamberlain (Hastings) against the then-Protector.

The story that Jane Shore and William, Lord Hastings plotted together with the queen appears to me to be most implausible. *The Dictionary of National Biography* observed that, 'Mr Gairdner's theory that she was employed as a go-between by Hastings and the queen is very reasonable.' I would suggest exactly the opposite. The queen and Hastings had a degree of recorded antipathy, especially in light of his rivalry with her sons and brothers, and had indeed lately argued about the size of Edward V's escort coming to London. That the queen consorted with her husband's favourite mistress is perhaps vaguely possible, since each may have retained a strong loyalty to the dead king. However, this seems extremely unlikely, and with Hastings' involvement, totally implausible. Indeed, when we look further into Gairdner's opinion, we find the following: 'We probably do not know, after all, the whole extent of the accusation against either the Queen of her [Jane]; and the fact that they were accused of acting in concert seems in itself to imply a better understanding than we should naturally expect between the widow and the mistress of King Edward.'[20] Perhaps here we can conclude with Thomas More that, 'For well they wist, that the queen was too wise to go about any such folly [i.e., enter into a conspiracy]. And also if she would, yet would she of all folk least make Shore's wife of counsel, whom of all women she most hated, as that concubine whom the king her husband had most loved'. Here again we see an example of Sir Thomas More implying two radically, indeed diametrically opposed, views at two differing parts of his narrative. I am here suggesting that the Woodville intrigues with Hastings' omission to tell his legitimate sovereign the truth about his nephews' status have here been inappropriately mixed together, and most probably intentionally so. I here sense the mind of Morton. To further understand the nuances of Jane's story, we need to consider her treatment in light of Richard's overall behaviour, and especially that toward women.

Sir Thomas More viewed Richard's treatment of Jane Shore as harsh and he painted the scene with sufficient pathos such that novelists, artists and playwrights throughout the centuries since have adopted the 'poor Jane' motif in both art and literature. She was portrayed as the friendless fallen female, who nevertheless was heroic in the face of public shame and adversity. Nowhere is this expression more richly illustrated than in William Blake's depiction of her penance. But is this characterisation correct?

If we examine Richard's general behaviour toward women, we find in a series of cases which can be documented, that Richard was very forgiving and generous toward them.[21] For example, following the execution of Lord Hastings, one might suspect that his wife and family would forfeit everything to the Crown, as was common practice. However, this is not so. Richard was generous not only to the memory of Hastings, as we have seen embodied in his chantry chapel at St George's, Windsor, but he was equally kind to his living family also. Richard was similarly generous to a number of women who for various reasons had either fallen foul of authority or had fallen on hard times. Why then this treatment of Jane?[22]

First and foremost, it is important to note the celerity with which her penance was imposed. To establish this, we have to appeal to the letter of Simon Stallworth of 21 June, and some inferences that may be tentatively drawn from it (and *see* Appendix I). In the letter, Stallworth said that Jane was already in prison.[23] As we know, Jane's downfall is associated with Hastings' execution on Friday 13 June. More noted that Richard, 'caused the bishop of London to put her to open penance, going before the crosse in procession vpon a sonday with a taper in her hand.' The only Sunday between Friday 13 June and Saturday 21 June (the date of the Stallworth letter) was Sunday 15 June. If the assumption holds correct that Jane did penance before entering prison, this sequence implies that she was caught up very shortly after Hastings' death and perhaps even on the very same day as part of the more general purge.[24]

It is clear that her goods were despoiled and, with this timetable, quickly condemned. For me, this argues that Jane had a very close association with Hastings and was viewed as sharing very heavily in his guilt. She was, of course, according to More, directly accused by the Protector himself. However, if Jane had truly plotted the death of Richard, the mere administration of penance and subsequent imprisonment seems to be a somewhat disproportionately small penalty for such a crime. According to More, Richard accused Jane, that alongside of Hastings, she was 'of counsel with the lord chamberlein to destroy him.' Hastings' penalty for this action was death and, presumably, Rivers, Grey and Vaughan suffered the same fate for the same aspiration, albeit as a part of a separate plot. Although Jane lost her property and was forced to walk in penance, her life was spared. What had she done to raise Richard's ire to such a degree and what happened to her after the famous walk with a taper?

My suggestion here has been, and remains, that Richard was aware of two, largely separate threats to his continued existence. That of the Woodvilles he knew about in part because of Hastings' earlier communications. Hastings was guilty of the sin of omission I have referred to earlier, essentially threatening Richard of the deprivation of his rightful position. I hypothesise here that Jane's assumed guilt was one of association. That is, she had been Edward's favourite and perhaps privy to some knowledge of his early contract with Eleanor Talbot. Although this is speculation, it would, as we have seen, certainly accord with Edward's general behaviour with respect to all other married women, and, of course, we have a record of him seducing Jane herself. If not through Edward then most probably through Hastings, she had known, or Richard had been told she had known, of the pre-contract. Although we can well imagine that Richard must have been somewhat unhappy with Mistress Shore and her role and influence in the life of his beloved brother, we cannot, as Thomas More endeavours to do,[25] cast Richard in the role of sanctimonious puritan, since he also had children and assumedly a relationship beyond wedlock. Portraying Richard as morally disapproving was another way to inflict a slur upon the now dead king. Jane Shore did penance not for her station in life but for her complicit knowledge. However, like the flaming passion of transient anger that induced Richard to execute Hastings, his similar disapprobation with Jane passed relatively quickly and she found herself in prison but not on the gallows. In fact, it is from prison that we next hear of her.

Jane's Tragic End?

Jane's phenomenal capacity to attract men of influence and stature was not bound by the happy confines of a court or elegant surroundings. Our next insight into Jane is provided by a letter of Richard himself to his Chancellor, John Russell, Bishop of Lincoln. It reads:

> By the King. Right reverend father in God etc. Signifying unto you, that it is showed unto us, that our servant and solicitor, Thomas Lynom, marvelously blinded and abused with that late wife of William Shore, now being in Ludgate by our commandment, hath made a contract of matrimony with her, as it is said, and intendeth, to our full great marvel, to proceed to effect the same. We for many causes, would be very sorry that he should be so disposed. Pray you therefore to send for him, and in that ye goodly may exhort and stir him to the contrary. And, if ye find him utterly set for to marry her, and none otherwise would be advertised, then, if it may stand within the law of the church, we be content, the time of the marriage being deferred to our coming next to London, that upon sufficient surety being found for her good a-bearing, ye do send for her keeper, and discharge him of our said commandment by warrant of these; committing her to the rule and guiding of her father, or any other, by your discretion in the mean season.
>
> To the right Reverend father in God etc. The Bishop of Lincoln our chancellor[26]

This letter, most probably written in later 1483, refers to Jane still within the confines of Ludgate prison and having had sufficient influence over the Solicitor-General, Thomas Lynom, to induce from or submit to a proposal of marriage. Richard very much wondered at this development, but he did not oppose it, 'if ye find him utterly set for to marry her ...' There were many potential implications of this letter. First, we might well assume that

Lynom had visited Jane in his official capacity and, unless he was totally dazzled be her in a single flash of 'love at first sight,' we might well assume that he has visited on multiple occasions; again, presumably between June and possibly October 1483. What was the initial purpose of such a visit or visits? Assuredly, this must have been in connection with the events at the Tower. Perhaps Richard was exploring the degree of her involvement with Hastings, or indeed any other plotters, if we are to follow the traditional notion of a conspiracy. Clearly, by this time, he must have largely absolved her of any malfeasance, since he stated that she may be released from prison by 'committing her to the rule and guiding of her father, or any other, by your discretion in the mean season.' In essence, Jane had been punished enough and could be released on parole if a sufficiently responsible individual will take charge of her.

Note also that this letter serves to provide reference to Jane's current state. Richard sought assurance from his Chancellor that any potential religious barriers to the match were not insurmountable, stating that, 'then, if it may stand within the law of the church, we be content, the time of the marriage being deferred to our coming next to London.' This confirms that Jane was now divorced and free to marry. After all, the person proposing to her was essentially the highest practicing legal official in the country. Surely Thomas Lynom would not have proposed marriage if any legal barrier remained? Richard also imposed a de facto cooling-off period. He dictated that the marriage be deferred until he was in London. Exactly why this was so is not clear. It may have been that he meant actually to attend the wedding if it had gone forward. To the best of our knowledge, the cooling-off period did not seem to have worked, as it appears Richard suspected it would not. Our information comes directly from the evidence of the will of Jane Shore's father.[27] This will was dated 24 September 1487 and contains the following quote:

> Also I bequeath to Thomas Lyneham gentilman xxs. To Elizabeth Lyneham my daughter a bed of arras with the velour tester and cortaynes [and] a stayned cloth of mary magdalen and Martha. Also I bequeath to Julyan Lyneham xls.

From this we may assume that the marriage occurred and that John Lambert was happier with his second son-in-law than his first by showing his appropriate testamental concern for his wife and their son and his grandson. Assumedly, this also meant some degree of gratification for Jane (Elizabeth) herself, who now had the son that she desired. Given her family connections with many rich relatives and the fact that Thomas Lynom seems to have done well, even after the death of Richard III, it seems hard to square More's account of the impoverished and bereft Jane of legend with that which seems to have been the implication of reality. It is not the first time upon which we have occasion to doubt More's veracity. Of course, the picture of women sinking from the highest ranks of the land into the lowest form of poverty, seems to be a much more attractive literary figure.[28]

There is an appealing but wholly misleading story that the London area of Shoreditch was named after poor Jane, who was supposedly found dead in a ditch in the area. The story is untrue. However, what was reported by More is that late in her life she had fallen very low from the exalted heights of Edward IV's company. Poignantly, More noted that, 'how much she is now in the more beggarly condition, friendless and worn out of acquaintance.' More decries this state, pointing out how much many influential people owed to her past kindness. However, if she was as he portrayed her, then she was a relatively unwelcome memory of a now past and disfavoured age. We get the impression of someone beggared by circumstances and neglected by those who should very much have reason to be grateful. It is the epitome of tragedy and it is in that light that Jane has been portrayed throughout the ages. But was this really her fate?

We know that Jane had three brothers and we can, to a degree, be sure that the individual shown in Figure 27 is a memorial brass of Jane (it is in the church of Hinxworth in Hertfordshire; for greater detail *see also* Figure 25).[29] This shows Jane, one of her brothers, John, and her daughter, but the full brass actually features Jane's father, John Lambert, and his wife, Amy, and the attributed date of creation is 1487. Thus, this might well show Jane in a happier state, especially if the brass had been commissioned earlier. Whatever the truth of her later poverty, Jane seems to have lived to a very old age for that time. We cannot say precisely how old she was, but, if, as has been speculated, she was born around 1450 or perhaps even as early as 1445,[30] then by the time of her death, again estimated to have occurred in 1527,[31] Jane could have been as old as eighty-two. At that age, she would have been living history. Indeed, her mere persistence to that age seems to argue against a life of the most abject poverty. It has also been suggested that Jane actually strewed flowers at the funeral of Henry VII in 1509. We know that she was a resident of London, at least for most of her lifetime, and had she been present as one of the populace in the streets this legend might well be true.

Her form of penance always carried the subtext of sexual infidelity or more general harlotry.[32] However, the confiscation of her property, the very public nature of the humiliation she was forced to endure and particularly the way these punishments seemed to follow very quickly after Hastings' fall of 13 June seem to argue for something very much more involved than simple sexual disapprobation on Richard's behalf. Indeed, his own explicit accusation and contemporary observations by Simon Stallworth confirm as much. Although most probably not present at the Tower of London that morning, Jane remains a pivotal player in Hastings' demise, and a very intriguing one at that, mostly due to the dearth of accurate information about her.

6

Robert Stillington, Bishop of Bath & Wells

a man of rather mediocre talents

An Introduction to the Bishop

In respect to the events surrounding the assumption of the throne by Richard, Duke of Gloucester, I, like others, have argued here that the fulcrum upon which the balance of judgment turns is the legitimacy of his claim to the crown of England. The document which argues for the legitimacy of this claim is the *Titulus Regius*.[1] It named Edward IV's pre-contract with Eleanor Butler as perhaps the primary reason[2] for the illegitimacy and thus the disinheritance of Edward's two sons, Edward V and Richard, Duke of York. By the time this pre-contract came to be at the centre of events in the summer of 1483, the two youngest of the three people involved in the pre-contract ceremony were already dead. It was of course the death of Edward IV himself on the 9 April of that year which had precipitated events.[3] The lady in question, Eleanor Butler, had died some fifteen years earlier, on 30 June 1468.[4] Thus, the only known witness to such events still alive at this critical juncture was the officiating priest, by then Bishop of Bath & Wells, Robert Stillington (*see* Figure 28).[5] Following the precedent of others, a brief assessment of his life, career[6] and subsequent actions in relation to the pre-contract is presented in this chapter to endeavour to understand his role in the making of Richard of Gloucester's critical decision.[7]

The Life of Robert Stillington

Robert Stillington has been treated rather dismissively by some modern historians. Kendall, for example, characterised him up as 'a man of rather mediocre talents not remarkable for strength of character.'[8] Given his most probable, relatively humble beginnings, his survival and periodic prosperity through the reigns of several sometimes antagonistic monarchs and his crucial role in the key events of the lives of some of those kings, Kendall's assessment might be viewed as somewhat harsh. Tentatively identified as a Yorkshireman,[9] we do not have the exact date of Robert Stillington's birth, which lacuna might support the contention that his origins were less than marked.[10] However, we do know that he graduated from the University of Oxford as a Doctor of Civil and Canon Law in 1442,[11] where he is supposed, perhaps erroneously, to have been a Fellow of All Souls' College.[12] It is most probable, although not certain, that he was over the age of twenty at that time,[13] and knowing that Stillington died in 1491 this would suggest that he lived to be at least seventy years old.[14] As we shall see, at the time of the pre-contract, around 1461, when Edward IV was only nineteen and Eleanor Butler a little older at approximately twenty-five, Robert Stillington, at just over forty, was not a young man, particularly by the standards of the day.

When involved in the disgrace and execution of George, Duke of Clarence in 1478, he was, assumedly, over fifty-six years of age and then, in 1483, as Richard III ascended the throne, Stillington at over sixty years of age must have been considered an elder statesman; all this at a time when average life expectancy was below the age of forty. Even adjusting for the fact that life expectancy figures were skewed by high infant mortality,[15] Robert Stillington was, at the critical points of his life, essentially an old man immersed in younger men's actions. Nor at the crucial time, in the summer of 1483, can he have been in the best of health, since we have evidence of earlier bouts of illness suggested by, for example, his inability to attend the opening of parliament in 1472.[16] Despite these respective advancements and adversities in his life, Stillington survived under six kings and served in an official capacity under at least four of these, receiving some degree of preferment from each. On the darker side, he was imprisoned by Edward

IV and suffered disgrace twice under Henry VII. The latter imprisonment suffered under the first of the Tudors should not be unexpected given the reported events surrounding Richard III's ascension to the throne. However, it is not Stillington's life *per se* which is of dominant interest here, but rather it is the insights that such a biographical survey permits into his critical actions in respect of the life of Richard III. With this overarching goal in mind, let us proceed to an abbreviated summary of the bishop's accomplishments.

Many of the specific details of his preferments and his appointments and grants can be found in modern sources[18] and I have drawn on these reports concerning his official appointments. Until 1461, Stillington primarily held ecclesiastical positions, the first of which appears to have been the post of Principal at Deep Hall in 1442. He had collected a number of such appointments, as, for example, when he became a canon of Wells Cathedral on 2 August 1445, which was followed on by his promotion to Cathedral Chancellor on 6 June 1447. Such appointments suggest an ambitious and able individual, especially in light of Stillington's suspected humble beginnings. Although from a landed family, he did not have the advantage of royal or noble birth and hence his early success must be attributed more to character than to connections.[19] This record of early achievement, such as his appointment as Archdeacon of Taunton on 20 April 1450, runs counter to Kendall's assessment of Stillington as a man of simply mediocre talents.[20] However, Kendall is talking largely of his achievements as an older individual and, on the much larger national stage which he later graced. Kendall does admit, however, that Henry VI was reputed to have said of Stillington that he possessed 'great cunning, virtues, and priestly demeaning.'[21]

Stillington's first obvious step toward wider pre-eminence was with his 1 November 1461 appointment by Edward IV as Keeper of the Privy Seal. From this start, he began to see diplomatic duty as an ambassador dealing with both Scottish and Continental concerns. We can presume that he accomplished such tasks satisfactorily, since the Calendar of Patent Rolls informs us that on the 20 January 1466 he was granted the custody of the temporalities of the Bishopric of Bath & Wells, later ascended to the vacant See itself, succeeding the late John Phreas (Free) as bishop.[22] His consecration by George Neville, Archbishop of York and the brother of 'Warwick the Kingmaker,' took place on 10 March in Westminster Abbey. This religious elevation was augmented some short time later on the 20 June 1467,[23] when Edward appointed him Chancellor of England, to succeed the same George Neville, who, as Warwick's brother, was dismissed following his involvement in the turbulence between the king and the Kingmaker.[24] Not unexpectedly, as a Yorkist adherent, Stillington's star declined with the readeption of Henry VI,[25] but rose again with Edward IV's return to the throne in 1471, when Stillington resumed his position as Chancellor.[26]

Stillington must have been a central figure in government at this time, but his influence also seems to have been a personal one, especially in generating a reconciliation between Edward IV and his brother George, Duke of Clarence, while also being appointed to the council of the young Prince of Wales, later to be Edward V.[27] Given the prince's age in 1473, the year of Stillington's appointment, it appears that this was something of an administrative rather than a pedagogical position. However, as we shall see, his role as intermediary and as friend to Clarence had much more immediate and serious implications. Following a bout of ill health which was recorded as having begun in September 1472, Stillington eventually resigned the office of Chancellor on 8 June 1473[28] and much speculation has surrounded the potential reason for this change. Some see this removal as evidence of reversal of royal favour, which perhaps might have come about because of his friendship with Clarence. Stillington's diocese overlapped with the heart of Clarence's main lands and there seems little doubt that they had contact during the period of 1470–1471, when Edward and his other brother Richard were in exile.[29] This generates the possibility that the friendship between Clarence and Stillington was more than a passing one, and the knowledge of the pre-contract (which event is purported to have occurred around 1461) would have potentially proved a crucial piece of information in the dispute between the brothers. However, it is also possible that ill-health prevented the bishop from accomplishing his duties at that time.[30] Given Stillington's knowledge about Edward's earlier association with Eleanor Butler, it would seem to be unwise for the king to antagonize the bishop and thus perhaps ill-health and incapacity was more likely the stimulus for this change. If it was disfavour, it does not appear to have been serious enough to cause a permanent rift. Stillington was subsequently appointed in late 1475 to seek the extradition of Henry Tudor by an appeal to the Duke of Brittany. Although unsuccessful, Stillington appears to have suffered little for the failure, either in terms of the disapprobation of Edward IV or, even later, after the turn of fortune at Bosworth in August 1485. Indeed, he seems to have been little persecuted by Henry VII in general, an individual not universally acclaimed for his tolerance. We shall explore Henry's uncharacteristic magnanimity toward Stillington later in this chapter. Despite this relatively benign treatment, Stillington later proved to be a supporter of the Simnel rebellion and, after its collapse following the Battle of Stoke, he sought refuge at the University of Oxford. Eventually, he was given up to the Tudor regime and was apparently imprisoned at or near Windsor, where he may have later died. Our primary point of departure here is, of course, the pre-contract itself, and it is to this that I now turn.

The Cleric and the Contract

Although there is a possibility that Edward IV and Eleanor Butler had already met some time previously, the occasion which appears most likely to have first brought them together concerns the rights to the manors of Griff and Great Dorsett in Warwickshire. Lord Sudeley had conveyed the manors to Eleanor and her husband Sir Thomas, but without royal licence. Upon the death of her husband Eleanor was constrained to petition the king for their return, since he had confiscated them for the Crown. It is uncertain where and when this meeting occurred, with Warwickshire, Gloucestershire, Norfolk and London all being viable candidates, as known locations of Edward IV in the summer and early autumn of 1461. We do not, at present, know this precise location, but we do know that the three people involved must have met together and apparently in a place that permitted a certain degree of privacy, since the report is that only these three people involved were present at the pre-contract. Of all the possibilities, the royal lodge at Woodstock in Oxfordshire would seem to be perhaps the most likely location, partly because of its proximity to Eleanor's lands.[31] As far as we are able to ascertain, evidence points to Stillington being the only witness to the fateful pre-contract between Edward IV and Eleanor Butler.[32] There are a number of informative works concerning the pre-contract[33] and what is of central interest here is Stillington's role in the event. Stillington himself was actually related to Eleanor Butler through his aunt Lady Lisle's (Joan Cheddar) relations to the Talbots.[34] Thus, given the reality of the pre-contract, Robert was marrying off one of his relatives to the king.[35] That this could form part of his later motivations during the turbulent summer of 1483 has not previously been explored in any great detail.

The overall sequence of events is rehearsed by Buck,36 who reported that: his [Edward's] affection was as general to others being a frank gamester, and one that would cast at all fairly set. Yet above all for a time, he loved the Lady [Eleanor Talbot] a very fair and noble lady, [daughter of John Talbot,] Earl of Shrewsbury; and [her mother was] the Lady Catherine Stafford, [daughter of Hum]phrey Stafford, Duke of Buckingham. [And this Lady E]leanor was the widow of Thomas, [Lord Butler,] Baron of Sudeley. And the king's [affection] was so strong, and he was so fervent and vehemen[t, and also at] that time so honest toward her as th[at he mad]e choice of her for his wife. And he was firmly and [sole]mnly contracted and also married to [her by] a reverend prelate, namely Dr. Thomas [Stillington, Bishop of B]ath, a grave and learned man and a counsellor of state, and much favour[ed] by the king, and often employed in great affairs (as I have partly intimated before). And this matter is witnessed by our Eng[lish] stories, and also by the honourable and veritable [histo]rian Philip de Commynes, and in these word[s;] … That is summarily in English thus: The Bishop of Bath, a privy Counsellor of [King] Edward, said that the king had plighted [his] faith to marry a lady of England, w[hom] the bishop named/viz, the Lady Ele[anor] Talbot/, and that this contract was made [in the] hands of the bishop. And he said that afte[rward] he married them, and no person being presen[t but] they twain and he. And he said also that [the king] charged him very strictly that he should not reveal this secret marriage to any man [living.] And this contract and marriage are related in the Act [of Parliament] aforesaid, and where it is di[s]ertly called a former marriage. And the king had a child by this lady.

As to the length of the subsequent relationship between Edward and Eleanor, we are not sure about the duration, and the rumour concerning a child from the union is repeated in a number of places.37 What is not in dispute is that, according to our current knowledge, the pre-contract did occur and Stillington was the priest involved.

Stillington and the Fall of Clarence

One of the questions that historians have raised over the years is the degree to which Stillington used his knowledge of this formal liaison, and in particular the way this secret information was involved in the eventual demise of George, Duke of Clarence.38 The final stage of this disputation between the two brothers has been described by Campbell,39 who observed:

Now began the fatal dissensions in the royal family which led to the destruction of the House of York, and the extinction of the name of Plantagenet. There is reason to think that the Chancellor did all that was possible to heal the dispute between the King and his brother, the Duke of Clarence. When the trial for treason came on in the House of Lords, the Duke of Buckingham presided as Lord Steward, and the King appearing personally as accuser, the field was left to the two brothers; 'no one charging Clarence but the King, and no one answering the King but Clarence.

To what degree Stillington was involved in the accusations of treason against Clarence is not easy to discover. The primary issue with Clarence was his continuing aspirations to assume Edward's throne,[40] and the dangerous nature of his growing threat is typified by his high-handed treatment of one Ankarette Twynho, a servant woman he suspected of having poisoned the Duchess Isabel. Clarence had her brought all the way from Somerset to Warwick and, in a court cowed by Clarence's power, she was found guilty and hanged on 15 April 1477. In this Clarence was seen to be assuming the rights of the king. It was part of a continuing sibling rivalry that had been simmering for almost a decade. For example, in relation to some earlier disputes between Edward, Clarence and Warwick the Kingmaker, the historian Habington,[41] speculating on knowledge of the pre-contract, had reported that:

> For had there been a just exception against this marriage, neither George Duke of Clarence, nor the Earl of Warwick, in their frequent calumnies against the King, being in open rebellion, had left it unmentioned.

In this context, Habington was very explicit that he was talking about the bar to the validity of Elizabeth Woodville's marriage to Edward on account of the pre-contract. As he noted, had the pre-contract been known at that time, there is little doubt that it would have been used in accusation, again suggesting that in the early 1470s it was still a secret pact.[42]

Following his high-handed treatment and pretensions to the throne, Clarence was himself arrested some two months later and imprisoned through the rest of the year of 1477, until he was required to answer the king's charges which followed the January Parliament, assumedly summoned primarily to indict the duke. In the squabble between the elder and the younger brother, the elder won and George, Duke of Clarence was dispatched on 18 February 1478.[43] From my perspective, Clarence had pressed the envelope one too many times and his execution was due predominantly to his never-ending ambition and was little contingent on knowing or relating anything about the pre-contract. Indeed, we can ask of what value would it have been to Clarence? Eleanor Butler had now been dead for almost a decade[44] and any accusation could be easily remedied by a simple ceremony. The threat of revelation essentially represented little or no threat to Edward at that time. Rather, it was Clarence's accusation of Edward's own illegitimacy that must have rankled. Edward having been born in France and George in Ireland, the issue of legitimacy must have involved the king, not his issue from Elizabeth Woodville.

It has often been suggested that Stillington revealed the pre-contract to Clarence. However, this assumption is based upon spatial and temporal contiguity and not on any hard evidence. For example, the proximity of some of Clarence's lands and Stillington's bishopric have suggested some degree of personal familiarity and this is supported by Stillington's efforts at reconciliation between the king and his brother. Similarly, the fact that March 1478 found Stillington in the Tower,[45] and had to pay 'a round sum for his ransom',[46] seems to suggest some degree of involvement.[47] The accusation that he was in prison for 'uttering words prejudicial to the King and his State' has most often been interpreted as his revelation to Clarence. However, whether his arrest dates from before or after Clarence's execution (18 February 1478)[48] or was simply contemporary with it is not known for certain. It may well have been possible that Stillington was implicated without ever having discussed the pre-contract. After all, as noted, it was not a major weapon in Clarence's armoury. This is potentially confirmed by the fact that by 20 June Stillington had secured a pardon, although he did not return to favour and held few appointments immediately after this time.[49] It is speculated that Stillington's pardon was contingent upon his silence or even active denial of the pre-contract, and some authors have suggested that the antipathy of the Woodvilles toward him was because of this critical knowledge that he held. However, we have no certain evidence of this and I believe this inference, although apparently a logical one, is, in actuality, flawed.

However, if for a moment we do assume that Stillington was in trouble for having revealed the pre-contract to George for his subsequent use in his arguments with his brother the king, why was his younger brother Richard apparently unaware of these accusations? For surely, George, in his attempt to bring his younger brother to his side of the argument, would have brought to light all he could of these circumstances in early 1478. This being so, Richard would have needed no reminding in early 1483, when he could have brought this issue to the fore himself as soon as he had entered London, and not continued with the normal processes which were to precede the coronation of his nephew, Edward V. Indeed, had Richard known, it would almost certainly have been recorded as such by the various contemporaries who commented on the events of the summer; particularly, we should expect to see evidence of Richard's insight in the *Croyland Chronicle* and perhaps Mancini's monograph also. The fact that we do not see this would seem to be important evidence that Richard knew nothing of the pre-contract until June 1483, when it became a pivotal issue in the succession.

Until and unless we have further evidence of Stillington's collusion in Clarence's treachery, we must consider the proposition unproven. Although the revelation of the pre-contract would seem to account for the general pattern of events in the spring of 1478, the threat of public revelation would seem to be essentially an empty one. It might well be that Stillington was 'swept up' in a general effort to quell the Duke of Clarence and his subsequent silence would be eminently understandable. After all, having dispatched his own brother, who could feel in any way safe broaching the king's anger?[50]

Stillington as the Source: the de Commines Evidence

In respect of the present hypothesis concerning Catesby and the revelation of the pre-contract, we have to examine a number of important propositions with respect to the more traditional notion that it was Stillington who revealed this startling information to the Duke of Gloucester. These respective issues can be stated separately and sequentially. First, was Stillington the source of Richard's information? Alternatively, did Stillington only act to confirm what had already been revealed to the Protector by someone else? In respect of these first two propositions, what contemporary sources do we have which speak to the issue? Further, if Stillington was the source, when was he purported to have revealed this, and what provenance do we have for such a dating? And finally, what was Stillington's reward for this crucial information which justified Richard, Duke of Gloucester's altering of the course of history and assuming the throne of England? Answers to these questions are vital in relation to the central hypothesis I have put forward here, since they go to the very heart of the matter.

Let us begin this sequence of evaluations by quoting an important note made by Hammond.[51] In this he states:

> It has been said that Commines is the sole contemporary source connecting Bishop Stillington with the pre-contract of Edward and Eleanor Butler. This is not in fact so, since from the contemporary report of a discussion of *Titulus Regius* by the Justices in the Exchequer Chamber at the beginning of the reign of Henry VII, and by the Lords in Parliament, it is clear that they thought that Stillington was the author, 'the Bishop of Bath made the bill.'

It is very important here to follow Hammond's observations closely, and so let us begin with the initial observation.

It is true that, among others, Levine has written that 'the only contemporary to say that Stillington told Richard about the pre-contract and claimed to have participated in its making is Commines ...'[52] Thus Hammond is most informative here, and we must first evaluate this traditional case of de Commines as the sole source before we pass on to the other evidence Hammond cites. It is worth stating in detail what de Commines[53] specifically had to say. In his first references to this issue, he reported:

> In short, the conclusion was this; by the assistance of the Bishop of Bath (who had been formerly King Edward's Chancellor, but falling afterward into disgrace, had been removed from his place, thrown into prison, and paid a round sum for his ransom), he executed his designs, as you shall hear by and by.
>
> This Bishop (Robert Stillington, Bishop of Bath and Wells) discovered to the Duke of Gloucester (Richard III) that his brother King Edward, had been formerly in love with a beautiful young lady and had promised her marriage, upon condition that he might lie with her; the lady consented, and, as the bishop affirmed, he married them when nobody was present but they two and himself. His fortune depending upon the court, he did not discover it, and persuaded the lady likewise to conceal it, which she did, and the matter remained a secret.

In a later passage in his sequence of books, de Commines reiterated the story, but with some embellishments:

> for King Richard, after his brother's death, had sworn allegiance to his nephew, as his King and sovereign, and yet committed that inhuman action not long after; and, in full Parliament, caused two of his brother's daughters to be degraded and declared illegitimate, upon a pretence which he justified by means of the Bishop of Bath, who, having been formerly in great favor with King Edward, had incurred his displeasure, was dismissed, imprisoned, and fined a good sum for his releasement. This bishop affirmed, that King Edward being in love with a certain lady whom he named, and otherwise unable to have his desires of her, had promised her marriage; and caused the bishop to marry them, upon which he enjoyed her person, though his promise was only made to delude her; but such games are dangerous, as the effects frequently demonstrate. I have known many a courtier who would not have lost such a fair lady for want of promise.
>
> This malicious prelate smothered his revenge in his heart near twenty years together, but it recoiled upon himself, for he had a son, of whom he was extremely fond and to whom King Richard designed to give a plentiful estate, and to have married him to one of the young ladies whom he had declared illegitimate (who is now Queen of England, and has two fine children). This young gentleman, being on broad ship by commission from King Richard, was taken upon the coast of Normandy, and upon a dispute between those that took him, he was brought before the Parliament at Paris, put into Petit Chastellet, and suffered to lie there till he was starved to death."

What we are to make of de Commines' latter observations on Stillington's purported son and a marriage to Elizabeth of York I leave, at this time, for future deliberations. Whether and how this would have acted as a reward for Stillington himself is difficult to decipher. However, there is more here concerning Stillington as the source, and especially if de Commines has been considered the sole source of this information for some prolonged interval of time. In particular, we need here to look at de Commines' specific use of language. A careful reading of the two quotations seems to indicate quite clearly that Stillington was the original source of information concerning the pre-contract. In fact, we read that, 'This Bishop discovered to the Duke of Gloucester …': the use of the term 'discovered'[54] here seems specifically to imply that it was Stillington's voluntary act that revealed the information to Richard. However, when we look a little further into the same text, more is revealed about this phraseology. Shortly after this quotation, de Commines used the term in the following quote: 'His fortune depending upon the court, he did not discover it, and persuaded the lady likewise to conceal it, which she did, and the matter remained a secret.' Here, the use is of the same word, but now we can read into this a different interpretation. In this sentence, the word 'discover' can mean advertise or broadcast the fact and in actuality it aligns much more with the modern use of the word uncover.

As we read further into de Commines' two passages, we also find that the Bishop 'assisted' Richard, in that he 'affirmed' the reality of the pre-contract. In the circumstances described, Richard 'caused two of his brother's daughters to be degraded and declared illegitimate, upon a pretence which he justified by means of the Bishop of Bath.' Here we have yet another description in which the bishop 'justified' Richard's action. I do not wish to belabour the point beyond what a reasonable interpretation will bear. However, the passages which describe Stillington as the primary source of the pre-contract, as opposed to someone who confirmed that the pre-contract had occurred, and whose authority was then employed by Richard to achieve a more general acceptance of the fact of the bastardisation, is not completely unequivocal. It can be interpreted in a number of potentially differing ways. Therefore, from the text alone, the idea that de Commines proves the source of a pristine accusation is not quite as clear as the traditional story might have us think.

However, there are other objections to de Commines as a source in general, beyond his own words. It has been noted that de Commines was 'unreliable,' inaccurate and slanderous toward 'English internal affairs.'[55] In respect of his own reporting, Lander has suggested that '[Armstrong] points out that [de] Commines himself stressed his ignorance of English affairs.'[56] Thus we have a source here of doubtful accuracy and this doubt is actually expressed by the original author himself. Indeed, it has further been suggested that de Commines may have even inferred Stillington's role here from what he was subsequently told about the Parliament of Richard which convened in early 1484, and some evidence he adduced from what was reported there. Furthermore, we must always remember that, of the three present at the pre-contract ceremony, Stillington was the only one alive at the time in question. Thus, it may be possible that de Commines inferred this role as the source of the revelation to Stillington as opposed to actually knowing of his actions directly. If this is so, it renders de Commines' identification as

Stillington as the source of the information potentially doubtful. In contrast, I contend here that Stillington only acted to confirm what Richard actually put to him. In providing this confirmation, Stillington subsequently became the public face of the pre-contract revelation. What I am questioning is whether he was the original source for this knowledge. It is evident that Wood also expresses doubts about Commines and indeed Croyland also as contemporary to the events of June. He noted, 'It is clear that Commines and Croyland both base their accounts not on the events of June but on the act of succession passed the following January which contains what is alleged to be a copy of the June petition.'[57] It is worth remembering that the Speaker of that latter Parliament, and a skilled and able lawyer himself, was one William Catesby. To garner further understanding of the accusation against Stillington we now need to turn to the other evidence that Hammond identified and subsequently to the reactions of Henry VII upon his assumption of the throne in the early afternoon of 25 August 1485.

Stillington as the Source: Later Evidence

Let us now return to Hammond's observations on other citations which identified Stillington as the source of the pre-contract and explore exactly what these respective sources said. In his brief note, which I have reproduced in full here, Hammond states that:

> It has been said that Commines is the sole contemporary source connecting Bishop Stillington with the pre-contract of Edward to Eleanor Butler. This is not in fact so, since from the contemporary report of a discussion of *Titulus Regius* by the Justices in the Exchequer Chamber at the beginning of the reign of Henry VII, and by the Lords in Parliament, it is clear that they thought that Stillington was the author, 'the Bishop of Bath made the bill' (*see* James Ramsey, *Lancaster and York*, Vol. 2, 1892, p. 488 and S.B. Chrimes, *English Constitutional Ideas in the Fifteenth Century*, 1936, p. 266, both citing the year book, Hilary Term, Henry VII, Appendix No. 75). The Lords thought he should be summoned before them, as the author of this notorious bill, but the King refused, saying he had pardoned him. It seems clear that his contemporaries thought the Bishop had told Richard about the pre-contract, or had invented it, since they would surely not have been so concerned if they had merely believed him to have drafted the bill on the orders of the King.[58]

This seeks to establish that, although de Commines may have been the traditional source for the accusation that Stillington revealed the pre-contract to Richard, it was by no means the only one and indeed if the citations in Ramsey and Chrimes to the same (almost contemporary) source are correct, this latter source[59] may have even been closer to events in time than de Commines' actual writing. So, let us explore this source in further detail. The observation by Hammond basically encapsulates what Chrimes has to say on the matter. Chrimes' last sentence is however, a little more informative. He states:

> All the justices in the exchequer chamber, by command of the king, discussed the reversal and destruction of the act which bastardized the children of Edward IV and his wife. This act was considered so scandalous that they were unwilling to rehearse it, and advised against its recital in the repealing act in order to avoid the perpetuation of its terms. 'Nota icy bien le policy' wrote the reporter. 'Nota ensement,' he continued, 'que il (i.e., the offensive act) ne puissoit ester pris hors del record sans act de la parliament pur l'indeminity et jeopardie d'eux qui avoient les records in lour gard.' The authority of parliament was needed to discharge them. The lords in the parliament chamber thought well of this counsel, and some of them wished to summon the bishop of Bath (Stillington), who had made the false bill, to answer for it, but the king said he had pardoned him and did not wish to proceed against him.

Ramsay is even terser on this matter and simply states, 'de Comines' assertions that the troth of Edward and Eleanor had been received by the Bishop of Bath was doubtless based on the mere fact that the case was got up by Stillington.' Ramsay cites the same source as that which was used later by Chrimes also. It should be carefully noted that these accusations concern the so-called 'Bill,' referring directly to the *Titulus Regius*, which was the subject of the conversation by the referenced lords. Stillington is accused of authorship here, although Ramsay goes further and accuses Stillington of the complete fabrication of the whole episode. It remains crucial to reiterate that this original source, used by both later authors, did not accuse Stillington of revealing the pre-contract to Richard. Rather, it accused him of authoring the bill in the Parliament of 1484, which took place some eight months after the events of June 1483 at the Tower. Thus neither of the close-to-contemporary sources that we have unequivocally points to Stillington as Richard's informant. It is true that both sources

heavily implicate him in these events, but the question of whether he was
the actual source remains, I suggest, unresolved by these documents. The
indication that Henry VII 'did not wish to proceed against him' is, in my
view, vitally important to the interpretation that we may impose on the
actions of Robert Stillington at this time.

The conclusion here is that Stillington certainly had something to do
with the bill, that being the *Titulus Regius* of Richard III of the Parliament
of early 1484. It may well have been this document which was also the
basis of de Commines' assertions. However, this latter reference, as we have
seen, certainly does not unequivocally accuse Stillington of revealing the
pre-contract to Richard in the summer of 1483, but only of complicity in
the bill passed in Parliament in early 1484. Thus from these initial sources
of information, it is at best a tentative assertion that Stillington acted in
the manner traditionally ascribed to him by historical commentators such
as Markham.

The revelation of the pre-contract and its implication was clearly no secret
some few decades later. The cited example of this is to be found in the letter
of Eustace Chapuys, an ambassador to the court of Henry VIII. He wrote to
his master, the Holy Roman Emperor, Charles V, on 16 December 1528. In
this missive, he was concerned with Henry VIII's treatment of his youngest
daughter, Elizabeth, later Elizabeth I. In the course of expressing this concern
he was to hark back to past times. Specifically, he recorded that:

> ... they say that you [Charles V] have a better title than the present King,
> who only claims by his mother, who was declared by sentence of the bishop
> of Bath [Stillington] a bastard, because Edward had espoused another wife
> before the mother of Elizabeth of York.[60]

The 'they' referred to in the quote of Chapuys' is his attribution of the
disgruntled populace of England, unhappy with a number of the policies
of the then current administration. By implication, he was suggesting that
circulation of the story of the pre-contract was one of public knowledge and
public rumour. However, it is probably the case that Chapuys' knowledge
was derived from the earlier observations of de Commines. After all, these
two were countrymen and it is possible, if not probable, that Chapuys
had Comines' text to hand. Of course, even if this were true, it does not
necessarily mean that there were not public mutterings and murmurings.
It is perhaps one of the sources of the great Tudor cruelty that they were so

fragilely established on the throne and were as a result spiteful, vengeful and oppressive of all those that they considered possible rivals, even including the old Countess of Salisbury.

However, there is one further wrinkle to this whole issue of Stillington as the source and it is derived from the observations of the *Croyland Chronicle*. Again, it is critical here to repeat the original words since they, like the other citations, are so important to follow accurately. Croyland said:

> and on the 26th day of the same month of June, Richard the protector, claimed for himself the government of the kingdom with the name and title of king; and on the same day in the great hall of Westminster he thrust himself into the marble chair. The pretext of this intrusion and for taking possession in this way was as follows. It was put forward, by means of a supplication contained in a certain parchment roll, that King Edward's sons were bastards, by submitting that he had been precontracted to a certain Lady Eleanor Boteler before he married Queen Elizabeth and, further, that the blood of his other brother, George, duke of Clarence, had been attainted so that, at the time, no certain and uncorrupt blood of the lineage of Richard, duke of York, was to be found except in the person of the said Richard, duke of Gloucester. At the end of this roll, therefore, on behalf of the lords and commonalty of the kingdom, he was besought to assume his lawful rights. It was put about then that this roll originated in the North whence so many people came to London although there was no-one who did not know the identity of the author (who was in London all the time) of such sedition and infamy.

Again, by tradition, this unnamed author has been assumed to be Stillington. It is my contention that the individual 'who was in London all the time' was Catesby, and not Stillington. As we have seen, the traditional sources which name Stillington refer to him as having made the bill. Like Wood, I see these references emanating from his role in the Act of Parliament. The 'parchment roll' of 26 June is a creation I believe it possible to attribute to Catesby's hand.

When was the Pre-contract Revealed?

Given this timetable of events, a very pertinent question arises here, and I shall use Mowat's words, who put it so succinctly:

Another pertinent question stems from the fact that those authors who accept that it was Stillington's disclosure of the pre-contract which sparked off events leading to Richard's assumption of the crown, assume that he revealed his secret early in June 1483: why did he delay so long after Edward IV's death? Is it possible that the Bishop himself was doubtful whether a contract and/or marriage entered into secretly, and witnessed only by himself, was a proper legal bar to the Woodville marriage?[61]

Given the traditional story, let us take for the moment the premise that Stillington was the source of the pre-contract revelation. Although I will again conclude by disputing this premise, for the sake of the argument here let us say temporarily that this is so. The question then naturally arises, as Mowat indicates, when did the actual revelation take place? In this, one relatively modern historian, Sir Clements Markham, offers what appears to be a candidate date which he identifies as the Council meeting of 8 June 1483. Again, it is important to hear Markham in his own words.[62] He says:

Up to this time affairs had gone smoothly. On June 5th the Protector had given detailed orders for his nephew's coronation on the 22nd, and had even caused letters of summons to be issued for the attendance of forty esquires who were to receive the knighthood of the Bath on the occasion. But now there came a change. Dr. Robert Stillington, Bishop of Bath and Wells, apparently on June 8, revealed to the Council the long-concealed fact that Edward IV was contracted to Lady Eleanor Butler, widow of a son of Lord Butler of Sudeley, and daughter of the first Earl of Shrewsbury, before he went through a secret marriage ceremony with the Lady Grey.

I can find no source earlier than Markham which identifies this as the crucial day on which the pre-contract was revealed. But it is worth noting that Markham is only saying 'apparently' here, and states no evidentiary basis for his speculation at this point, other, presumably, than his own intuition as to the timing of events. However, Markham's immediate intuition is directly countered by Kendall's observation, which, in contrast, is backed up by fact. Kendall reports: 'Writing on June 9th to an acquaintance in the country, Simon Stallworth, a servant of the Lord Chancellor's reports that there is nothing new since he has last written, sometime before May 19th.' Now we must weigh in the balance here Markham's intuition against the null evidence implied in the Stallworth letter. In my view, the preponderance of the evidence that we have must argue against Markham's speculation. One further point also militates against the Markham proposition. The 8th was a Sunday and in other citations the Council meeting is purported to have occurred a day later, on Monday 9th.[63] This interpretation might actually strengthen Markham's proposition, but again the Stallworth letter is somewhat against it. There is, however, the small point of the cessation of the writs of the Privy Seal that again may be indicative here. We cannot thus rule out the possibility of the revelation taking place on the 9th out of hand. However, we must say that case for the 8th is doubtful and, similarly, the case for the 9th at present can at best be considered unproven. However, there is more.

A little further into Markham's text we read what appears to be the definitive passage. It reads: 'There was a prolonged sitting of the Lords Spiritual and Temporal in the Council Chamber at Westminster, on June 9th Bishop Stillington brought in instruments, authentic doctors, proctors, and notaries of the law with depositions and diverse witnesses.'[64] The authority that Markham cites for this observation is Grafton.[65] At first blush this would seem to put paid to all that I have espoused in the present text. For if Stillington revealed the pre-contract to the Council meeting on the 9th, there can be no way that it was actually Catesby performing this self-same function on the 13th. However, when we delve a little deeper here we find an instance of one of the most frustrating aspects of Ricardian research. For it turns out that the original passage in Grafton's *Chronicle* is some form of fictionalised account of a conversation between the Duke of Buckingham and Bishop Morton wherein, parenthetically, the duke is highly eulogistic of the bishop and his abilities. Upon closer reading, we find that the 'he' referred to in the passage cited by Markham is actually Richard, Duke of Gloucester, and not Stillington at all. Also, Grafton provides no dating of this meeting. Thus Markham transposes the individual involved and derives the dating from his own unsupported interpretation. This form of unbound speculation, if not outright misidentification, makes subsequent interpretation more than difficult,[66] especially if one accepts Markham's statements at face value. I find in light of these facts that I am justified in rejecting what Markham has suggested. I fail to find any creditable evidence here that Stillington presented anything to the Council on that date, or indeed at any other time. I have thus proposed here that the revelation actually took place on the morning of the 13th, some four or five days later, and that the informer involved was not Stillington at all but Catesby.

I have further suggested that Catesby benefitted enormously from his act. However, supposing the traditional account to be correct and that Richard owed his throne to Stillington, let us see how the bishop was rewarded for this signal and indeed unique service to his new king.

The Tower and Beyond

If Stillington was actually the original source of Richard's information concerning the pre-contract and its crucial implications, he received precious little reward for effectively elevating the Duke of Gloucester to the throne. For example, even Kendall notes that 'Resentment against Edward for the loss of high office, a desire for revenge upon the Woodvilles may have urged him (Stillington) to make his declaration. No discernible reward did he receive from Richard …'[67] Stillington did take part in the coronation of Richard III, where he was noted as performing the ceremony of hallowing the king and queen.[68] Again, interpretation of this participation very much depends upon how one sees Stillington. If he did confirm the pre-contract then he would have understood that Richard was the rightful king. If he did not, or in actuality the pre-contract was only confabulation, then his actions at the coronation must have been of the highest order of hypocrisy.[69] As is evident from the tenor of the present text, I tend toward the former interpretation.[70] Thus, I believe he must have seen Richard as his rightful king, but, again, we see very little evidence of any tangible reward for Stillington in the short years of Richard's reign up to the time of Bosworth.[71] However, if Richard did not reward him, on the up side, Henry did not punish him to any significant extent either.

Regime change is an unsettling event and the days following the unexpected victory of Henry VII at Bosworth must have been quite dramatic for those who lived through them. Often the immediate actions of the new regime betray their most critical fears and some of the dictates of the new monarch can be viewed with this perspective in mind. It seems Henry was very anxious to secure at least two individuals who very much concern us here. Although we do not know where Stillington was on 22 August 1485, we do know that a warrant was issued for his arrest the next day in Leicester.[72] It must have been pursued with some dispatch by Rawdon and his colleagues who were sent after the Bishop, since we understand that five days later Stillington was detained in prison in York and was 'sore crased by reason of his trouble.'[73] He certainly should have been. Not only had he taken part in efforts to extradite the one-time Earl of Richmond, now Henry VII, he was also the putative source of information on the pre-contract which bastardised Elizabeth of York, whom Henry was sworn to marry in an attempt to unify the country and solidify his own very shaky claim to the crown. We know that Henry took great pains to suppress the *Titulus Regius*, the central concern of which must have been the notation of the the pre-contract.[74] All this would militate strongly against the continued health and well-being of Robert Stillington who, at the very best, seemed to be looking at a long term of imprisonment. After all, as the reputed author of the bill and the source of the revelation of the pre-contract to Richard, Duke of Gloucester, he must have surely been viewed as a very dangerous individual indeed to the new monarch. Yet where do we next meet Stillington? Puzzlingly, he is officiating at the coronation of Henry VII. This indeed is one of the central mysteries of Robert Stillington's story. Why was he treated so leniently by an individual who would earn a reputation for exactly the opposite sort of behaviour?

In respect of Henry's actions following Bosworth, we can compare his respective treatment of Catesby and Stillington. Here we find eminent differences. Catesby was executed even before Stillington was detained. If the reason were jealously on behalf of others in Richard's realm it is difficult to see how Catesby had so offended the new King Henry VII if all he had done was work assiduously for the former king. Many had done so and even fought for Richard that day at Bosworth; these individuals were not beheaded, and some were not even punished. It may be that their noble birth and high station saved them, for Henry would need the nobility as all of his predecessors had. However, if Stillington was truly the source of the revelation of the pre-contract, surely he would have seen a much harsher punishment. The contrasting harshness to Catesby and the relative leniency to Stillington suggest that the culpability of the former (at least in the new regime's eyes) was much greater. For me, it argues that Catesby was the source and Stillington the confirmation, and their respective levels of punishment reflected this. Of course, Stillington's clerical status may also have been instrumental in him avoiding execution, but it is hard to see how it could act as a shield against a harsh sentence. From the perspective I have created, Stillington's plea to Henry would have been that he was acting as a neutral churchman, answering to the then king as his duty dictated. I believe Henry accepted this explanation and excused Stillington any greater punishment on the promise of the same degree of loyalty to his own monarchy.[75] Despite this degree of reconciliation, I do not argue that Stillington became either favoured by, or friends with, the new king. I believe that he had earned and suffered at least a degree of Henry's disapprobation and, of course, Stillington was Yorkist to the last.

Some authors argue that Stillington's exclusion from Henry VII's first Parliament signifies the disgrace that he was in, yet we find that on 22 November 1485, just two months after Bosworth, Stillington was granted a full pardon.[76] The only material penalty that he suffered was the deprivation of the deanery of St Martin. In the act repealing the *Titulus Regius*, Stillington was indeed accused of 'horrible and haneous offences ymagined and doune by him against the King.' Despite this rhetoric, very little in the way of real punishment was visited upon the good bishop. One would think that given this history of close shaves with the power of the throne, Stillington would have suspended his political activities and, at the age of at least sixty-five, retired to his religious calling. Yet this was not the case. He was directly involved with the Lambert Simnel rebellion. It was Stillington who himself had at least confirmed the existence and effect of the pre-contract, so presumably in 1487, in supporting Simnel, he understood that his previous actions had invalidated the claim of the pretender, whether he was purported to be Edward V or his younger brother, Richard, Duke of York. Was it because as a Yorkshireman he was loyal to the Yorkist party from first to last and sought to support what he wished or knew to be the last viable remaining male heir of the House of York? Even today, Yorkshiremen in general are known for their stubbornness and indeed their loyalty. Was this the last act of a faithful servant who must have known that he had little time left? Until we discover further evidence, this will remain just one of the many mysteries of the long-lived bishop.

After the defeat at the Battle of Stoke on 16 June 1487, four years to the day after the young Richard, Duke of York had been escorted from Westminster Abbey to the Tower, Stillington took refuge within the University of Oxford. At first the university authorities refused to give up the bishop, but eventually, under pressure from the king, he was delivered up, and imprisoned at Windsor in October 1487. Some three and a half years later, in May 1491, Stillington died, still a prisoner.[77] His body was taken for burial at Wells Cathedral in a chapel which he himself had had caused to be built. By all accounts it was a splendid structure,[78] but sadly it no longer stands today, having been pulled down some time early in the reign of Edward VI.

7

Return to the Tower

Forbade to wade through slaughter to a throne.[1]

When was the Fateful Decision Made?

Any comprehensive and compelling account of Richard III and his assumption of the throne of England must explain where and when he made the fateful decision to depose his young nephew, Edward V, and to become king himself.[2] As I have indicated in the opening chapter, one's opinion on this matter very much dictates how one views Richard in general, with an adverse assessment directly corresponding with earlier estimates.[3] In my preceding arguments, I have proposed that the window which brackets this decision is actually a fairly small one. I believe the evidence we have supports the contention that the change in Richard's mind from de facto Protector to aspiring monarch came on that momentous day of Friday 13 June 1483 at the Tower of London. I do not wish to assert necessarily that the whole of his decision process was played out in just one single, critical moment. However, I do think that the pivotal revelation of the pre-contract and the consequent understanding by Richard that his nephews were therefore ineligible to inherit, stemmed from information presented to him on the morning of that day.[4] The subsequent securing of the young

Richard, Duke of York from sanctuary sprang from this understanding and therefore Richard's actions of Monday 16 June immediately following the execution of William, Lord Hastings three days earlier are eminently understandable in light of this timeline of events. The following then, is my version of the happenings of that day in the Tower of London and my associated observations upon how the present explanation of this course of events serves to address a number of issues whose previous explanations have been in my view, at best, less than satisfactory.

The Letters of 10 and 11 June 1483

While it will clearly always be possible to read different interpretations into the actions of Richard, Duke of Gloucester as Protector, I believe it is fair to say that there is no substantive documentary evidence that he overtly sought to secure the throne before the fateful meeting on 13 June. In this I think we have to agree with Wood[5] that the citation of the York letter of 10 June and the Neville letter of 11 June actually represent evidence for, rather than against, this interpretation. If Richard was planning some form of coup to occur on the 13th, he clearly must have known that an appeal for troops, issued on the 10th and dispatched at the earliest possible moment on 11 June cannot have got to the north much earlier than 14 June. Further, such troops could not have reasonably been expected to have reached the capital until about the 19th, even at their best rate of progress. Again, Wood's interpretation that the summons was most probably meant to bring aid and leverage to Richard in order to influence the decisions of the form of Parliament which was proposed to take place on the 25th is certainly a reasonable one. Such force may well have been to back his claim to retain his status as Protector.[6] This is a far more plausible interpretation of these letters than seeing them as a direct part of a plot for the throne and especially as preparatory to Hastings' demise only two days later on the 13th. This being so, it suggests that by the time Ratcliffe left for York and other parts north, Richard had no more malevolent intention than that of sustaining the status quo in terms of his own safety and security. In terms of what Richard must have known had happened to Humphrey, a previous Protector and Duke of Gloucester, this course of action would seem to be a wise precaution. The letter, in my view, provides at best marginal evidence that Richard aspired to the throne at this precise juncture and reasonably tangible evidence that he did not.

Troops in the Capital

One of the major considerations of any actions taken at this time must have thus centred around the number of troops that Richard can realistically have commanded, called upon and relied upon in and around the capital. De Blieck's point is very well made here.[7] Any pre-meditated move radically to alter the on-going course of events must have been founded upon the belief that such a decision could be backed up by force if necessary. Presumably there were Woodville forces as well as those of Lord Hastings, the Duke of Buckingham and those supporters Richard had brought south with him, all in and around the capital at this time. However many London-based troops Richard actually did command at that time, he clearly thought that he needed more support and thus the 10 June summons to those of his affinity in the north. The latter appeal argues for his recognition that, at this point he did not have enough strength present. Stallworth's fear was expressed in his letter of the 21st, where he noted: 'Yt is thought ther schalbe xx thousand of my lord protectour and my lord of Bukyngham men in London this weeke.' This observation was clearly rumour, but Stallworth's general tenor suggests at least some, if not many, forces were in and around the capital already. His ruminations were confirmed, when following Hastings' execution, 'All be lord chamberleyne mene be come my lordys of Bokynghame menne.' While Richard and Buckingham had men present, it was unlikely these were enough for a carefully considered, planned, pre-emptive strike. And even if this were so, would such a strike have taken the form of the actions that we know occurred on the 13th? A fully thought-out plan would, most probably, not have been primarily directed at Hastings. This being so, it furthers the idea that the events of 13 June were reactive and not pre-meditated in nature. Thus, although I do not think with the present information that we have that we can fix, with absolute certainty, the point where Richard decided to take the crown itself, we can say with some confidence that the expected course of events in respect of Edward V's ascension to the throne very much changed that Friday morning in the Tower.

Strawberries and Treason

Our account of the fateful morning meeting that day comes primarily from Thomas More, and when we say More, I think it is fair to reinforce the probability that this version of events is fairly heavily influenced by Morton.[8] Since we have then to distill our explanation through the filter of one of Richard's most virulent enemies, I think I have to declare my bias here. In my view, Morton was a very astute and clever individual.[9] In using More in part as his de facto mouthpiece, he did not seek to provide a totally false account.[10] Such an effort at deception would have been too obvious to too many individuals, some of whom would still have been alive and able to comment on any evident fabrications. Providing specific detail could, such as the case of the citation of Elizabeth Lucy, be liable to lose vital credibility. Rather, I think he sought to present a fairly accurate account, but one salted with misdirection at crucial points in order to sway subsequent opinion. I think, therefore, the basic account of the Council meeting is fairly accurate, but cleverly manipulated.[11]

Croyland, in his *post hoc* interpretation of the day's events, adjudges Richard to have been 'shrewd' in splitting the Council that day. However, this may well have been a simple matter of expediency. There was a country to run and a king to be crowned and, as again Stallworth noted, much business to be accomplished, especially in relation to the coronation. If Richard did plan this division with a mind to what subsequently occurred, he must have known something by the 12th and yet, apparently, not on the 11th, since he had held over Ratcliffe's departure from the day before, as evidenced by the Neville letter. I cannot dismiss this degree of perhaps one day's foreknowledge as at least a potential possibility. However, as I shall argue, it is the emotion which is expressed and precipitate action taken on the 13th that implies that what changed Richard's mind happened that very morning.

Sir Thomas More reports that at the start of the Council meeting there was an affable tenor to proceedings and the Protector himself was in good spirits. But now something must have happened. It is not clear whether Richard was called away from the meeting (which is what I suspect happened) or whether he himself initiated a short break. I am inclined to the former interpretation, although I am a firm believer in strawberries. This small point about strawberries, so insignificant in itself, seems to me to have the ring of truth about it.[12] It may well be that Richard used this as a 'time-filler' to cover what he might have anticipated would be only a short interruption. Since I believe he had not yet received the crucial revelation, I read no malevolence into the request, but one that roughly equates to the modern idea of a morning coffee break.

I think the interruption was made at the behest of Catesby. It is my thesis that on that morning, Catesby provided Richard with evidence, and perhaps indeed written evidence,[13] of the existence of the pre-contract. I think this evidence came from Catesby's direct association with Eleanor Butler through his father and step-mother,[14] and his own personal relationship. I suspect the written evidence was something that he had retained since the time of the pre-contract itself, now some decades earlier; after all, he was a lawyer. Further, I think Catesby told Richard that he had not revealed this to him earlier either on the tacit or explicit orders of Lord Hastings, who at some juncture in the past had told Catesby to remain silent on the issue. I believe that this was the knowledge which Hastings had shared with his friend and former king, Edward IV. It left Richard in a terrible quandary. If the information was true, he was rightful King of England and one of his oldest allies and comrades in arms, William, Lord Hastings had kept the fact from him. It was, I believe, this betrayal by the absence of an action which left Richard in a white heat of anger. It was this anger that spilled over when he re-entered the council chamber. In the interim interval of about an hour, I think Richard had been very busy. He must have assembled a body of armed men who waited outside the chamber for the crucial signal (*see* Figure 24). The signal was to be a banging on the council table, at which the armed men were to take up the cry of 'Treason.' It was also clear that some thought had been given as to who would be arrested and detained from those present in the council chamber. Overwhelmingly angry as he was with Hastings, there were others in that room who had no love for the Protector and from whom Richard understood that he himself needed subsequent protection.

On Hastings' Surprise

Although we read of the dark dreams and forebodings on behalf of some of those members of the Council,[15] I see this as *post hoc* rhetoric by commentators seeking some sort of coherent account of events. I think the overwhelming impression that we get of Hastings' reaction to the sudden happenings of that morning is one of almost complete surprise. For example, only a short time before, Croyland talks of 'Hastings bursting with joy.'[16] The empirical question which derives from this observation, and other allied commentaries, is why Hastings should be surprised? If Hastings had indeed been plotting in a conspiracy against Richard, and further if Catesby had earlier approached him about his acquiescence to Richard's ascent of the throne and Hastings had replied in the fierce negative, why would Hastings have been so surprised by these events? The fact that he was is surely attested to by the fact that he had little or no support present within or close to the Tower, at least sufficient to provide him any personal protection. Most certainly Richard was able, fairly easily, to detain and execute him in short order, and one wonders whether this would have been possible had there been a large contingent of Hastings' men around?

When the Protector first returned to the council chamber, it was only Hastings who had the courage to reply to Richard's angry inquisition. This act by Hastings does not argue for a guilty conscience about nefarious and conspiratorial actions planned with others or the reticence of having denied Catesby's overtures. Rather, I think it reflects the fact that Hastings suspected little or nothing of the coming storm. Indeed, from Hastings' perspective, he had done nothing wrong. On the contrary, with respect to the Protector, he had helped him on several recent occasions, most notably in circumventing a Woodville dominance following Edward IV's death. He did not then realise that his sin was fundamentally one of omission in not telling Richard of the pre-contract.[17] It was, I believe, not with respect to other plotting as has always been inferred in traditional accounts of the motivation involved, but critically a betrayal by omission. Richard saw treason in his silence. I also tend to think Richard was so incandescently angry because he saw Hastings' betrayal as that of a friend. This could well be the reason why Hastings paid the ultimate price that day while others who could certainly not have been counted as Richard's friends were, in contrast, spared.

Of course, it could well be that Catesby orchestrated the whole situation. He could have informed Richard that Hastings was opposed to his ascendancy to the throne but this does not accord with what I have noted earlier about the suddenness of the Protector's transformation on that morning. It does, however, argue that Catesby must have actively considered his strategy in relation to Hastings' downfall.[18] Had Richard spared Hastings, he might well have risen again to prominence and Catesby's position as his betrayer would have been precarious indeed. If this move was part of a larger Catesby strategy to remove one of his old mentors and barriers to the greater expansion of his lands in the Midlands, it was a hazardous enterprise indeed. As we shall see, Richard would later most certainly have been very glad of the military experience of his former comrade-in-arms at Bosworth,[19] and thus More's observation that the Protector was 'loath to lose him'[20] does indeed ring true here. As I have observed, we often understand, and can sometimes even respect, an enemy whose actions seek to damage or destroy us. However, in regard to betrayal, as I have noted earlier, we rarely forgive a friend.

Crossed Plots and Withered Arms

Perhaps the most unsatisfactory facet of the traditional account of the notion of the plotting against Richard is that it links together Hastings and Edward IV's queen dowager, Elizabeth Woodville.[21] I view this reported association as classic misdirection on behalf of More[22] and his shadowy sponsor, the Parson of Blokesworth. In my view, there is not one plot involving a collaboration of these two individuals but actually two separate issues here. I think each has become bound up in the single association with reference to 'withered arms,' and it is important to separate and explain these two distinct lines of threat. Most cleverly, More advanced a story on behalf of Richard which his readers will understand is manifestly false. Specifically, he reported:

> Then said the protector, 'Ye shall see in what wise that sorceress, and the witch of her counsel, Shore's wife, with their affinity, have by their sorcery and witchcraft wasted my body.' And therewith he plucked up his doublet sleeve to his elbow upon his left arm, where he showed a weerish, withered arm, and small, as it was never other. And thereupon every man's mind sore misgave them, well perceiving that this matter was but a quarrel. For well they wist, that the queen was too wise to go about any such folly. And also if she would, yet would she of all folk least make Shore's wife of counsel, whom of all women she most hated, as that concubine whom the king her husband had most loved. And also no man was there present, but well knew that his arm was ever such since his birth.[23]

However, now More can deny this assertion as a patently false claim and in so doing he can denigrate Richard accordingly.[24] I suggest that Richard's original observations were not physical but rather metaphorical in nature. The 'withered arms' he spoke of referred to his armorial bearings or position in society. We do know that Richard himself was keen on these identifications, having himself founded the College of Arms.[25] Thus, what Richard was referring to were the separate efforts to reduce his authority and rightful position.[26] In respect of the first threat by Elizabeth Woodville and those of her affiliation, the reference is to their attempt to remove or abrogate Richard's role and power as Protector of the realm. Indeed, Richard had been aware of this effort most probably from before the time that he left York. It was Hastings himself who had, in the early stages, kept him apprised of this threat. As Protector, Richard would have had certain rights and privileges which would have accompanied this position and efforts to remove them would indeed have 'withered his arms.' Although the accusation in More is directed toward the queen,[27] I think Richard was most probably concerned with all of the members of the Woodville affiliation, and perhaps at the forefront of his mind on that day was the 'Pontefract Three.' Their fate, as Richard now understood, was to be viewed as those who had plotted not just against the Protector of the realm but actually against their rightful king. It was in light of this that they were subsequent judged, an issue to which I shall return.

I am the first to admit that this reinterpretation is indeed contentious[28] and appeals to symbolism rather than known fact, a strategy of which I generally have a poor opinion.[29] However, it must be remembered that the alternative is to accept that Richard accused one of his erstwhile friends and one of the more powerful members of the aristocracy of physical damage through witchcraft when much of the known evidence indicates that Richard had no such deformity. While neither proposition is supported by direct evidence, it does appear to me that the invocation of witchcraft, which suggests an irrational action on behalf of the Protector, clearly provides an opportunity to slander Richard. It is one, of course, that the fabulists and playwrights have found too appealing to ignore over the years.

Now, on a totally distinct front came the inaction of Hastings, whose omission had reduced Richard, not from his role as Protector, but rather from the throne itself. Again, this silence on behalf of Hastings had threatened to exclude Richard from his now rightful position as King of England. As monarch he would have had pre-eminent rights and privileges and so Hastings' inaction here had also truly 'withered his arms.' What More (and assumedly Morton) appear to have done is to take the two separate issues (the curtailment of the office of Protector and the exclusion from Richard's place as monarch) and have tied these strands together to cause confusion. In so doing they have caused subsequent historians to seek to explain a most unlikely alliance between Hastings and Elizabeth Woodville[30] (and, as we know, also Jane Shore), which is surely unsatisfactory at best and at worst simply untenable.[31]

To complete the misdirection, More (and Morton?) have framed these accusations by Richard as though he claimed he was physically damaged. Although he may have used the idea of arms as metaphorical representation of physical damage, it is doubtful whether he would have presented an outright falsehood for his enemies to exploit. It was a clear tactic indeed to turn a metaphor into a statement of physical reality and then to tie two actions into a single strand, so clever that it has persisted now for more than five centuries. In all of this misinformation, it is not only the queen and Hastings who were specified, but subsequent commentators have included nearly all of those who were detained that day. Most interesting and most incongruous of all is the purported association between Elizabeth Woodville and her husband's favorite mistress, Jane Shore. It is to this element of the story that I now turn.

The Role of Jane Shore

Richard, as Duke of Gloucester and subsequently as King of England, had a record of dealing very considerately and indeed generously with almost all of the women with whom we know he had interactions.[32] In contrast, Jane Shore apparently got what appears to be rather harsh treatment. It was not simply the public penance imposed upon her but it was the spoilage of her goods and holdings that reduced her personal wealth significantly and was presumably a major factor in her purported descent into the poverty which More later reports. Neither Henry VII nor his son, nor those who had previously benefited from her intercession and beneficence, apparently saw any need to alleviate her from this state. Following Mr Lynom's proposal, Jane and he seem to have married. However, this followed her personal punishment by Richard. Was this level of retribution merely a result of her having been Edward's mistress

1. The Great Hall of Middleham Castle. Said to be Richard's favourite residence, Middleham was most probably where he first received news of his brother's untimely death. (*Photograph by the Author*)

2. Sheriff Hutton Castle, North Yorkshire. This was where Anthony Woodville, Earl Rivers was taken after his arrest at Northampton and it was here on 23 June 1483 that the *Testamenta Vetusta* tells us that he made his Will. Shortly thereafter, he was transferred to Pontefract (Pomfret) Castle and there executed. (*Photograph by the Author*)

3. Elizabeth Woodville, widow of Edward IV. The standard interpretation of William, Lord Hastings's demise has him in a conspiracy with the dowager queen to do away with Richard, Duke of Gloucester. Given their reputed antipathy towards one another, this standard interpretation bears careful re-analysis. If Hastings was not plotting with the queen, why did Richard have him executed with such dispatch?

4. The Cely Letter from the critical period of June 1483. From Hanham, A. (1975) (ed.), *The Cely Letters 1472–1488*. (pp. 184–5). Oxford University Press: London.

5. John Talbot, first Earl of Shrewsbury (*c.* 1387–1453).

6. Margaret Beauchamp (1404–67). This image depicts the second wife of John Talbot, the first Earl of Shrewsbury, in prayer.

7. Sir William Catesby, father of William Catesby 'the Cat'. Taken from the representation of the brass in the church at Ashby St Ledgers. (*Photograph by the Author*)

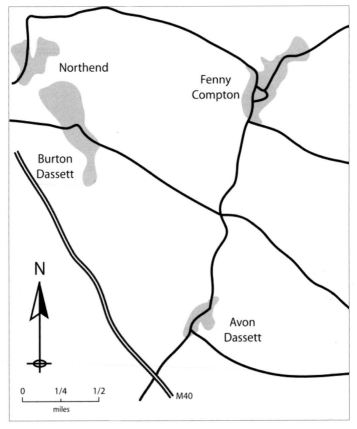

8. Burton Dassett (Great Dorset) and Avon Dassett are in extremely close proximity to Fenny Compton. This proximity and the resulting convenience is most probably the reason why Lady Eleanor Butler, the incumbent of Great Dorset returned the Manor of Griff to her father-in-law Lord Sudeley in apparent exchange for the rights to the manor of Fenny Compton.

9. The brass of Sir Richard de la Bere, son of Joan Barre and Sir Kynard de la Bere, in Hereford cathedral. Sir Richard is famous there for having twenty-one children. (*Photograph by the Author*)

10. All Saints' Church, Burton Dassett. (*Photograph by the Author*)

11. Could this representation of the Madonna contain something of the facial features of Eleanor Butler? (*see* also Figure 33)

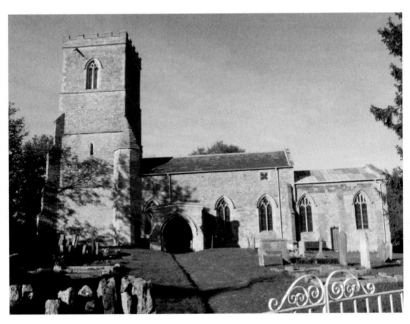

12. Grafton Regis Church. Was this the site of the bigamous second marriage of Edward IV with Elizabeth Woodville? (*Photograph by the Author*)

13. The Church of the Blessed Virgin Mary and St Leodegarius is shown on the right while the Gatehouse of the Manor of Ashby St Ledgers, the home of the Catesby family is shown on the left. Both Sir William and his son are buried in the church. The gatehouse is purportedly one of the locations which played a pivotal role in the genesis of the Gunpowder Plot which sought to assassinate James I. (*Photograph by the Author*)

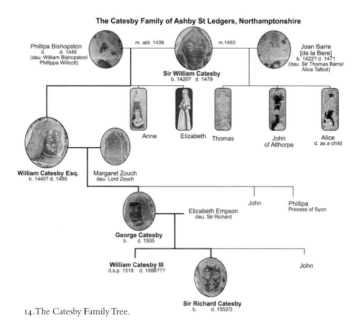

The Catesby Family of Ashby St Ledgers, Northamptonshire

Phillipa Bishopston
b.   d. 1446
(dau. William Bishopston/
Phillippa Willcott)

m. abt. 1439

m. 1453

Joan Barre
[de la Bere]
b. 1422? d. 1471
(dau. Sir Thomas Barre/
Alice Talbot)

Sir William Catesby
b. 1420? d. 1479

Anne   Elizabeth   Thomas   John
of Althorpe

Alice
d. as a child

William Catesby Esq.
b. 1440? d. 1485

Margaret Zouch
dau. Lord Zouch

John

Phillipa
Prioress of Syon

Elizabeth Empson
dau. Sir Richard

George Catesby
b.   d. 1505

William Catesby III
d.s.p. 1518   d. 1598???

John

Sir Richard Catesby
b.   d. 1552/3

14. The Catesby Family Tree.

15. The floor brass of Sir William Catesby (father of the 'Cat') in the Church of the Blessed Virgin Mary and St Leodegarius at Ashby St Ledgers, Northamptonshire. (*Photograph by the Author*)

16. A letter from Richard III to William Catesby. The full text and associated information is provided in Appendix V. (*By permission of the Folger Shakespeare Library*)

Left: 17. The full brass of William Catesby, also showing his wife, Margaret Zouche 'of whom I have ever been true of my body', as Catesby noted in his Will. She was the only person to act as his executor following his execution.

Above: 18. The head of William Catesby. Note the scored line across the neck. (*Photograph by the Author*)

Below: 19. The name plate of the tomb of William Catesby and his wife Margaret. Note the different lettering and absence of a capital letter for Margaret's name as well as the irregular spacing. It is strongly suggestive that this was added later and, overall, the name plate is a poor piece of work. (*after Bertram, 2006*)

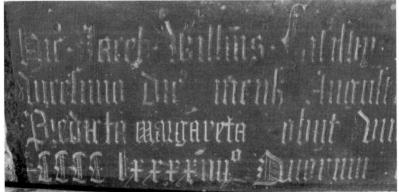

20. Note how the new plate has been cut into the fabric of the original memorial. (*Photograph by the Author*)

21. Garter Stall Plate of William, Lord Hastings in St George's Chapel at Windsor Castle.

22. The Council Chamber of the White Tower of the Tower of London. (*Photograph by the Author*)

23. The entry of the armed party to the Council Chamber in art. (*Drawn by G.F Sargent and engraved by J.C. Varrall*)

24. It was most probably through this doorway, and/or its companion in the same wall a little further to the north, that the armed group of men came into the Council Chamber crying 'Treason' at the agreed signal. (*Photograph by the Author*)

25. The brass of Jane Shore from Hinxworth Church in Hertfordshire. (*Photograph by the Author*)

Above left: 26. This portrait of a young woman from Eton College is purported to be that of Jane Shore, who is thought to have interceded with King Edward in restoring some of its lands and possessions after Parliament had annulled the gifts of Henry VI who had founded the institution.

Above: 27. The brass of the Shore family in Hinxworth Church, Hertfordshire. Jane and her daughter are featured on the lower right. (*Photograph by the Author*)

Left: 28. The coat of arms is that of Robert Stillington (1420?–1491), the Bishop of Bath & Wells, and is taken from the article by Greensmith (1977). The specific description given was: 'Quarterly 1 and 4; Silver, 3 Leopard's faces all gold, 3 blue fleur-de-lys.' They are here shown impaled with the arms of the See of Bath and Wells.

STILLINGTON

29. The Abbey of Croyland at which the second continuation was created. The identity of the second continuator still continues to be debated. (*Photograph by the Author*)

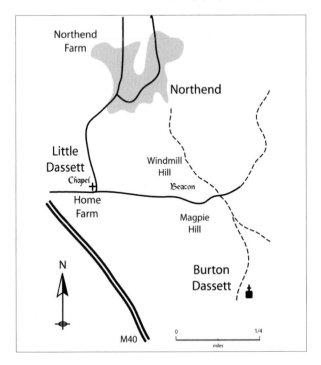

30. The purported Templar chapel in the Little Dassett area. Note its location on this map immediately below the label for Little Dassett and above Home Farm.

31. The Tower on the Burton Dassett hills.

32. Details of the wall paintings showing a part of the sequence of the Passion of Christ from the Church of the Blessed Virgin Mary and St Leodegarius at Ashby St Ledgers. The manor of the artist of this work bears a strong resemblance to that of the work in All Saints' Church, Burton Dassett. (*Photograph by the Author*)

33. The arch above the nave of All Saints' Church, Burton Dassett showing some of the existing wall paintings. Like those in Ashby St Ledgers, these are fragile representations and in certain need of maintenance and restoration. The figure to the left of the apex of the arch is thought to be the Virgin Mary and it is her face which might represent the features of Eleanor Butler. *See also* Figure 11 (*Photograph by the Author*)

34 & 35. The roof structure of the churches of Burton Dassett (*left*) and Ashby St Ledgers (*right*). Such structures have probably been replaced and repaired on many occasions over the years, however, the similarity between them and their distinction from many others church roofs is certainly interesting. (*Photographs by the Author*)

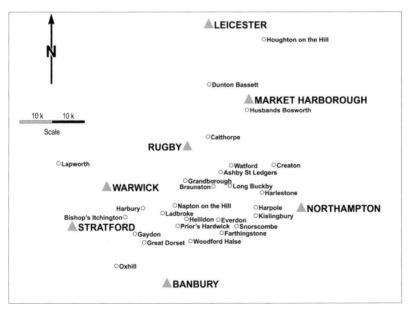

36. The landholdings of William Catesby prior to 13 June 1483.

37. The lands acquired by William Catesby after 13 June 1483.

38. The combined land holdings of William Catesby at the time of his death.

and having been subsequently passed perhaps from Dorset to Hastings after Edward's death? If so, it seems harsh treatment indeed for a woman whose fate was so controlled by a series of powerful men.

I do not see Jane's punishment as solely related to her sexual history. Thus, I cannot cast Richard in the role of prude here, especially given his knowledge of his brother's behaviour in such matters in general and his own history of illegitimate children.[33] Rather, I see in this punishment a much closer association between Jane and Hastings. In particular, I believe Richard suspected or indeed was told, again perhaps by Catesby, that Jane had been privy to the pre-contract. It is most likely that she was included as part of Hastings' downfall, since after all her punishment proceeded from that time. However, it is also possible that Edward himself had told her of his pledge to Eleanor Butler. Thus, I see Jane Shore's punishment as proceeding from the same anger that engulfed Hastings. However, this emotional storm obviously wore itself out, for Richard in his communication concerning Lynom provided evidence that at a later time he was willing to forgive Jane, albeit that she would be supervised by responsible family members in relation to her actions. In this light, Jane's downfall is not a result of her sexual activities but rather her knowledge of the politics of inheritance. I think this a more reasonable explanation for the destruction of her personal wealth, although, as I have noted, her penance does imply punishment for transgressions of a sexual nature as well. More's subsequent account seems one very much of myth and tragedy, rather than adhering to actual events. Again, it is here in creating a tragic figure for literary exploitation that we can view More's dissertation as both art and propaganda intermixed with historical observation. That we are, today, frustrated by this amalgam reflects upon our own division of knowledge and at least some of the criticism directed at More may well be anachronistic in nature.

The Motivations of William Catesby

When we look at the motivations of William Catesby that day, I think the issue is clear. He had seen, during his formative years, how the political winds could favour an individual one moment and destroy them the next. As a strong affiliate of Hastings, perhaps he anticipated that the supremacy of Edward V would prove most harmful to his own personal prospects. It is my belief that he bided his time and picked the moment to strike very well indeed, from his point of view.[34] His actions elevated him to the highest standing with the new monarch, while at the same time removed the one individual whose place and possessions stood directly in the way of his advancement.[35] From Catesby's perspective, the events of 13 June were exceptionally beneficial and he received a whole panoply of honours and rewards (*see* Appendix VI and Figures 36, 37 and 38). During Richard's reign he was arguably the second most powerful man in the realm, especially so after Buckingham's fall. Contrast this with the dearth of reward to Stillington and again we must suspect that Catesby did his new liege lord a signal service; since, when we examine it objectively, this was not a bad achievement for a relatively unknown lawyer from Northamptonshire. Indeed, I would argue that his rise was almost unprecedented.[36] However, these actions and achievements rebounded on him badly, directly following the debacle of Bosworth.

I am fairly sure that Catesby himself was at Bosworth. The primary reason for this is the celerity of his execution, so quickly following the day of the battle. However, as a lawyer, I do not think he actually fought himself. Rather, I think he was put in charge of the hostage, Lord Strange, with orders to execute him if the Stanley forces attacked Richard. As Strange survived, we can assume that Catesby hedged his bets here; after all, it would have been easy to kill Strange before Richard returned to his camp, assuming the king had been triumphant. Catesby expected some reward or at least commutation of punishment for this act. He lamented this in the famous line in his will: 'My lordis Stanley, Strange and all that blod help and pray for my soule for ye have not for my body as I trusted in you.' However, I think he also saved Stanley on that fateful day in the Tower.[37] I think he told Richard of the Hastings betrayal but told him Stanley was not directly privy to the pre-contract. It was this action by Catesby that saved Stanley that day. Again, he expected some degree of reciprocation two years later. As we know, he did not get it.

The second line in Catesby's will reads: 'I doubt not the King will be good and gracious Lord to them, for he is called a full gracious prince. And I never offended him by my good and Free Will; for god I take my juge I have ever loved him.' This has always been taken as a desperate piece of 'toadying' on behalf of an individual on the verge of execution. However, as we understand from a recent text,[38] William's mother-in-law, Elizabeth St John, was the maternal half-sister of Margaret Beaufort, the mother of Henry VII. In such circumstances, William and Henry would have been cousins by marriage. It was perhaps this relationship to which William was appealing and perhaps relying on. Although he himself was evidently disappointed in such hopes, his son George did eventually manage a reversal of the attainder, so perhaps William was looking to the future, even at this moment of his greatest terror.

In all I should say that Catesby was unlucky in his eventual fate. As he stood alongside his king, facing the rag-tag forces of Henry Tudor, he, like Richard, must have been fairly confident of success, and in his role as king's counsellor, he may even have been anticipating securing even more lands and possessions from those who would have forfeited them that day had Richard won. As we know, this never happened, and Catesby, like Richard, passed into myth and legend, largely shaped by Shakespeare and his dramatically and politically motivated stage production.

The Proclamation, the Parchment Roll and the Act

Following immediately upon the execution of Hastings and in the subsequent days, we seem to have a number of critical documents in circulation, and it is important to consider each of these and their potential author(s). The first is an observation of Thomas More's and, as with all of More's work, we have to look very carefully at what he says to try to distill any underlying truth and subsequent understanding. This story is purpose-designed to try to persuade readers that Hastings's execution was not an impulsive act but rather a pre-meditated one. Specifically, More reported:

> Now was this proclamation made within two hours after that he was beheaded, and it was so curiously indited [elaborately composed] and so fair written in parchment in so well a set hand, [professional] and therewith of itself so long a process [narration], that every child might well perceive that it was prepared before. For all the time between his death and the proclaiming could scant have sufficed unto the bare writing alone, all had it been put in paper and scribbled forth in haste at adventure. So that upon the proclaiming thereof, one that was schoolmaster of Paul's, of chance standing by and comparing the shortness of the time with the length of the matter said unto them that stood about him 'Here is a gay, goodly cast [trick] foul [basely] caste away for haste.' And a merchant answered him that it was written by prophecy.[39]

I view this as classic More misdirection. If Richard had needed to palliate the public opinion, the heralds would have rendered a verbal oration.

True, they may have read from a document, but it need not have been an elegantly written one. Of course, we have no evidence of this document, other than More's account, written some decades later. The story with its little vignette of the schoolmaster and the merchant appears to me to be one concocted very much to distract subsequent readers from the sudden immediacy of the act. In this manner, it serves to denigrate Richard in at least two ways. In respect of this parchment, as a final and parenthetical comment here, I believe it is very dangerous process to omit evidence altogether, however contentious. Like choosing which observations one will accept and which one will discard, it is fraught with peril. However, I think the stories of the merchant and the schoolmaster, around the parchment, are largely of More's invention or embellishment at the very least. There is, however, the further possibility that the author of the actual document, which I take to be a real proclamation, was William Catesby.[40]

The parchment is not the only document that appears around this time, for shortly after the week of the 13th, the Croyland continuator commented on another parchment roll (*see* Figure 29). Again it is important to quote the original source[41] directly; thus Croyland noted that:

From that day [16 June] both these dukes showed their intentions, not in private but openly. Armed men in frightening and unheard-of numbers were summoned from the North, and Wales and from whatever other districts lay within their command and power and on the 26th day of the same month of June, Richard, the protector, claimed for himself the government of the kingdom with the name and title of king; and on the same day in the great hall of Westminster he thrust himself into the marble chair. The pretext of this intrusion and for taking possession in this way was as follows. It was put forward, by means of a supplication contained in a certain parchment roll, that King Edward's sons were bastards, by submitting that he had been pre-contracted to a certain Lady Eleanor Boteler before he married Queen Elizabeth and, further, that the blood of his other brother, George, duke of Clarence, had been attainted so that, at the time, no certain and uncorrupt blood of the lineage of Richard, duke of York, was to be found except in the person of the said Richard, duke of Gloucester. At the end of this roll, therefore, on behalf of the lords and commonalty of the kingdom, he was besought to assume his lawful rights. It was put about then that this roll originated in the North whence so many people came to London although there was no-one who did not know the identity of the author (who was in London all the time) of such sedition and infamy.

As I have noted elsewhere, the author of this parchment roll is usually considered to have been Stillington, but it is my hypothesis that the author of this essentially 'legal' document was Catesby. If we dissect what Croyland says here, we can see that it nowhere contradicts the theory I have offered. In several places it actually confirms it. While it is clear that the Croyland author does not approve of this process, he makes it clear that there were specific attempts to show how Richard was exercising a legal right to the throne. It has been argued, largely on the basis of speculation, that the statements in this parchment roll did not match what was eventually included in the act which ratified Richard's right to the throne. Unfortunately, since we do not possess this parchment roll, much as we should like to, such debates continue to be speculation until further evidence is discovered.

Why did Stillington Reveal the Pre-contract?

One of the issues that is rarely considered to any great degree is: if he did actually do so, why did the bishop reveal the pre-contract? Also, again on the supposition that it was Stillington, why wait until some time presumably around 9 June? The traditional version has it that his motivation for this was 'revenge.' But revenge on whom? If it was Edward IV, he was already dead and the revenge could only have been on his progeny. If it was then indirect revenge on Edward IV through his son, we must remember that Stillington was a member of Edward V's Council and, as an old man, why would he do this to a youngster that he presumably knew to some degree and had a hand, albeit a small one, in raising? Further, Edward V had grown up largely separated from his father, and was the revenge motive enough for such a tired, sick old man?

We know Stillington was a staunch Yorkist supporter and had been all his life. If he were the source of the revelation he was acting against at least part of the family he had followed all his life. Some have said that Stillington didn't want to see a minority rule, but Edward V was rising thirteen and would be a fully mature monarch in his own right in only a couple of years; surely this was not a viable motive? And, as Mowat has noted, why did he wait until June, with all the preparations for the coronation going ahead?

It makes no sense: if he was going to tell Richard he could have told him on 5 May, the day after the entry into London, when the Duke of Gloucester could have then immediately sent for troops, rather than waiting until 10 June. The problem here is that if we view Stillington as the source, we are presented with significant problems in establishing a motive. However, such interpretational difficulties are totally obviated if Stillington changes from the source of the knowledge of the pre-contract to simply confirming that what was put to him by Richard was true. It is quite natural that Stillington's name has become associated with this revelation, as he was the only one of the three people present at the ceremony left alive and the inference is a natural one. Further, as a prior Chancellor of England and a leading member of the clergy, it is natural to associate his authority with so weighty a matter. However, the inside 'fixer' of events here seems to be the Speaker, William Catesby. I suspect that it was his influence that directed matters and I suspect that this was generally quite well known, as is evidenced by Henry Tudor's reaction immediately following Bosworth. One of the clinching factors in securing this argument is a brief assessment of who benefited following Richard's ascension to the throne. If it was Stillington who helped Richard to the position of ultimate authority in the realm, he received precious little, if any, reward. However, if, as I have proposed, it was Catesby, the reward was, as we have seen, indeed commensurate with the service (and *see* Appendix VI: The Offices and Lands of William Catesby).

Betrayal as a Common Denominator

The key to understanding Richard and his actions immediately following Edward's death is his abhorrence of betrayal. If we look at the men taken that June day in the Tower, the common denominator was their individual act of betrayal, the antithesis of loyalty.[42] Thomas Rotherham had already shown his hand earlier in relation to the queen and Richard had no trust there. With respect to Stanley, as Kendall notes, 'When he [Richard] was but seventeen years old – in the spring of 1470 – he had experienced Stanley's capacity for disloyalty, when that shift lord had been the husband of Warwick's sister.' The case of John Morton is also not hard to understand. Lancastrian at heart, his betrayals were multiple, changing sides whenever convenient, but a traitor to the house of York in the end. With him, Richard would have had few qualms about detainment. However, it was the betrayal of his friend and comrade Hastings that was deepest of all. I see no evident conspiracy here. Having dispatched Hastings it was a prudent move to detain those guilty of disloyalty also. Mere spatial and temporal proximity do not necessarily connote any causal connection. I think much of this putative conspiracy is created in the monograph of Sir Thomas More from whole cloth.

With respect to Rivers, Grey and Vaughan, they had plotted against Richard, as per the Stony Stratford episode: they were thus guilty of treason against the king, since Richard had been king in fact since the day Edward IV died (if the pre-contract were true). He did try to have them executed, but the Council refused and he abided by this decision – but when he knew it was treason against a king and not just betrayal of the Protector, on 13 June, he took immediate steps to have the execution warrants sent north, most probably early the following week.[43]

On Murdering the Relatives of Edward IV

I want to start these final considerations by bringing up a point that, in my view, is rarely given enough emphasis. Richard III did not have two nephews in the Tower at one time, he had three. Also, we know as certainly as we know anything of these times that Richard did not kill at least one of these nephews. Our certain knowledge extends to the fact that Henry VII did, in fact, execute one of these three boys. That it was Edward, Earl of Warwick, son of George, Duke of Clarence means that his demise has received much less publicity than the sons of Edward IV. However, the fact remains that one of the nephews of Richard III was certainly murdered by Henry VII who has, of course, been implicated in the murder of the other two boys also.[44] Parenthetically, we should also note that Henry VII's son, Henry VIII, executed Margaret Pole, Countess of Salisbury who was the daughter of George, Duke of Clarence and sister of Edward, Earl of Warwick. Thus, like his father before him, Henry VIII was also certainly involved in the extinction of Clarence's children.

In the end, almost everyone will want to know how the present information provides the 'solution' to the mystery of the 'Princes in the Tower' I am sorry to disappoint, but it does not really address this issue.[45] Until history uses much more sophisticated techniques such as concept maps and advanced simulation models, we shall only take diminishingly small steps toward the goal of solving such a mystery. Even if we are able to use such powerful tools, we need to be able to distill methods which will tell us whether the problem is, or is not, soluble. And we shall want to be able to specify what additional information it is that will allow an eventual solution and whether it will be feasible that such 'new' information can or will ever be distilled. All this is in the future, but for the present, we must try to provide a synopsis for what the present observations say about the persistent mystery of the two boys and their disappearance from the Tower of London.

The first point is that the sequence I have described tends to support the contention that the boys were illegitimate and thus barred from ascending the throne of England. This being so, Richard, Duke of Gloucester had no immediate need to have them murdered. Indeed, one can argue that under the circumstances they stood in almost exactly the situation as Edward, Earl of Warwick, the son of Richard's brother, George, Duke of Clarence, who was also before Richard in line for the throne but barred because of a different impediment, that of Clarence's attainder. It would seem that those who accuse Richard of 'nephewcide' must also therefore, accuse him of evident inconsistency. After all, why murder two inconvenient nephews and leave the third alive. Let me be very explicit on this point: I do not think that the proposition I have advanced in this work rules out Richard as being behind any purported murder. After all, his dispatch of William, Lord Hastings, Earl Rivers and others certainly demonstrates that Richard was a man of his times, and these were dangerous times. I do not think that we can, with any certainty, rule out the possibility of his involvement. It is just when we come down to a full and complete analysis of the existing information, there is no evidence of murder, and with the frustrating and possible exception of the 'bones' in Westminster Abbey, precious little evidence of any untimely death at all.

Richard and his Motivations

After all this discussion, there is one individual, quite obviously the key person in all of these events, whom we have encountered here really only in outline. The central question is: what of Richard in all these events? I think it best to judge him by his actions, certainly not by the opinion of biased commentators. When we do this we see that Richard was no paragon of untrammeled virtue, but then neither was he the cartoon tyrant that popular history has rendered him. As I have observed, he was a man of his times. With respect to the executions he approved, the four primary examples we have encountered in this text have, as I have emphasised, a common motivational factor: betrayal. Colyngbourne, as an additional example, is also a straight case of treason[46] and Buckingham was executed because of his betrayal in his mysterious act of rebellion. It is doubtful if Colyngbourne sought to see the king, but we know Buckingham did apply for this privilege, which was summarily denied. If we apply these same motivational sources to the case of Hastings I think we see the consistent pattern I have observed. Hastings' 'betrayal' was all the more painful because Richard saw him as an ally. Thus the celerity of his punishment was in proportion to the perceived degree of betrayal. Colyngbourne's case took several months to mature. Buckingham's case took several days following his capture. However, Hastings' rate of dispatch was more in the order of mere minutes. To an extent, Hastings' betrayal extended to Jane Shore, but as a woman and only an indirect participant Richard dealt severely but not terminally with what he must have seen as being a betrayal of his brother and, indirectly, of himself. The rapidity of the execution of Hastings argues strongly for an act committed in the heat of anger. I am persuaded that Richard regretted his action, and especially two years later on the road to Bosworth where the old warrior Hastings may have helped tip the balance of the battle.

It is a demonstrable fact that Richard could strike for the purpose of political expediency. The events of Stony Stratford show this clearly. Arguably an act of self-defence in the grander scheme of things, Richard was quick to dispatch those who sought his destruction. With respect to the princes, I think it is a question of whether Richard saw them more as his brother's sons or as the queen's Woodville heirs. I tend to think the former. Betrayal was so wounding to Richard because he himself was so loyal. To him, his motto was not simply words but rather a principle by which to live. He had been fiercely loyal to his eldest brother, following him into exile and even siding with him against his other brother George, Duke of Clarence in a direct family dispute. This, despite being closer to George during his formative years. His loyalty to Edward never swerved in life and I think, as a man of this principle, he would have distained to harm his brother's sons in death. I think he would have thought it simply below him. However, as rightful king, of political experience he would have been worried about factiousness and my best present estimate is that he would have quietly sent them out of harm's way. I think Richard was rather straight-laced, compared at least to his partying brother. The somewhat dour northerner may well have been relatively unpopular in the more sophisticated south, a propensity that continues to the present day.[47] Despite all that occurred, I think Richard still viewed his nephews as a family responsibility and would have, as far as possible, protected them. I think the reason that the subsequent Tudor regime lived in a state of fear, and the reason Elizabeth Woodville eventually reconciled herself to Richard, was that they both knew this fact.

8

Summary and Narrative

A Narrative of Eighty-eight Days

In the early days of April 1483, while still at his northern estates, Richard heard the distressing news that Edward the king had died. Although not completely unexpected, this news was naturally upsetting, especially to one who had been such a loyal supporter throughout his whole life of his idolised elder brother. Arranging for services of remembrance for the dead king, Richard pledged his allegiance to Edward's son, and had his retainers do likewise. He sent comforting words to Elizabeth Woodville, the grieving widow. She was clearly not absolutely prostrate with grief since before he left the north Richard heard from William, Lord Hastings of various Woodville machinations. Perhaps aware that his brother had made him Protector, he would have certainly been apprised of that fact fairly quickly and the Woodville actions were thus not merely against him personally, but they also showed disrespect for the last wishes of his recently deceased brother and monarch. Such actions showed scant regard for Edward's memory and it must have been a wary Duke of Gloucester who at last set out from Yorkshire for London.

Efforts had apparently been made to co-ordinate the respective journeys of Richard and his nephew. Not only known by written evidence but the simple geography of the respective routes, Edward's retinue made an obvious and expressed effort to meet with Richard at a mutually agreeable site, which was evidently Northampton. Possibly Richard saw these arrangements as a litmus test of the intentions of the wider Woodville diaspora? Would Rivers and his companions follow the agreed arrangements to the letter? Would they do as they had promised? Whatever the reason, it appears that Rivers and members of the new king's party deviated from the agreement. Spurred on by Hastings' warnings[1] and the now express antipathy of the recently met Duke of Buckingham, Richard interpreted the missed meeting at Northampton as evidence of Woodville double-dealing and he moved quickly to secure his situation. He assumed control of the person of the king and had Rivers, Grey and Vaughan sent to various strongholds in the north which he himself controlled. While I suspect that it might have been the desire of the king and those of the Woodville family to stay at the family home in Grafton Regis for the night that created this situation, it is evident that in failing to satisfy Richard about this Rivers had made a tactical mistake. It was one for which he and his colleagues would pay dearly.

With the young king safely in his charge, Richard now proceeded to London. Here, he assumed his rightful position as Protector and de facto leader, his actions negating the idea of a council of equals, which was never his brother's intent. In this role he put in motion the preparations for his nephew's coronation. The absurd date of 4 May, which the Woodvilles had argued for, was revised in light of the scale of the actual preparations needed. Despite his move to cement his position at Northampton, Richard was still aware of the efforts of other members of the Woodville clan to undermine his protectorate and overthrow him personally. In light of these dangers, he sent to those of his affiliation in the north for reinforcements. After all, he did not know his nephew very well and instability may well have followed the coronation when the new king would begin to have a much greater say in matters. The coronation, now scheduled for late June, was to have some form of parliament to follow. It was against these contingencies that Richard called for reinforcements. For surely, if Richard could have retained the reins of government for the few short years it would take his nephew to come to maturity, he could stabilise the country against internal conflicts while educating his young nephew in the role of royal leadership. This would give Richard time to emphasise his own role as bulwark of the northern marches and to see Edward V move beyond the status of Woodville puppet into a king in his own right. This strategy was put into place and, up to 13 June, proceeded accordingly.

The Fateful Day

Then, on 13 June, Catesby revealed the pre-contract to Richard, about which Hastings has previously sworn Catesby to silence. However, it was not too late to prevent the coronation and the assumption of the throne by a 'bastard slip'. Catesby acted at this crucial moment almost completely for reasons of his own. The timing was indeed critical; only a few more days and the course of events would have been unalterably fixed. The revelation left Richard in a terrible quandary. I do not believe Richard would have taken Catesby solely at his word, but Catesby had documentary proof, saved from the time when he knew Eleanor Talbot very well indeed.[2] It may have even been during this fateful hour that Richard solicited Stillington either to confirm or deny the validity of this pre-contract. In confirming what Catesby had revealed, Stillington became the living evidence of the pre-contract and subsequently the public face of its validity. Now events moved very quickly. Perhaps Buckingham was summoned and apprised of the situation; perhaps he was already present; but something had now to be done. Richard was livid with Hastings, and a party of armed guards was assembled. Richard must have also wanted to know who else was party to this information, who else had known? Catesby now moved to have some of his rivals removed or neutralised; primarily John Forster was arrested and others were implicated, including individuals Richard knew that he could not trust.

After this fateful hour, the Protector returned to the council chamber. What should happen to those whose actions would cause the death of the Protector? Unaware of his danger, since his act was one of omission, Hastings was the only one to speak up and declare that they who countenanced such an action deserved death. In Richard's eyes, he condemned himself out of his own mouth. No wonder Richard was so incensed. This was a man he had fought alongside, a man who was his brother's best friend and ally, a man he trusted to the utmost and now his pejorative silence concerning the pre-contract had put Richard in peril of his very life. Richard's anger was palpable; so much so that he called for Hastings' immediate execution – a hasty, and eventually ill-advised, act. The other 'conspirators' were rounded up. Despite a blow being aimed at Stanley during the melée and indeed finding its mark, he was not seriously injured and Catesby spoke up for him. Catesby's reassurance returned Stanley to favour and three weeks and two days later he would attend Richard's coronation. Ever suspicious of Morton, Richard had him removed and imprisoned, but he was much less harsh with Rotherham than the other cleric suspected of betrayal. As well as Foster and Oliver King, Richard's anger fell upon Jane Shore, an intimate of the now-dead king, and the now-dead Lord Hastings as well. She was another thought to be cognisant of the pre-contract and its implications and her own silence was deserving of some punishment. However, calm again quickly reasserted itself and her guilt was palliated but not dismissed. Richard was now king by right of succession, but not by acclamation or by general recognition. Somehow, his legitimacy must be established in the mind of the nobility, the public and its most influential members. The coming weekend must have been one of great thought and of strategy as to how to achieve this. Of course, regime change would not be easy.

On Monday 16th, Richard looked to secure the young Duke of York from Westminster Abbey. What was important was the control of all of the critical pieces on the political chess-board, and the young boy in the Abbey was the key element currently beyond Richard's influence. Having achieved this, his first aim, Richard must now have planned his steps carefully. Revealing the evidence of the pre-contract to the Council was only one step. Many individuals were already very aware of Edward IV's propensity for the ladies and his pattern of behaviour in seducing women must have been generally known. The testimony of Stillington must have been very influential, but as to exactly how and when this testimony was rendered is still unclear. Perhaps the vacillations over the stating of Richard's various rights to the crown are evidence of the uncertainty at this time, although by January 1484 the reason was clearly stated. However, it is evident that by late June, Richard and those of his persuasion had begun to convince the greater public of the veracity of his claim. Worried by a minority rule, it was not unlikely that this news was acceptable to many who feared the instability that a child king would create. Others must have been wary of a Woodville-dominated administration and so favoured Richard accordingly. Indeed, Richard was much more of a known quantity. A proven leader in peace and in war with a reputation for fair government, he must have looked a fairly appealing candidate to a neutral observer, especially the good burghers of the capital, ever-mindful of their profits. It was thus unsurprising that the blandishments of Shaa and Buckingham met with somewhat receptive ears and at least tacit if not acclaimed acceptance.

The degree of subsequent acquiescence is reflected in the attendance at Richard's splendid coronation on 6 July, by which time the whole transition had been accomplished. Richard himself lived by his motto and, with the notable exception of his brother Clarence, he seems to have found it very hard to forgive any form of direct betrayal. Hastings was dispatched because of his implicit betrayal. Rivers, Grey and Vaughan paid a similar price for a similar but more active offence; this when Richard realised that their treachery at Northampton had been against their rightful king and not just the Protector (although they owed their allegiance to Richard as Protector in any case). It is indeed sad then that two years later, in the moments of his critical need at Bosworth, he was in the hands of men like Stanley, for whom the idea of loyalty was ever servant to expediency; word and oath always being sacrificed to benefit and gain. The impression of Richard with which we are left with is a man in whom trust and loyalty were very strong motive forces. That he was undone by men of lesser integrity remains one of the tragedies of history.

A Final Conclusion

When one looks to distill any pattern or causal sequence in history, it is inevitable that one features the actions, motivations and inferred intentions of some individuals while at the same time minimising the role, influence and effect of others, even if only by omission of detail and emphasis.[3] In what I have presented here, I have certainly featured a small group of people while not emphasising the role of significant others such as Henry Stafford, Duke of Buckingham, Lord Stanley, Bishop Morton, Elizabeth Woodvillle, Edward V and Archbishop Rotherham, all of whom were key players, and whose actions I have recorded but not brought to the fore. Of course, this means that the actual tapestry of events is somewhat distorted, since, for the individuals noted above, their own motivations and concerns were to the fore of their own consciousness and they would have reacted according to these different lights.[4] Thus, I ask the reader to see my account as an embedded one and whose primary observations are still immersed in the panoply of life as lived during the tumult of the summer of 1483.

Richard's brother, and arguably the centre of his loyalty and allegiance, died in early April 1483. Less than three months later, Richard himself wore the crown of England. During that time, a named king had been deposed, four influential lords had been executed and prominent individuals arrested, imprisoned and removed from the centres of power. Yet no battles had been fought and no major uprising had occurred in this spectacular transfer of power. Was Richard thus the ultimate in cunning and heartless ambition? Or, was he a man of his times, reacting to the uncertainties of events which faced him from April to early July? The eventual answer will always belong to history, but I see him in the latter light, a basically loyal and honourable man caught in the *Realpolitik* of his times. From this vantage point his actions are logical and, for him, reasonable. History should render on him, if not a favourable, at least a fair judgment.

Reference Materials

Original Sources

Bacon, F. *The History of the Reign of King Henry the Seventh*. J. Weinberger, Cornell University Press: Ithaca, NY, 1996.

Bruce, J. (ed). *Historie of the Arrival of Edward IV*. Camden Society: London, 1838.

Commines, P. de *Memoirs*. Henry G. Bohn: London, 1855.

Davies, R. (ed.) *Extracts from the Municipal Records of the City of York*. J. B. Nichols & Son: London, 1843.

Ellis, H. *Polydore Vergil's English History*. Camden Society: London, 1844.

Fabyan, R. *The New Chronicles of England and France*. Ed. H. Ellis, 1811.

Gairdner, J. (ed.). *Letters and Papers Illustrative of the Reigns of Richard III and Henry VII*. Longman, Green, Longman & Roberts: London, 1861.

Gairdner, J. (ed.). *The Paston Letters 1422–1509 A.D.* PRO: London, 1872.

Horrox, R. & Hammond, P. W. (eds). *British Library Harleian Manuscript 433*. Alan Sutton, for the Richard III Society: Upminster, Essex, 1979.

Mancini, D. (Ed. and trans. C. A. J. Armstrong). *The Usurpation of Richard III*. 1984.

Pronay, N. & Cox, J. (eds.). *The Crowland Chronicle Continuations: 1459–1486*. Alan Sutton, for the Richard III and Yorkist History Trust: London, 1986.

Thomas, H. and Thornley, I. D. (eds). *The Great Chronicle of London*. 1983.

Warkworth, J. *A Chronicle of the First Thirteen Years of the Reign of King Edward the Fourth*. Camden Society: London, 1839.

General References

Abbott, J. *History of King Richard the Third of England*. Harper & Brothers: New York, 1858.

Abbott, J. *Margaret of Anjou*. Harper & Brothers: New York, 1900.

Aleyn, C. *The historie of that wise and fortunate Prince Henrie of that name the Seventh, King of England. With that famed Battaile, fought betweene the sayd King Henry and Richard the theird named Crookbacke, upon Redmoore neere Bosworth. (Thomas Cotes for William Cooke, and are to be sold at his shop, neere Furnivalls Inne gate in Holbourne)*. London, 1638.

Ashley, M. *British Kings & Queens*. Carroll & Graf, 2002.

Baldwin, D. *Elizabeth Woodville*. Sutton: Stroud, Gloucestershire, 2002.

Buck, G. (ed. A. N. Kincaid). *The History of King Richard the Third*. Alan Sutton: Stroud, Glos, 1982

Cheetham, A. *The Llife and Times of Richard III*. Weidenfeld & Nicholson: London, 1972.

Chrimes, S. B. *Henry VII*. Yale University Press: New Haven, CT, 1999.

Clive, M. *The Son of York*. Knopf: New York, 1974.

Colwell, T .M. 'Why Richard III.' *The Ricardian*, 151 (2000), 161–178.

Cunningham, S. *Richard III: a Royal Enigma*. National Archives: London, 2003.

Dockray, K. *Richard III*. Alan Sutton: Stroud, Glos, 1988.

Drewett, R. & Redhead, M. *The Trial of Richard III*. Alan Sutton: Stroud, Glos, 1984.

Edwards, R. *The Itinerary of King Richard III 1483–1485*. Alan Sutton, for the Richard III Society: London, 1983.

Fahy, C. 'The Marriage of Edward IV and Elizabeth Woodville: A New Italian Source.' *English Historical Review*, 76 (1961), 660–672.

Fields, B. *Royal Blood: Richard III and the Mystery of the Princes*. Regan Books: New York, 1998.

Gairdner, J. *History of the Life and Reign of Richard the Third*. Cambridge University Press: Cambridge, 1898.

Goodman, A. *The New Monarchy: England 1471–1534*. Blackwell: Oxford, 1988.

Green, R. F. 'Historical Notes of a London Citizen, 1483-1488.' *English Historical Review*, 96 (1981), 585–590.

Halsted, C. A. *Richard III*. Longman, Brown, Green & Longman: London, 1844.

Hammond, P. W. & Sutton, A. F. *Richard III: The Road to Bosworth Field*. Constable: London, 1985.

Hanham, A. *Richard III and his Early Historians 1483-1535*. Oxford: Clarendon Press, 1975.

Helmholtz, R. H. ' The Sons of Edward IV: A canonical assessment of the claim that they were illegitimate.' In P. W. Hammond (ed.). *Richard III: Loyalty, Lordship and Law* (pp 91-103). London, 1986.

Hicks, M. A. *False, fleeting, perjur'd Clarence*. Alan Sutton: Stroud, Glos, 1980.

Hicks, M. *Anne Neville: Queen to Richard III.* Tempus: Stroud, Glos, 2006.

Horrox, R. *Richard III: a Study in Service.* Cambridge, 1980.

Jacob, E. F. *The Fifteenth Century 1399-1485.* Oxford, 1961.

Jenkins, E. *The Princes in the Tower.* Barnes & Noble: New York, 1978.

Kendall, P. M. *Richard the Third.* W. W. Norton: New York, 1955.

Kendall, P. M. *The Yorkist Age.* W. W. Norton: New York, 1962.

Kendall, P. M. (ed.). *Richard III: The Great Debate.* W. W. Norton: New York, 1965.

Kingsford, C. L. (ed.). '*Citizens of London.*' *Chronicles of London.* Oxford, 1905.

Knecht, R. J. ' The Episcopate and the Wars of the Roses.' *Birmingham History Journal,* VI (1957–1958), 108–131.

Lamb, V. B. *The Betrayal of Richard III.* Sutton Publishing: Stroud, Glos, 1990.

Lander, J. R. 'The Treason and Death of the Duke of Clarence.' *Canadian Journal of History,* 2 (1967), 1–28.

Lander, J. R. *Crown and nobility, 1450-1509.* Edward Arnold: London, 1976.

Lindsay, P. *The Tragic King: Richard III.* Robert . M. McBride & Co.: New York, 1934.

Littleton, T. & Rea, R. R. *To Prove a Villain.* MacMillan: New York, 1964.

Manning, J. A. *The Lives of the Speakers.* Willis: Covent Garden, London, 1851.

Markham, C. R. *Richard III: His Life and Character.* Smith, Elder & Co.: London, 1906.

More, T. (ed. R. S. Sylvester). *The History of King Richard III.* Yale University Press: New Haven, CT, 1976.

Myers, A. R 'The Character of Richard III.' *History Today,* 4 (1954), 511–521.

Myers, A. R. 'Hastings.' *History Today,* 1954, 710.

Okerlund, A. *Elizabeth Wydville: the Slandered Queen.* Tempus: Stroud, Glos, 2005.

O'Regan, M. 'The pre-contract and its effect on the succession in 1483.' *The Ricardian,* 54 (1976), 2-7.

Pendrill, C. 'Richard III.' In S. J. Hunt (ed.). *A History of Fotheringhay.* (pp. 17-19) Fotheringhay Church Restoration Committee: Peterborough, 1999.

Pollard, A. J. *The Wars of the Roses.* St Martin's Press: New York, 1988.

Pollard, A. J. *Richard III and the Princes in the Tower.* Sutton Publishing: Stroud, Glos, 1991.

Potter, J. *Good King Richard?* Constable: London, 1983.

Richardson, G. *The Hollow Crowns.* Baildon Books: Shipley, England, 1996.

Richardson, G. *The Deceivers.* Baildon Books: Shipley, England, 1997.

Richardson, G. *The Lordly Ones.* Baildon Books: Shipley, England, 1998.

Richardson, G. *The Popinjays.* Baildon Books: Shipley, England, 2000.

Richardson, G. *A Pride of Bastards.* Baildon Books: Shipley, England, 2002.

Rosenthal, J. T. 'The training of an elite group: English Bishops in the Fifteenth Century.' *Transactions of the American Philosophical Society,* 60 (5) (1970), 1-54.

Roskell, J. S. 'The Office and Dignity of Protector of England, with special reference to its origins.' *English Historical Review,* 68 (1953), 193-233.

Roskell, J. S. *The Commons and their Speakers in English Parliament 1376-1523.* Manchester, 1954.

Ross, C. *Richard III.* University of California Press: Berkley, CA, 1981.

Saul, N. *Richard II,* New Haven, CT: Yale University Press, 1997.

Scofield, C. L. *The Life and Reign of Edward IV*. Frank Cass & Co.: London, 1967.

Seward, D. *Richard III: England's Black Legend*. Penguin: London, 1982.

Speed, J. *The Historie of Great Britaine*. Humble: London, 1632.

St Aubyn, G. *The Year of Three Kings*. Athenaeum: New York, 1983.

Strachey, J. (ed.). 'Parliamentary Record,' Act of Attainder, *Rotundi Parliamentorum*, 1767-83, volume VI.

Walpole, H. *Historic Doubts on the Life and Reign of King Richard III*. Faulkner, Leathley & Smith: Dublin, 1768.

Weir, A. *The Princes in the Tower*. Ballantine: New York, 1992.

Williams, N. *The Life and Times of Henry VII*. Weidenfeld & Nicholson: London, 1973.

Williamson, A. *The Mystery of the Princes*. Alan Sutton: Gloucester, 1981.

Wise, T. & Embleton, G. A. *The Wars of the Roses*. Reed International: London, 1983.

Chapter 1: The Path to the Throne

Carpenter, C. (ed.). *Kingsford's Stonor Letter and Papers. 1290-1483* (pp 159-160). Cambridge: Cambridge University Press, 1996.

Davies, R. *Extracts from the Municipal Records of the City of York*. J. Nichols & Son: London, 1843.

de Blieck, E. *Analysis of Analysis of Crowland's Section on the Usurpation of Richard III*. http://crowland.netfirms.com/.2003.

De Commines, P. *The Memoirs of Phillip de Commines, Lord of Argenton*. Bohn: London, 1855.

Edwards, R. *The Itinerary of Richard III 1483-1485*. Alan Sutton, for the Richard III Society: London, 1983.

Gairdner, J. *Letters and Papers Illustrative of the Reigns of Richard III and Henry VII*, London: HMSO, 1861.

Green, R. F. 'Historical Notes of a London Citizen 1483-1488.' *English Historical Review*, 96 (1981), 585-590.

Hancock, P. A. 'On the Trail of King Richard III.' *Ricardian Register*, 29 (1) (2004), 8-10.

Hancock, P. A. 'On images of the "Princes in the Tower."' *Ricardian Register*, 30 (1) (2005), 4-18.

Hancock, P. A. ' No Richard Rhyme nor Reason.' *The Medelai Gazette*, 14 (3) (2007), 16-22.

HMSO. *The Tower of London* (p. 6), HMSO: London, 1974.

Kendall, P. M. *Richard III: The Great Debate*. W. W. Norton: New York, 1965.

Levine, M. 'Richard III – Usurper or Lawful King?' *Speculum*, 34 (1959), 391-401.

Mancini, D. *The Usurpation of Richard III*. Trans. C. A. J. Armstrong. Alan Sutton: Gloucester, 1989.

Markham, C. R. *Richard III: His Life & Character* (pp 93-102). Smith, Elder, & Co.: London, 1906.

More, T. *The History of Richard III.* Ed. R. S. Sylvester. New Haven, CT: Yale University Press, 1976.

Myers, A. R. 'The Character of Richard III.' *History Today*, 4 (1954), 511-521.

Pollard, A. J. *The Middleham Connection: Richard III and Richmondshire 1471-1485.* (p.1). Old School Arts Workshop: Middleham, 1983.

Pronay, N. & Cox, J. (eds.). *The Croyland Chronicle Continuations.* Alan Sutton, for the Richard III Society: London, 1986.

Richmond, C. 'The Princes in the Tower; The Truth at Last.' *Ricardian Register*, 26 (3) (2001), 10-18.

Smith, G. 'Hastings and the news from Stony Stratford.' *Ricardian Bulletin*, Summer 2006, 48-49.

Strickland, A. *Lives of the Bachelor Kings of England* (p. 143). Sempkin, Marshall, & Co.: London, 1861.

Wigram, I. 'Research Report.' *The Ricardian*, 7 (1963), 9-10.

Williams, B. 'Richard III and Pontefract.' *The Ricardian*, 86 (1984), 366-370.

Wood, C. T. ' On the Deposition of Edward V.' *Traditio*, 31 (1975), 247-286.

Wood, C. T. 'If Strawberries Were Ripe on June 13, Was October 2 Really Richard III's Birthday?' Paper given at the 1993 Meeting of the American Branch of the Richard III Society

Worth, S. 'Richard & the Parson of Blokesworth.' *Ricardian Register*, 26 (3) (2001), 4-7.

Chapter 2: Eleanor Talbot, Lady Butler

Ashdown-Hill, J. 'Lady Eleanor Talbot: New evidence: New answers; New questions.' *The Ricardian:* 16 (2006), 113-132.

Ashdown-Hill, J. ' Edward IV's Uncrowned Queen. The Lady Eleanor Talbot. Lady Butler.' *The Ricardian*, 11 (1997), (139), 166-190.

Ashdown-Hill, J. 'Further Reflections on Lady Eleanor Talbot.' *The Ricardian*, 11 (1999), (144), 463-467.

Ashdown-Hill, J. ' The Inquisition Post Mortem of Eleanor Talbot, Lady Butler, 1468.' *The Ricardian*, 12 (2002), (159) 563-573.

Ashdown-Hill, J. ' Lady Eleanor Talbot's Other Husband.' *The Ricardian*, 14 (2004), 62-81.

Ashdown-Hill, J. ' The Endowments of Lady Eleanor Talbot and Elizabeth Talbot, Duchess of Norfolk, at Corpus Christi College, Cambridge.' *The Ricardian*, 14 (2004), 85-86.

Ashdown-Hill, J. 'The Go-between.' *The Ricardian*, 15 (2005), 119-121.

Ashdown-Hill, J. (2009) 'Eleanor: The Secret Queen,' The History Press: Stroud, Gloucestershire

Baker, E. 'Notes on the paintings in Burton Dassett Church.' In F. O'Shauhnessy, Undated.

Barker, J. ' Sir Thomas Le Boteler.' *The Ricardian*, 45 (1974), 6-8.

Bertram, J. *The Catesby Family and their Brasses at Ashby St Ledgers*. Monumental Brass Society: Burlington House: London, 2006.

Campbell, J. *Lives of the Lord Chancellors* (pp 333-335). Murray: London, 1868.

Hancock, P. A. 'On the Trail of King Richard III.' *Ricardian Register*, 29 (1) (2004), 8-10.

Hargreaves, J. W & Gray, J. B. *The Passion Series of Wall Paintings in the Church of the Blessed Virgin Mary and Saint Leodagarius, Ashby St Ledgers, Northamptonshire*. JR Press: Daventry, undated.

O'Regan, M. 'The Pre-contract and its Effect on the Succession in 1483.' *The Ricardian*, 54 (1976), 2-7.

O'Shaughnessy, F. *The Story of Burton Dassett Church*. In possession of the author. Undated.

Phillips, G. *The Templars and the Ark of the Covenant*. Bear & Company: Rochester, VT, 2004.

Routh, P. 'In Search of Lady Eleanor Butler.' *The Ricardian*, 32 (1971), 4-7.

Smith, M. 'Reflections on Lady Eleanor.' *The Ricardian*, 142 (1998), 336-339.

Sutton, A. ' Richard III's "tytylle & right": A new discovery.' *The Ricardian*, 57 (1977), 2-8.

Tristram, E. W. ' Wall-paintings in Ashby St Ledgers Church.' Northampton & Oakham Architectural & Archeological Society, in *Associated Architectural Societies Report and Papers*, 38 (1926–1927), 352-360.

Vane, G. H. F. (ed.). ' Will of John Talbot, First Earl of Shrewsbury.' *Transactions of the Shropshire Archaeological Society*, (3rd Series) 4 (1904), 371-378.

Chpter 3: William Catesby, Esquire of the Body

Badham, S. & Saul, N. 'The Catesbys' Taste in Brasses.' In J. Bertram (ed.), *The Catesby Family and their Brasses at Ashby St Ledgers* (pp 36-75). Monumental Brass Society: London, 2006.

Bertram, J. (ed.). *The Catesby Family and their Brasses at Ashby St Ledgers*. Monumental Brass Society, Headley Brothers: Ashford, Kent., 2006

Brindley, D. *The Collegiate Church of St Mary, Warwick; The Beauchamp Chapel*. R. J. L. Smith & Associates: Much Wenlock, Shropshire, 2001.

Dickson, J. 'William Catesby.' *The Medelai Gazette*, 4 (3) (1997), 24-28.

Dickson, J. M. *William Catesby: 'Gras de Hower Gyd.'* Richard III Foundation: Las Vegas, NV, 2007.

Foss, P. *The Field of Redemore: the Battle of Bosworth, 1485*. Kairos Press: Newton Lindford, 1998.

Gairdner, J. *History of the Life and Reign of Richard the Third*. Cambridge: Cambridge University Press, 1898.

Hammond, P. W. 'The Cat, the Rat, etc.' *The Ricardian*, 50 (1975), 31.

Hammond, P. W. ' Colyngbourne's Rhyme.' *The Ricardian*, 67 (1979), 145-146.

Hancock, P. A. 'Solem a tergio reliquit: the Troublesome Battle of Bosworth.' *Ricardian Register*, 27 (2) (2002), 4-10.

Hillier, K. 'William Colyngbourne.' *The Ricardian*, 49 (1975), 5-9.

Hutton, W. *The Battle of Bosworth Field*. Nichols, Son & Bentley: London, 1813.

Ives, E. W. *The Common Lawyers of Pre-Reformation England*. Cambridge: Cambridge University Press, 1983.

Jones, M. K. *Bosworth 1485*. Tempus: Stroud, Glos, 2002.

Kendall, P. M. *Richard III*. W. W. Norton: New York, 1955.

Kleineke, H. 'The Catesby Family and their Brasses at Ashby St Ledgers: Book Review.' *The Ricardian*, XVII (2007), 108-109.

Leach, C. A. ' A Mess of Strawberries'. *The Ricardian*, 29 (1970), 21-22.

Morris, M. ' Catesby Brasses at Ashby St Ledgers.' *The Ricardian*, 39 (1972), 28-32.

Nicholas, N. H. *Testamenta Vetusta*. Nichols & Son: London, 1826.

Payling, S. '"Never desire to be grete about princes, for it is dangeros": the Rise and Fall of the fifteenth-century Catesbys' (pp 1-17). In: Bertram, J. (ed.), *The Catesby Family and their Brasses at Ashby St Ledgers*. Monumental Brass Society, Headley Brothers: Ashford, Kent, 2006.

Puplick, C. ' The Parliament of Richard III.' *The Ricardian*, 36 (1972), 27-29.

Richardson, G. 'The Cat, the Rat and the Dog.' *Ricardian Register*, 23 (4) (1998), 4-10.

Roskell, J. S. ' William Catesby, Counsellor to Richard III.' *Bulletin of the John Rylands Library*, 44 (1959), 145-174.

Serjeantson, R. M. ' The Restoration of the Long-lost brass of Sir William Catesby [at Ashby St Legers].' *Association of Architectural Societies*, XXXI (1912), 519-24.

Stephen, L. & Lee, S. (eds) *The Dictionary of National Biography* (pp 1193-1194). Oxford: Oxford University Press, 1917.

Sutton, A. F. 'Colyngbourne's Rhyme.' *The Ricardian*, 67 (1979), 145-146.

Sutton, A. F. & Hammond, P. W. (eds). *The Coronation of Richard III*. Alan Sutton: Gloucester, 1983.

Thorne, S. E. (ed.). *Readings and Moots at the Inns of Court in the Fifteenth Century* (p. lvii), Selden Society, Bernard Quaritch: London, 1954.

Williams, D. T. 'The Hastily Drawn-up will of William Catesby, Esquire, 25th August, 1485.' *Transactions of the Leicestershire Archeological and Historical Society*, 51 (1975), 43-51.

Chapter 4: William, Lord Hastings

Atreed, L. 'Hanham redivivus:' A salvage operation. *The Ricardian*, 65 (1979) pp. 41-50.

Chrimes, S. B. *Lancastrians, Yorkists and Henry VII*. Macmillan: London, 1964.

Coleman, C. H. D. 'The Execution of Hastings: A Neglected Source.' *Bulletin of the Institute of Historical Research*, 53 (1980), 244-247.

Craig, J. (1953). *The Mint: A History of the London Mint from A.D. 287 to 1948.* Cambridge: Cambridge University Press.

Davis, M. A. 'Lord Hastings Dies.' *The Medelai Gazette*, 13 (2) (2006), 26-32.

Donno, E. S. ' Thomas More and Richard III.' *Renaissance Quarterly*, 35 (3) (1982), 401-447.

Dunham, W. H. ' Lord Hastings' Indentured Retainers 1481-1483.' *Transactions of the Connecticut Academy of Arts and Sciences*, 39 (1955), 1-175.

Hamilton Thompson, A. ' The Building Accounts of Kirby Muxloe, 1480-1484.' *Transactions of the Leicestershire Archaeological Society*, II (Parts 7 and 8) (1919–1920).

Hammond, P. 'Research notes and queries.' *The Ricardian*, 39 (1972), 10-12.

Hanham, A. 'Lord Hastings and the Historians.' *English Historical Review*, 87 (1972), 233-248.

Hanham, A. 'Hastings Redivivus.' *English Historical Review*, 90 (1975), 821-827.

Hillier, K. ' William, Lord Hastings and Ashby-De-La-Zouch.' *The Ricardian*, 100 (1988), 13-17.

Keay, A. *The Elizabethan Tower of London: The Haiward and Gascoyne Plan of 1597.* Topographical Society: London, 2001.

Moorhen, W. E. A. ' William, Lord Hastings and the Crisis of 1483: An Assessment. Part 1.' *The Ricardian*, 122 (1993), 446-466.

Moorhen, W. E. A. ' William, Lord Hastings and the Crisis of 1483: An Assessment. Part 2 (Conclusion).' *The Ricardian*, 123 (1993), 482-497.

Ross, C. *Edward IV.* University of California Press: Berkeley, CA, 1974.

Thompson, J. A. F. ' Richard III and Lord Hastings – A Problematical Case Reviewed.' *Bulletin of the Institute of Historical Research*, 48 (1975), 22-30.

Turner, D. H. (1983) *The Hastings Hours.* Thames and Hudson: London

Weissbruth, C. A. ' Inquiry.' *The Ricardian*, 31 (1970), 12.

Wigram, I. ' The Death of Hastings.' *The Ricardian*, 50 (1975), 27-29.

Wolfe, B. P. ' When and Why Did Hastings lose his Head?' *English Historical Review*, 89 (1974), 835-844.

Wolfe, B. P. 'Hastings Re-interred.' *English Historical Review*, 91 (1976), 813-824.

Woodhead, P. *The Sylloge of Coins of the British Isles: Schneider Collection, English Gold Coins and their Imitations.* Spink & Sons: London, 1996.

Chapter 5: Jane Shore

Anon. *The History of Jane Shore.* printed by Henry Blake and Co: Keene, New Hampshire, 1794.

Barker, N. & Birley, R. ' The Real Jane Shore.' *Etoniana*, 125 (1972), 391-397.

Brown, R. D. '"A talkative wench (whose words a world hath delighted in)": Mistress Shore and Elizabethan Complaint.' *The Review of English Studies*, 49 (196) (1998), 398-415.

Crossland, M. *The Mysterious Mistress: The Life and Legend of Jane Shore*. Sutton Publishing, Stroud, Glos, 2006.

Davis, M. A. 'Lord Hastings Dies.' *The Medelai Gazette*, 13 (2) (2006), 26-32.

Fahy, C. ' The Marriage of Edward IV and Elizabeth Woodville: A New Italian Source.' *English Historical Review*, 76 (1961), 660-672,

Helgerson, R. *Adulterous Alliances: Home, State and History in Early Modern European Drama and Painting*. University of Chicago Press: Chicago, 2000.

Johnson, W. S. *The History of Jane Shore (Compiled from Authentic State papers)*. W. S. Johnson, Charing Cross: London, 1830.

King, S. *The unfortunate concubine; or, history of Jane Shore, Mistress to Edward IV, King of England; showing how she came to be concubine to the King with an account of her untimely end*. S. King, Publisher: New York, 1821.

Paget, G. *The Rose of London – Jane Shore*. Hutchinson: London, 1934.

Rowan, D. F. ' Shore's Wife.' *Studies in English Literature, 1500-1900*, 6 (3) (1996), 447-464.

Rowe, N. *The Tragedy of Jane Shore*. Players Press: London, 1995.

Scott, M. M. *Re-presenting Jane Shore: Harlot and Heroine*. Ashgate: Aldershot, England, 2005.

Seward, D. *The Wars of the Roses*. Viking: New York, 1995.

Shepard, A. C. '"Female Perversity," male entitlement: The Agency of Gender in More's *The History of King Richard III*.' *Sixteenth-Century Journal*, 26 (2) (1995), 311-328.

St Aubyn, G. *The Year of Three Kings*. Atheneum: New York, 1983.

Stephen, L. & Lee, S. (eds). *The Dictionary of National Biography* (pp 147-148). Oxford: Oxford University Press, 1917.

Sutton, A. 'William Shore, Merchant of London and Derby.' *Derbyshire Archeological Journal*, 106 (1986), 127-139.

Sweeney, J. 'Eleanor Butler, Queen to Edward IV?' *The Medelai Gazette*, 3 (3) (1996), 18-19.

Thompson, C. J. S. *The Witchery of Jane Shore*. Grayson & Grayson: London, 1933.

Chapter 6: Robert Stillington

Anon. 'False, fleeting, perjured.' *The Ricardian*, 25 (1969), 17.

Brindley, D. *The Collegiate Church of St Mary Warwick*. R. J. L. Smith & Associates: Much Wenlock, Shropshire, 2001.

Campbell, J. *Lives of the Lord Chancellors and the Keepers of the Great Seal: From the Earliest Times till the Reign of King George IV*. John Murray: London, 1868.

Campbell, W. *Materials for a History of the Reign of Henry VII* (p. 172). London: Macmillan, 1873.

Cassan, S. H (1829) *Lives of the Bishops of Bath and Wells*, C. and J. Rivington: London

Chrimes, S. B. *Henry VII*. Yale University Press: New Haven, CT, 1999.

Clive, M. *The Son of York*. Knopf: New York, 1974.

De Comines, P. *The Historical Memoirs of Philip de Comines*. Ed. W. McDowall.

Fleet Street, London, 1855.

Edwards, R. *The Itinerary of King Richard III 1483-1485.* Alan Sutton, for the Richard III Society: London, 1983.

Foss, E. *A Biographical Dictionary of the Judges of England* (p. 632). London, 1870.

Greensmith, L. T. ' Coats of Arms of some Ricardian Contemporaries.' *The Ricardian*, 56 (1977), 20-22.

Habington, T. *History of Edward IV.* Cotes, Holborne: London. 1640.

Hairsine, R. C. 'The Changing View from Oxford: I. Vivat rex in eternum.' *The Ricardian*, 53 (1976), 16-22.

Hairsine, R. C. 'The Changing View from Oxford: II. Most Christian Prince.' *The Ricardian*, 54 (1976), 14-23.

Hairsine, R. C. ' The Changing View from Oxford: III. Our Most Dread Sovereign.' *The Ricardian*, 55 (1976), 13-24.

Hammond, P. W. 'Research Notes and Queries.' *The Ricardian*, 52 (1976), 27-28.

Hammond, P. W. ' Stillington and the Pre-contract.' *The Ricardian*, 54 (1976), 31.

Hampton, W. E. ' A Further Account of Robert Stillington.' *The Ricardian*, 54 (1976), 24-27.

Hampton, W. E. 'Bishop Stillington's Chapel at Wells and his family in Somerset.' *The Ricardian*, 56 (1977), 10-16.

Hancock, P. A. ' The Polarizing Plantagenet'. *Ricardian Register*, 26 (4) (2001), 4-7.

Hicks, M. A. *False, fleeting, perjur'd Clarence.* Alan Sutton: Gloucester, 1980.

Hicks, M. A. 'The Middle Brother: False, fleeting, perjur'd Clarence.' *The Ricardian*, 72 (1981), 302-310.

Hicks, M. A. (1981). 'Clarence's Calumniator Corrected.' *The Ricardian*, 74, 399-401.

Hicks, M. A. 'False, fleeting, perjur'd Clarence: A Further Exchange, Richard and Clarence.' *The Ricardian*, 76 (1982), 20-21.

Jacob, E. F. *The Fifteenth Century 1399-1485.* Oxford: Clarendon Press, 1961.

Jex-Blake, T. W.'Historical Notices of Robert Stillington; Chancellor of England, Bishop of Bath and Wells.' *Proceedings of the Somerset Archeological and Natural History Society*, 20 (Part II) (1894), 1-18.

Kendall, P. M. *Richard the Third.* W.W. Norton: New York, 1955.

Knecht, R. J. ' The Episcopate and the Wars of the Roses.' *Birmingham History Journal*, VI (1957-1958), 108-131.

Lander, J. R. ' Edward IV: The Modern Legend: And a Revision.' *History*, 41 (1956), 38-52.

Levine, M. 'Richard III: Usurper or Lawful King?' *Speculum*, 34 (1959), 391-401.

Lingard, J. *The History of England from the First Invasion by the Romans to the Accession of William and Mary in 1688.* 6th edition, 10 volumes, Charles Dolman: London, 1855.

Markham, C. R. (1891). 'Richard III: A Doubtful Verdict Reviewed.' *English Historical Review*, 6 (22), 250-283.

Maxwell-Lyte, H.C. (1937). *The Registers of Robert Stillington, Bishop of Bath and Wells 1466–1941*, Somerset Records Society, Taunton, Somerset.

Mowat, A. J. 'Robert Stillington.' *The Ricardian*, 53 (1976), 23-28.

Ramsay, J. *Lancaster and York*. Oxford: Clarendon Press, 1892.

Richardson, G. *The Deceivers*. Baildon Books: Shipley1997.

Riley, J. C. *Rising Life Expectancy*. Cambridge: Cambridge University Press, 2001.

Rosenthal, J. T. ' The Training of an Elite Group: English Bishops in the Fifteenth Century.' *Transactions of the American Philosophical Society*, 60 (5) (1970), 1-54.

Roskell, J. S. *The Commons and their Speakers in English Parliaments 1376-1523*. Manchester: Manchester University Press, 1965.

Scofield, C. L. *The Life and Reign of Edward IV*. London, 1923.

Smith, M. ' Edward, George and Richard.' *The Ricardian*, 77 (1982), 49-49.

Somerset Record Society *The Register of Robert Stillington, Bishop of Bath and Wells 1466-1491*. 1937.

Vergil, P. *English History* (p. 117). Ed. H. Ellis. Camden Society: London, 1849.

Wigram, I. 'Clarence still perjur'd.' *The Ricardian*, 73 (1981), 352-355.

Wigram, I. 'False, fleeting, perjur'd Clarence: A further exchange, Clarence and Richard.' *The Ricardian*, 76 (1982), 17-20.

Wood, C. T. 'The Deposition of Edward V.' *Traditio*, 31 (1975), 247-286.

Chapter 7: Return to the Tower

Anon. 'Foundation of the College of Heralds.' *The Ricardian*, 25 (1969), 9.

Hammond, P. W. ' The Deformity of Richard III.' *The Ricardian*, 62 (1978), 35.

Hammond, P. W. 'The Illegitimate Children of Richard III.' *The Ricardian*, 66 (1979), 92-96.

Hammond, P. W. & Weeks, M. 'The Deformity of Richard III.' *The Ricardian*, 61 (1978), 21-24.

Johnson, D. 'The Real Reason why Hastings Lost his Head.' *The Ricardian Bulletin*, Winter 2007, 38-41.

Leach, C. A. ' A Mess of Strawberries.' *The Ricardian*, 29 (1970), 21-22.

McArthur, R. P. ' Thomas Stanley.' *The Medelai Gazette*, 7 (1) (2000), 22-26.

Pitfield, F. P. *Bere Regis Church, Dorset*. Thomas Williams Educational Trust, Dorset Publishing Co.: Sherborne, Dorset, 2000.

Pollard, A. J. ' North, South and Richard III.' *The Ricardian*, 74 (1981), 384-389.

Sweeney, J. 'Cecily Neville: The Rose of Raby.' *The Medelai Gazette*, 4 (1) (1997), 14-18.

Chapter 8: Summary and Narrative

Wood, C. T. 'The Deposition of Edward V.' *Traditio*, 31 (1975) 247–286.

Appendix I

The Cely, York and Stallworth Letters

The Cely Letter

The text of the Cely Letter reads:

Ther ys grett romber in the Reme/The Scottys has done grett yn Ynglond/ Schamberlayne ys dessesset in trobell. The Chavnseler ys dyssprowett and nott content/The Boshop of Ely ys dede/Yff the Kyng, God ssaffe his lyffe, wher dessett/The Dewke of Glosetter wher in any parell/Geffe my Lorde Prynsse, wher God defend, wher trobellett/Yf my Lord of Northehombyrlond wher dede or grettly trobellytt/Yf my Lorde Haward wher slayne. De Movnsewr Sent Jonys.[1]

A modern translation of this text reads:

There is great rumour in the realm, the Scots have done great [harm] in England, the Chamberlain is deceased in trouble, the Chancellor is desperate and not content, the Bishop of Ely is dead, if the King, God save his life, were deceased, the Duke of Gloucester were in any peril, if my Lord Prince, whom God defend, were troubled, if my lord of Northumberland were dead or greatly troubled, if my Lord Howard were slain.[2]

The two primary things to note about this manuscript are, first, that it appears to be more of a memorandum that a letter *per se*; second, it appears to reflect some accurate information, e.g. Hastings is dead, but equally some inaccurate information, e.g. Morton is dead. The rest of the text is largely doom and gloom and it is replete with conditional 'ifs.' Another interesting issue is the reference to the king, the Duke of Gloucester as well as 'my Lord Prince.' Given the nature of the observations, we can place this writing with reasonable accuracy and must perhaps believe that the Lord Prince was Richard, Duke of York. The general tenor of uncertainty is obvious; however, there may be yet more to glean from this communication.

The York Letters

The two relevant letters of the time were written by Richard, Duke of Gloucester to his loyal supporters in the city of York. They have been published in Davies, R., *Extracts from the Municipal Records of the City of York*, J. Nichols & Son: London, 1843. The first of written on 5 June 1483 and delivered to York by Brakenbury on 14 June. It reads:

The Duke of Gloucester, brother and uncle of King, protector and defensor, Great Chamberlain, Constable and Admiral of England. – Right trusty and well-beloved, we greet you well, and whereby your tres of supplication, to us delivered by your servant John Brackenbury, we understand that by reason of your great charges that ye have had and sustained, as well in the defense of this realm against the Scots as otherwise, your worshipful city remains greatly in poverty, for the which you desire us to be good means unto the King's grace for an ease of such charges as you yearly bear and pay unto his highness, we let you wit that for such great matters of business as we now have to do for the weal and usefulness of the realm, we as yet do not have convenient leisure to accomplish this your business, but be assured that for your kind and loving dispositions to us at all times showed, which we cannot forget, we in goodly haste shall so endeavor us for your ease on this behalf as that ye shall verily understand we be your especial guide and loving lord as your said servant shall show you, to whom it will like you him to give further credence; and for ye diligent advice which he hath done to our singular pleasure, unto us at this time we pray you to give him laud (praise) and thanks, and God keep you. Given under our signet, at the Tower of London, the 5th day of June

– To our right trusty and well-beloved the Mayor, Aldermen, Sherriff, and Commonalty of the City of York.

The second, a much more urgent communication, was written by Richard on 10 June 10th 1483 and was delivered to York by Richard Ratcliffe on 15 June. It reads:

The Duke of Gloucester, Brother and Uncle of the King, protector, Defender, great Chamberlain, Constable and Admiral of England. – Right trusty and well-beloved, we greet you well, and as you love the well of us, and the well and surety of your own self, we heartily pray you to come unto us to London in all the diligence you can possible after the sight hereof, with as many as you can make defensibly arrayed, their to aid and assist us against the Queen, her blood adherents and affinity, which have intended and daily doth intend, to murder and utterly destroy us and our cousin the Duke of Buckingham, and the old royal blood of this realm, and as it is now openly known, by their subtle and damnable ways forecasted the same, and also the final destruction and disinheritance of you and all other inheritors and men of honor, as well of the north counties as other countries that belong (to) us; as our trusty servant, this bearer, shall more at large show you to whom we pray you give credence, and as ever we may do for you in time coming fail not, but haste you to us hither. Given under our signet, at London, the 10th day of June. – To our right trusty and well-beloved John Newton, Mayor of York and his Brethren and the Committee of the same and every thane.

The Stallworth Letters

The two relevant letters of the time were written by Simon Stallworth to Sir William Stonor. These letters, among many others, have been published in Carpenter, C. (ed.), *Kingsford's Stonor Letter and Papers, 1290-1483* (pp 159-160), Cambridge: Cambridge University Press, 1996. The first, which was written on Monday 9 June 1483, reads:

Master Stoner, after dew recommendacons, I recommend to youe. As for tydyngs seyns I wrote to yove we her noun newe. Be Quene keps stylle Westm., my lord of zorke, my lord of Salysbury with othyr mo wyche wyll nott departe as zytt. Wher so evyr kanne be founde any godyse of my lorde

Markues it is tayne. Be Priore of Westm. Wasse and zytt is in a gret trobyll for certeyne godys delyverd to hyme by my lord Markques. My lord Protector, my lord of Bukyngham with all othyr lordys, as well temporale as spirituale, were at Westm. in be councel chambre from x to ij, butt per wass none bat spake with be Qwene. Ber is gret besyness ageyns be coronacion, wyche schalbe bis day fortnyght as we say. When I trust ze wylbe at London, and ben schall ze knove all be world. Be Kyng is at be towre. My lady of Glocestre come to London on thorsday last. Also my lord commendys hyme to yove, and gave me in commaundement to wryte to you, and prayes you to be god Master to Edward Jhonson of Thame; He wass with my lord, and sued to be made a denyson for fer of be payment of bis subsidy: and my lord send to Jeves be clerke of be corone and sawe be commissione and schewyde to hyme bat he schold pay butt vj s. viij d. for hymeself: and so wer he better to do ben to be mayde denyson, wyche wold coste hym be third parte of his goods. And as for suche as have trobyld with in be lordchype of Thame my lord wylbe advysyd by you at your commyng for be reformacion, yf ze take note or ze come: for he thynkess bat bei schalbe punished in examplee of othyr. And Jhesu preserve yove. In haste from London by be handys of your servande, be ix day of June.

Simon Stallworthe.

To the right honorabille Sir William Stoner, knyghte.

The second, which was written on Saturday 21 June 1483, reads:

Worschipfull Sir, I commend me to you, and for tydynges I hold you happy that ye ar oute of the prese, for with huse is myche trobull, and every manne dowtes other. As on Fryday last was the lord Chamberleyn hedded sone apone noon. On Monday last was at Westm. Grret plenty of harnest men: ther was the dylyveraunce of the Dewke of Yorke to my lord Cardenale, my lord Chaunceler, and other many lordes Temporale: and with hym mette my lord of Bukyngham in the myddes of the hall of Westm.: my lord protectour recevynge hyme at the Starre Chamber Dore with many lovynge wordys: and so departed with my lord Cardenale to the toure, wher he is, blessid be Jhesus, mery. The lord Liele is come to my lord protectoour, and awates upon hyme. Yt is thought ther schalbe xx thousand of my lord protectour and my lord of Bukyngham men in London this weeke: to what intent I knowe note but to keep the peas. My lord haith myche besynes and more then he is content with all, yf any other ways wold be tayn. The lord Arsbyschop of Yorke, the

Byshop of Ely ar zit in the toure with Master Olyver Kynge. (I suppose they schall come oute neverbelesse). Ber ar men in ther placese for sure kepynge. And I suppose bat ber shall be sente menne of my lord protectour to beis lordys places in be countre. They ar not lyke to come oute off ward zytt. As for Foster he is in hold and meue fer hys lyke. Mastres Chore is in prisone: what schall happyne hyr I knowe nott. I pray you pardone me of mor wrytyng, I ame so seke bat I may not wel holde my penne. And Jhesu preserve you. From London be xxj day of June be handys of your serand.

Simon Stallworthe.

All be lord chamberleyne mene be come my lordys of Bokynghame menne.

To the right worschipfull Ser Willm. Stoner, knyht.

Appendix II

On the Date of the Death of William, Lord Hastings

Modern historical research has tended to move away from what is seen as the more traditional, somewhat hidebound, litany of dates approach to history that was dominant in the late nineteenth and early twentieth centuries. Understandable though this trend is, dates are important. In the present context, the date of the execution of William, Lord Hastings is absolutely pivotal. If what I have suggested is correct, it is really quite critical that Hastings was beheaded on Friday 13 June 1483, in the first rush of Richard's anger. and not one week later on 20 June after a whole week for calmer deliberation.

In some sense, this concern over dating looks to be a non-issue. The date of Hastings' execution is given by the *Crowland Chronicle*[1] and there appear to be no contemporary records which contradict this information. This certainty might have persisted but for the protestation of Clements Markham, who, in 1891, argued that Hastings was actually executed one week later.[2] For Ricardian apologists this suggestion has some appeal, since it would tend to suggest that Richard had given Hastings the benefit of due process before dispatching him, instead of the summary execution which appears to argue for Richard's more malevolent motivations. Markham's position is not merely one of wishful thinking: he based his proposition on the Stallworth letter,[3] which was dated Saturday 21 June and referred to the execution as occurring on Friday last, the implication taken by Markham being that the preceding Friday was in fact 20 June.[4]

This proposal tended to languish, most probably because it was an interpretation (and one which we shall see for which there is an evident explanation), and especially because no corroborative evidence could be found. This all changed in 1972 when in her article[5] Alison Hanham cited a passage in the Acts of the Court of the Mercers' Company[6] which could be interpreted as indicating that William, Lord Hastings was still alive on Sunday 15 June, two days after his execution date. Her observations induced a response by Professor Wolfe,[7] who cited an impressive array of contradictory evidence which seemed to confirm the original date. Although Hanham had argued that some of the extant documents could have been altered, one of the primary sources of confirmation came from the building records of Kirby Muxloe castle.[8] Thanks to the great tradition of English workmen downing tools as soon as it looked like they might not be paid, we can see the most mobile of the workmen, the master masons, leaving Hastings' unfinished structure after only working on Monday 16 June 1483. From this we may infer that news of Hastings' demise reached the outskirts of Leicester sometime either during the weekend or on the Monday itself.

The dispute, however, did not stop at this juncture. Hanham had included her re-dating in her own text, 'Richard III and his Early Historians,'[9] which had appeared before she had the opportunity to see and reply to Wolfe's original article. This turned out to be an important sequence of events, since her argument persuaded Wood to include this revised date in his very influential article.[10] It has been suggested that this re-dating had only limited effect on what Wood proposed, but this is not so, especially in relation to the interpretation of the critical event of the release of Richard, Duke of York from sanctuary[11] in Westminster

After having the opportunity to examine Wolfe's original response, Hanham returned with her own response,[12] which focused primarily upon Wolfe's specific arguments rather than bringing any new information to the fight. As this interchange was proceeding, others were also prompted to reply to Hanham's original observations. Thompson's article[13] supported the interpretation of Wolfe and thus reconfirmed the original dating on 13 June. Much of the dispute revolved around the interpretation of the citation in the Acts of Court. Unfortunately, we only posses a sixteenth-century copy of the lost original and some concern was aired about the problems of copying and original dating. The most comprehensive evaluation of this issue was presented by Sutton and Hammond,[14] who concluded that, while copying mistakes were obviously possible, perhaps the most telling piece of evidence was that the meeting of the Court of the Mercers' Company would have had to have happened on a Sunday, which would have been a very exceptional circumstance. It was concluded that the entry had actually referred to a meeting that had occurred on that date but in an earlier year than 1483.

In respect of the interchange between Hanham and Wolfe, Wolfe contributed the final word,[15] but there followed another observation by Coleman[16] which focused on the 'Black Book' of the Exchequer. As Chamberlain of the Exchequer, Hastings' death was recorded on 13 June, and this added to the collective weight of evidence which re-affirmed the date which the *Crowland Chronicle* first established. There were also a number of commentaries on this issue which provided useful information,[17] and indeed, there remains a concise summary of the controversy by Hammond which is on the present Ricardian website.[18]

It is natural that we tend to see the world in terms of 'winners' and 'losers,' and if we have to view it in this manner then Alison Hanham comes out as a 'loser.' But this is a very limited perspective. As Atreed[19] so trenchantly reminds us, Alison Hanham made a significant contribution to scholarship with her observations on this matter and, although the traditional date of Friday 13 June 1483 stands as the day that Hastings lost his head, it is primarily thanks to Hanham that we have now assembled the present body of information which supports this contention. I fully concur with Atreed's assessment that we have much for which to thank Hanham. From my present perspective, the critical necessity to establish the notion that Richard acted in the first flush of anger is very much bolstered by the information which emerged in this process of debate.

Appendix III

The Manor
of Great Dorsett

Introduction

The manor of Great Dorsett was once just that – great. It was, at the time that Eleanor and her husband were granted title, one of the more important centres in the Midlands of England (*see* Figure 30). Today, it is a small Warwickshire[1] backwater, passed in mere moments by those on the adjacent M40 motorway and given scant attention. We know that this downgrading happened as a function of the policies and actions of those who inherited the manor following the time of Eleanor and her husband. It is probable that there was no issue from Eleanor's marriage to Sir Thomas,[2] since it appears the manor reverted to her father-in-law, Sir Ralph, after Eleanor's death. Sir Ralph had been a Bodyguard and eventually Standard Bearer to Henry VI, and was at one time Lord Treasurer of England.[3] His property was apparently divided between his two sisters.[4] The manor passed to one sister, Joan, and, through her marriage to Sir Hamon Belknap, who had been treasurer of Normandy when Ralph himself was treasurer of England, it then passed through the Belknap family until it came into the possession of Sir Edward Belknap, whose actions so reduced its subsequent circumstances.[5] The proposition is that Great Dorsett consisted of a number of settlements, including the modern-day, Avon Dassett, Little Dassett, Temple Herdewyke and

Northend. Today, Northend is a small village in and of itself, as is Avon Dassett further south, down the escarpment. What was most probably the centre, Burton Dassett, is now just a small collection of farm buildings and All Saints' church, set almost in splendid isolation.[6]

The present-day Burton Dassett Country Park shows almost exactly why Eleanor and her husband would have wanted to unify the manors of Great Dorsett and Fenny Compton. Burton Dassett is on the hills and provides excellent terrain for sheep farming and wool production, which was one of the major commercial propositions of that and earlier times. In contrast, Fenny Compton is in the vale below the hills. It provides excellent, sheltered land for arable farming. The combination of these two properties and their physical proximity would have made them very profitable propositions indeed. However, there were and are many other advantages of this site. One of the primary advantages was the presence of a regular market. At one time, because of this market facility, the area was known as Chipping Dassett, where the name Chipping refers directly to the market function (e.g. Chipping Campden, Chipping Norton, etc., a naming convention that persists in other countries, e.g. Linkoping in Sweden). This market would have brought in a good revenue and we can also see from the geographical location why this is so. The Burton Dassett hills stand in a most strategic position with respect to the lower West Midlands. From the top of the hill where the present tower stands (*see* Figure 31), one can get a wide, panoramic view of the surrounding countryside. In an era of far less sophisticated communications and one which emphasised more the value of location, this dominating hill would have had additional value. It is indeed a little strange that no Norman Castle ever appears to have been erected here, perhaps because of the local over-dominance of Warwick not many miles away.

The connection with Temple Herdewyke is one of the more intriguing aspects of the Eleanor Butler story. We can see on the following map (*see* Figure 30) that just above the location identified as 'Home Farm' is a site labeled 'Chapel'. It is the contention of Graham Phillips that this is a Templar chapel of extraordinary importance. As is well known, the Order of the Knights Templar was suppressed by Phillip the Fair of France in 1308. Indeed, it may well have been from this action that we derive our folk superstition about Friday 13th (it being also coincidental that William, Lord Hastings also died on Friday 13th). Phillips' suggestion is that an influential member of the Templar order secreted Templar treasure around this location. He also suggested that Sir Walter Ralegh purchased part of this property through his wife Elizabeth Throckmorton in order to look for the buried treasure. I leave it to others to further assess the veracity of this letter which I have been unable to substantiate.

The Link to Ashby St Ledgers

Much of the present text is about the relationship between Eleanor Butler and the Catesby family and the two respective locations (Great Dorsett and Ashby St Ledgers) that they occupied at this time. Therefore, any link that can be found between the two geographical locations might well help to bolster the present case. Given the era which we are considering, virtually the only buildings standing in each location around at the time are the respective churches of All Saints at Burton Dassett and the Blessed Virgin Mary and St Leodegarius at Ashby St Ledgers. And here we find most probably associated paintings in each location (*see* Figures 32 and 33 respectively). Subject to the on-going efforts at restoration, Ashby St Ledgers can claim to have possibly the best display of early church paintings in the whole of England. It is also a reasonable possibility that much of this work was conducted during the lordship of Sir William Catesby, since we know that he spent significant amounts of his resources on this church around this time.[7]

Some of the paintings in All Saints' church in Burton Dassett are thought to be by the same hand. Thus, for example, Baker concludes that:

> This series is unusual in that a Doom which symbolizes the gates of Heaven and that one must be judged before one can enter Heaven. However, there is a painting of similar subject and style in Ashby St Ledgers (near Daventry in Northants.) Ashby has three Passion series, all by different painters, the centrally placed painting is very similar in style to the painting here and could be the work of the same painter.

As always, painting style is a matter of personal perception, but if we take the linkage between the two to be a reasonable one, the respective pictures were painted at roughly the same time – which their form seems to support. Then what is the other common between the two locations? It will be no surprise if I suggest that this is Eleanor Butler. Whether it is possible that Eleanor encountered the painter on a visit to Ashby St Ledgers and subsequently sponsored some similar work at Burton Dassett, or whether the artist was at this latter location and Eleanor encouraged further work at Ashby we cannot say. However, given her age, I am inclined to suspect the former sequence (of course, we must always remember the most likely thing is that there was no such connection). However (*see* Figure 11), if the painter was commissioned by Eleanor to beautify All Saints' church, it might not be too much of a stretch that part of the face of what has been identified as the Virgin Mary bears some resemblance to Eleanor? After all, artists have done this before, and indeed since. There is one final similarity between the two churches that is relatively uncommon in other places and that is the internal design of the roofing as illustrated in Figures 34 and 35.

Lady Eleanor's Motivation

Why did Eleanor Butler not press her claim to the throne? Elizabeth Woodville certainly did, and the Talbots outranked the Woodvilles in terms of the nobility of England. Could it have been that Eleanor was ill; after all, she died not too long after this time on 30 June 1468? However, perhaps there was something more than illness behind her curious reticence. We have then to ask what could have been more valuable to Eleanor than a kingdom. The only feasible answer I can imagine is something to do with her religion. It was Eleanor that perhaps Edward was referring to when he commented on the holiest harlot in his kingdom. What could there have been at Great Dorsett or Dorsett Magna that she valued so much that she would be willing to give away a kingdom for it? If we needed further evidence of her religious devotion we can see this in her later life, when she retired to a house of religion rather than marry again. Could she have been the guardian of some form of religious treasure and did she sacrifice herself to Edward to retain that treasure?

The idea that there was a great Templar treasure at Temple Heredwyke, which was part of the Great Dorsett demesne, has been put forward by Phillips.[8] Like other such speculations, Phillips' text looks to link historical personages to legendary riches. In the present case, the argument revolves around the linkage between the Boeteler family and their early Templar connections.[9] Phillips even suggests that Sir Walter Ralegh has his wife (Bess Throckmorton) purchase Temple Heredwyke in order to search for the purported treasure. We should remember that the Catesby family were directly associated with Eleanor and one of William Catesby's very first royal appointments was to a commission to examine the disposal of the Boeteler lands after both Eleanor and her husband had died and the property had reverted to her father-in-law, who himself then subsequently died without issue. As with all such speculation, it is most tempting to hypothesise a relation between William and this fabled treasure, and perhaps the disfigurement of his brass might have something to do with such intrigues. Alas, there is no hard evidence to support such contentions, seductive though they may be. At present, we must await this evidence before travelling down such a tempting path.

Appendix IV

The Letter of Sir William Catesby of 15 September 1452

The letter is held at The National Archives, under entry PRO SC1/51/147, and reads as follows:

William Catesby to Master John Assheby:

Right trusty and my right special friend I recommend me to you as heartedly as I can and thank you in my most tender wise of your great kindness that I have found with you at all times. And forasmuch as Sir John Barre has moved to my lady of Shrewsbury that there might be writing of such communications as be appointed between my lady Dame Joan and me, which me thinks needs not, because, as for the jointure, as soon as the marriage is done estate shall be made to her in all goodly haste possible, and as for she desires to have 'Sic[er]teyn' for her own finding which is a place I wene of value 20 marks she shall not need to mistrust me for she shall have that and more too for me. Nevertheless, I pray you that you will speak with her and if it shall please her that these points or any other that I agreed to shall be put in writing I will agree thereto with right a good will to her pleasure, how be it it shall never need her to mistrust me, and this I am agreed with my lady of Shrewbury and with Sir John Barre to make writing indented between my lady of Shrewsbury and me of as many points as my lady Dame Jane will desire that she and I were agreed of and that you will say unto her that

I prayed her that she would write to my lady of Shrewsbury her intent by the bringer of this, also that it may please her to send me word either by writing or by mouth by the bringer of this her intent. And as for the marriage me thinks that the Sunday fortnight Trinity Sunday is over is a good day, for I shall not 'mow attend arft' for divers causes which I shall tell her and to which day my lady of Shrewsbury and her brother both be agreed to and she would the same and that it may be kept 'privey' because it shall be do prively and that she will send to me measures of such garments as she will have made and other stuff for other things that she will have made as 'Tyr[us]'. And that you will say to her that it please her to give credence to my servant Edmund the bringer of this of such thing as he shall speak with her, me and Jesus have you in his keeping.

Written in haste at London Friday after Holy Rood day.

Your true friend William Catesby.

Appendix V

The Letter from Richard III to William Catesby

The text of the letter reads:

Richard by the grace of god King of England and of Fraunce and Lord of Irland. To o[ur] trusty and Right welbeloued Counsaillo[ur] William Catesby oon of the squiers for oure body: greting[.] For asmoche as we of oure grace esp[ec]ial / and for certain causes and considerac[i]ons vs moeving haue yeuen and graunted vnto you alle suche wood as is growing within the Grove called the peche conteynyng sex acres in the [par]isshe of Nuthurst being now in the holding of oon Davy Tussingh[a]m, whiche he[re]tofor[e] belonged vnto o[ur] Rebell s[ir] William Noreys and by reasou[n] of his Rebellioun and atteyndre is co[m]men to our handes. We therefor[e] yeue vnto you and suche [per]sones as by you shalbe deputed and assigned full powar and autorite [?] by thise presents, for to felle and cary alle the said wood being in the Grove aforsaid at yo[ur] pleas[irr] w[ith]oute any lette or interupcio[n] of any oure officers or soubgiettes Receyuyng thise oure l[ett]res / whiche we wol to be yo[ur] sufficient warrant and discharge at all tymes herafter Yeuen vnder oure signet at oure Castell of Kenelworth' the xxviij[th] Day of May The secunde yere of our Reigne.

The question of dating has come somewhat to the fore, since the second year of Richard's reign by the calendar would be 1484, yet in the following text it is noted as 1485. As the monarch's reign was most probably dated from the coronation, the year 1485 is likely to be correct.

The full text in modern English can be found in Preston, J.F. & Yeandle, L., *English Handwriting 1400-1650* (pp8–9), Pegasus Press: Ashville, NC, 1999. The original text is held at in the Folger Shakespeare Library in Washington, DC, reference Folger MS. X.d.92 (*see* Figure 16).

What is much less commonly known is that the following notation is made on the reverse of this letter:

> This writing was showed forth unto William Knight at the time of his examination taken at Henley-in-Arden the 25th day of September, 1640 before us – William Barnes, John Parsons.

What this examination of William Knight was about in 1640, why the interrogators had this paper and what its significance may have been, I have not yet been able to ascertain. It is the subject of an on-going investigation.

Appendix VI

The Offices and Lands of William Catesby

The Offices of William Catesby

Rather than trying to provide an exhaustive listing of all of the offices that William Catesby held over the course of his life, this appendix is only concerned with how he specifically benefitted from the execution of William, Lord Hastings.[1] Thus, it is principally confined to the offices and rewards he received following Hastings' execution on 13 June 1483. Even that restriction provides significant scope since, as we shall see, Catesby reaped numerous rewards, many of which derived directly from Hastings' demise.

Very shortly after 13 June, Catesby began to see manifest rewards for his service to the Protector, Richard, Duke of Gloucester. Among the first of these was a position he clearly coveted, that of Constable of Rockingham Castle and Master Forester of the Forest of Rockingham. As is evident from analysis of his land holdings, Rockingham occupied a prime place in Catesby's ambitions. Around the same time he was also named both Chamberlain of the Exchequer and Steward of the holdings of the Duchy of Lancaster in Northamptonshire. Each of these offices had previously been held by Hastings, and the latter appointment brought him great influence in the area of his own existing family hegemony. Also, on 30 June, before Richard had even been formally crowned, Catesby was also named Chamberlain of Receipts.

Chamberlain of Receipts was another of those offices which the hapless Hastings had previously occupied. Added to this, Catesby was now the Steward of the Manors of Rockingham, Brigstock and Cliffe (assumedly the modern-day King's Cliffe). As if these were not rewards enough, Catesby was also appointed to the much more prestigious position of Chancellor of the Exchequer on 30 June 1483. In respect of the latter appointment, Payling has the following to say:

> Clearly he (Catesby) was an important figure before the political murder of Hastings in 13 June but he had become much more so in its aftermath. In the first days of the new reign he was appointed to two offices not usually the preserve of men of his rank: on 27 June he was named the chamberlain of the Exchequer previously held by Hastings, and, three days later, he became chancellor of the Exchequer. With these offices went places in the royal household and upon the royal council, and soon after he added another of Hastings' offices, that of steward of the duchy of Lancaster lordships in Northamptonshire.[2]

Here then is a wealth of accumulated evidence of Catesby's direct benefit, not only from Hastings' vacated offices but also from the highest administrative positions in the land. Payling's observation bears reiterating, that Catesby also thus became an immediate member of the inner circle, that being the Royal Council. Again, just two days after Richard assumed his leadership, Catesby was also Chancellor of the Earldom of March.[3] It is clear that Catesby had gone from being a legally capable individual, but just one of the followers of Lord Hastings, to the leading professional administrator in the land. Little wonder that Collingbourne, thus impressed by Catesby's meteoric rise, later placed him first in his insulting couplet.

These various offices and appointments, and the celerity with which they were awarded, very much supports my contention that it was Catesby who revealed the pre-contract and at the same time precipitated the death of Hastings. This contention is supported by the fact that this profusion of honours and appointments came to him right at the very start of Richard's reign. Other honours also followed for Catesby in the first months of the new reign. On 16 August he was named Deputy Butler to the ports of Bristol, Exeter and Dartmouth and on 25 September of the same year he became Steward of the Duchy of Lancaster's lordships in High Ferrers,

Daventry and Peverell's fee of the estates in Northamptonshire. Each of these appointments was associated with his relationship with Lovell.

This is by no means an exclusive listing of all of Catesby's offices and influence, nor of his appointments to legal positions and various commissions. Neither does it emphasise his parliamentary seat nor arguably his most critical role as Speaker of the Parliament scheduled for November 1483 but subsequently convened in January 1484. However, it does give a useful account of not merely the rewards Catesby received, but the critical timing of those rewards immediately following Richard's assumption of power. They stand in stark contrast to the lack of reward received by Stillington, it being arguable that the unfortunate cleric received absolutely no personal reward from Richard whatsoever. I think, in in answer to the question *cui bono*, Catesby was the one on the receiving end and the unprecedented reward of someone outside Richard's close circle argues for the rendering of a unique service. There is, of course, another very tangible way in assessing Catesby's reward and this can be found in the form of the accumulation of lands and influence on lands following the happenings of 13 June. It is to these acquisitions that I now turn.

The Lands of William Catesby

As with the offices of William Catesby, one of the most interesting comparisons that can be made is between his holdings prior to 13 June 1483 and the lands and influence he accumulated after this pivotal date. It is this division which is presented here. There are, however, important caveats with respect to this present comparison. First, I should be very explicit and note with care that this is not an exhaustive but an illustrative listing. Although a complete evaluation awaits future scholarship, the present comparison relies on a number of present sources and I am happy to acknowledge each of these.[4] The principal way in which this comparison can be made plain is to provide a map-based representation of Catesby's holdings either side of 13 June, and then distill what we may from the pattern that emerges. I have done this in Figures 36, 37, and 38.

Of the general trends which can be distilled from this overall pattern, some are indeed self-evident. These patterns certainly show that Catesby was enlarging his holdings and, if we compare the lands represented on Figure 36 that had taken his family well over a century to accumulate, then his own additions, which accrued in approximately two years, are enormous in comparison, see Figure 37. It is not only the size of his accumulations which are telling but also their spatial distribution. For example, it is clear that Catesby focused considerable effort at 'in-filling' around his already-established holdings, *see* Figure 38. We shall return to the specific case of the manor of Welton after we have noted the general pattern. As well as in-filling, Catesby expanded his lands consistent with the valley of the River Nene. He extended the boundary of his holdings both east and west, but his primary acquisitions were to the north in Leicestershire. It will, by now, come as no surprise that Leicestershire was the heartland of Lord Hastings holdings. Thus what we see here is a systematic and coherent plan to generate a cohesive, inter-linked domain of contiguous land holdings. In general, Catesby had done very well in looking to put this strategy into effect.

Perhaps the most evident example, especially of this in-filling policy, comes in respect of his dealings for the manor of Welton. It is also representative of Catesby's rapaciousness, a characteristic of which he himself was well aware as we shall also see. In respect to his dealings concerning Welton, we can again cite Payling,[5] who reports:

He also used the influence of the office [Speaker] to secure a goal of his own. In the aftermath of the usurpation he had taken a bond in the massive sum of 700 marks from Richard Hawte, a kinsman and supporter of Edward V, as security for his good behavior; he then pressed Hawte into agreeing to surrender two of his manors in Kent to Thomas Peyton, the owner of the Manor of Welton, which neighbored Ashby (St Ledgers), who also happened to be Hawte's son-in-law; in return Peyton undertook to give Welton to Catesby. These arrangements were threatened by Hawte's involvement in Buckingham's rebellion; if he were attainted then the two manors in Kent would fall to the Crown and the agreement would be undone. To prevent this, William as speaker had inserted into the act of attainder against the Buckingham rebels a proviso exempting the two manors and Welton was surrendered to him.

Here we can see evidence of a number of facets of Catesby's behaviour. Even a brief glance at the map will show that Welton lies right in the heart of the Catesby domain and he must have schemed for this transfer fairly extensively. Obviously he took advantage of Hawte's (Haute) misfortune, but essentially he traded two of his family manors, which arguably would have gone to Peyton anyway, for the coveted manor at Welton. Here Catesby himself risked almost nothing to secure his desired aim. When this arrangement was threatened, Catesby used his legal skills and position to perpetuate the arrangement with the connivance of the law.

This incident does not represent a 'one-off,' but rather seems to have been part of a general pattern. In respect of the efforts at in-filling, we can also cite the case of Long Buckby (Bukby). Again, this was a property within only two to three miles of Catesby's own centre at Ashby St Ledgers and, again Catesby seems to have schemed to get it. It has been noted that somehow, and here we are unsure of the mechanism, Catesby obtained land that was in this location. It has been noted that this land in the time of Henry III was in the possession of one Hugh Revell. Somehow Catesby was successful in obtaining it, but it is clear that this transaction preyed on his conscience. The evidence that we have for this lies in Catesby's will, in which he himself stated:

> Item: that the executors of Nicholas Cowley have the lond again in Evertoft withoute they have their C li. Item: in like wise Revell [6] his lond in Bukby.

The suggestion here is that Catesby, in his 'hasty' will, was trying to put right each of the suspect dealings that had helped him accumulate the domain we have seen. In this case we see that he was returning the Long Buckby lands to the Revell family, who had held them for an extensive period of time, notably since the reign of Henry III. The other cases cited in his will attest to a similar attack of conscience; the Welton lands were not mentioned, although they might conceivably come under his command to 'restore all londs that I have wrongfully purchased.' In places where Catesby could not force or cajole the private owner to part with their property, as was the case with Church lands, he used his undoubted influence with the king to help secure his design. Thus, in the case of Stanford-on-Avon, we can see this tactic come to fruition. Again, it is important to note the geographic context here. Stanford-on-Avon is not so close to Ashby St Ledgers as either Welton or Long Buckby; however, it does lie a few miles to the north, immediately adjacent to the properties of Catthorpe, Lilibounre and Clay Coton, for which Catesby had already manoeuvered. Critically, it also lay directly on the path of his manifest expansion into Leicestershire. Thus we find Roskell observing that, 'it was at the King's instance that on 5 October, 1483, the abbot of the said Yorkshire Benedictine house of Selby gave Lovell and Catesby a grant for their lives (in survivorship) of the office of steward of the manor of Stanford [on-Avon] (Northants.) near where Catesby's own estates were on the ground.' Roskell is very helpful here, but Stanford-on-Avon was not near Catesby's estates; it now lies packed within them, another of the dominoes to fall in Catesby's progressive march to dominion.

Thus, we can say that Catesby accumulated more lands and holdings during his brief two years of influence than his family had in the previous 100 years of effort (compare Figure 36 vs. Figure 37). When these were all lost in the aftermath of Bosworth, his family was impoverished and took more than a decade to recover even some of its traditional holdings. The Catesby family never again secured such influence, although with one of the direct descendants of William Catesby leading the 'Gunpowder Plot' more than a century later, the name Catesby did remain in the public eye, albeit one that connoted sedition and infamy.

A Listing of the Lands

As I have noted, the present assessment is illustrative only. It presents a listing of lands where Catesby had some influence and some investment. That association could range from directly owning all the lands in the manor to some association with a group who benefitted from revenues from the whole or even part of some location. The latter include monies received from revenues, claims on resources and the like. For example, in 1485, Catesby had a grant from King Richard of 100 oaks, to be taken from the king's old park at Tanworth, and Earlswood in Tanworth. These were not possessions *per se*, but rights and advantages associated with various locations. It may be helpful for those in the future to list these here and to cite the provenance for such observations. I start with reference to some original public records.

In the Reign of Henry VI

Piece Details: SC 6/949/15
In Northamptonshire the lands of Margaret and William Catesby: Welton, Harlestone and Heyford, Watford, Creaton, Hinton, Braunston, Ashby, Stanford, Stormsworth, and Yelvertoft:, Hellidon, Hinton. 25 to 26 Hen VI 27 to 28 Hen VI 30 to 31 Hen VI 37 to 38 Hen VI 38 to 39 Hen VI 3 to 4 Edw IV

8 to 9 Edw IV 14 to 15 Edw IV [14 to 15 Edw IV] 16 to 17 Edw IV 17 to 18 Edw IV 20 to 21 Edw IV 21 to 22 Edw IV 22 Edw IV, to 1 Ric III.

Piece Details: SC 2/207/30

In Warwickshire, Description of Courts: Court of William Catesby and others. Places: Grandborough (Grendburgh); Ladbrooke (Lodbrok). 25, 26 Hen VI.

Piece Details: E 40/4369

Letter of attorney by John Talbot, Viscount de Lisle, William, lord of Lovell, knights, Henry Grene, Thomas Tresham, Robert Catesby, the elder, esquire, William Bryten, vicar of All Saints', Northampton, John Gervys, rector of Bukkeby church, John Verney, rector of Lodbrok church, John Wattson, rector of Rodburn church, and John Prudde, authorising Edmund Newnham and Thomas Mettley to deliver to William Catesby, knight, and Joan his wife, full seisin of the manors of Grenburgh, Lodbrok in Grenburgh, and Lodbrok, the advowson of the church of Lodbrok, with lands &c., 25 June, 31 Henry VI.

Piece Details: SC 6/860/24

Dorstone (Lands of [? Lady Joan Catesby]): [Hereford] Description of Officer. 32 to [33] Hen VI

In the Reign of Edward IV

Piece Details: SC 6/1117/16

(Lands of William Catesby; Receipts attached):Leamington: [Warwick] Coventry, Fee in: [Warwick] Combe, (Rent paid by Abbot of Combe) Fee in: [Warwick] Braunston: [Northampton] Buckby: [Northampton] Towcetter: -- Medbourn: [Leicester] Granborough (Crenneborough): [Warwick] Radburn: [Warwick] Warwick: [Warwick] Description of Officer: Receiver, 20 Edw IV

Piece Details: E 40/4575

Sale by John Hathwyke, to William Catesby, for 200l. of the manor of Oxsshile, and the advowson of the church there: Warw.

4 January, 21 Edward IV.

In the Reign of Richard III

Piece Details: E 40/4306

Grant by William the abbot, and the convent of St Mary's, Combe, to William Catesby, esquire of the king's body, of a yearly rent of 26s.8d., for his life, with licence of entry into the lands and tenements of the lordship of Herburbur', in case of non-payment of the said rent.

3 February, 1 Richard III.

Piece Details: E 40/4786

Demise by John, lord Le Scrop, knight, and Dame Elizabeth his wife, for her life, to William Catesby, esquire of the king's body, of the manors of Berughy, Oneley and Gretton, with lands and tenements in Hayngworth: also letter of attorney authorising Thomas Aynesworth and William Lytylhay to deliver seisin of the premises: N'hamp.

16 February, 1 Richard III.

Item Details: C 47/10/28/19

Private papers of the Earl of Ormond: Bond of Thomas Ormond and William Boleyn, knights, to William Catesby for 40 pounds , 2 Ric III Feb 8

Piece Details: E 40/4776

Grant by Thomas Peyton, grandson of Thomas Peyton late of Esilham and of Margaret his wife, daughter and heiress of Ellen, daughter and heiress of John Malorre and Joan his wife, to William Catesby, esquire of the king's body, and John Catesby, esquire, of Olthorp, of the manor of Welton, and of all the lands &c., 14 February, 2 Richard III.

Piece Details: E 40/4496

Grant by John Pratte of Henley, to William Catesby, esquire, of all his right in a pasture called 'Henleys' in Lapworth. Warwickshire, Last day of May, 2 Richard III.

Piece Details: E 42/540

Recovery by William Catesby, Esquire of the King's Body, and John Catesby of Althorp (Olthorp), esquire, of the manor of Welton, and lands there, against Thomas Peyton: Northampton shire. 2 Ric III

Piece Details: E 210/571

Grant by William Catesby of ... , to William Catesby, knight, of Aschby Legers, Roger Wike of Bylsworth, Thomas ..., Thomas Barker of ..., and Elizabeth Catesby, the grantor's daughter, of all his lands &c. in Fodyngworth, co. Leicester, and Sylson, co. 20 ... , 2 Richard III.

In the Reign of Henry VII

Item Details: E 150/1111/4

Catesby, William, attainted: Warwick , 1 Henry VII.

<u>Piece Details: E 42/521</u>
The king to John Halwell, Knight of the Body to the King: Grants of land in Silsworth and Braunston late of William Catesby, esquire, attainted of high treason: Northamptonshire., 7 Hen VII.
<u>Piece Details: E 40/5059</u>
Release by John Halyghwell, knight, to George Catesby, son and heir of William Catesby, of all his right in land in Silesworth: Northamptonshire, 18 December, 11 Henry VII.

Centre for Buckinghamshire Studies

22 August 1485 (NB: date of Bosworth). [D-X731/1/2] Feoffment 22 August 3 Richard III
1. Richard Maryet of Shiryngton [Sherington], gentleman
2. John Catesby, knight, William Catesby, esquire of the king's body, Robert Tate and John Tate, aldermen of London, John Tate son of John Tate, lately mayor of London, Thomas Kebeel, William Lane, John Legerdon, clerk, John Ardys, Simon Sakavile, Robert Yonge, Richard Wolfe
The manor of Sherington called Caves, with all its land and rights
Witnesses: Michael Ardys, John FitzJohn, chaplain, Henry Rande, John Coyte. At Sherington

Cambridge University, King's College Archive Centre

Wootton Lease: Date: 3 February 1485 (1484/5)
Lease of Wootton manor by Walter Field, Provost of King's College to Sir William Catesby. Seal attached.

Northamptonshire Record Office

Date: [1484]
Rental, houses, shops and lands at Northampton of Wm. Catesby showing payments to the chapel of the Blessed Virgin Mary in All Saints and to the bailiff of Northampton; also rental for Tylbroke, Bedfordshire.

Date: [1484], Rental, lands of Wm. Catesby at Long Buckby, Murcote & Shutlanger

Warwickshire Records Office

Gift with warranty from Richard Boughton, esq., to William Catysby, knight, William Catysby the younger, esq., John Huggeford, William Harper esq., John Harper esq., Richard Harper, John Danton, William Dyxwell, Master John Wymark, William Stanerton, John Dyve the younger, and Thomas Ley, of his manor of Browneswover, with all appurtenances. To have and to hold to the aforesaid, their heirs and assigns forever, of the chief lord of the fee, for the customary services. He appoints as attorneys John Norton and Henry Bene, to deliver seisin on his behalf. Given at Bruneswover 1st May, 15 Edward IV. Witnesses: William Hylle, chaplain, John Rose of wover, the aforesaid John Coke of the same, William Overton and many others.; Seal: round; device: deer's head; red; tag.; Endorsed: charter of Richard Boughton made to William Catesby and others, of the manor of Brownsover: 1st May, 1475.

Manor of Oxhill: in 1482 the manor was sold for £200 to John Catesby of Lapworth.

Date: 12 February, 1481: Letter of attorney of Guy Fairfax knight and royal justice, Richard Pigot servant and law of the king, William Catesby, esq., and Thomas Kebell, appointing John Chancy and William Brett to receive seisin of the manors of Astwell with all the lands, tenements etc., belonging to it in Astwell, Wappenham and Falcutt from Thomas Billyng and Thomas Lovett (NB: each of these are small hamlets that are close to the village of Helmdon in Northamptonshire).

In Leicestershire: Catthorpe, Dunton Bassett, Husbands Bosworth, Swinford.

In Northamptonshire: Great Everdon, Hellidon, Silsworth, Snorscombe, Ashby St Ledgers.

Lands Reported in Payling (2007)

1. Tilbrook, Bedfordshire (acquired between 1476-1483)
2. Oxhill (acquired between 1476-1483)
3. 5/1/1482. ninety-nine-year lease on church/rectory, Ashby St Ledgers
4. Radbourne (acquired by great-great-grandfather, also William)
5. Ladbrooke (by marriage in early fourteenth century)

12 February 1481

Letter of attorney of Guy Fairfax knight and royal justice, Richard Pigot servant and law of the king, William Catesby, esq., and Thomas Kebell, appointing John Chancy and William Brett to receive seisin of the manors of Astwell with all the lands, tenements etc., belonging to it in Astwell, Wappenham and Falcutt from Thomas Billyng and Thomas Lovett. These are small hamlets that lie around the village of Helmdon in Northamptonshire.

Notes

Setting the Scene

1. From Shakespeare, *As You Like It*, II.VII (1599).
2. See Nayha, S. ' Traffic deaths and superstition on Friday the 13th.' *American Journal of Psychiatry*, 159 (2002), 2110-2111; and also Radun, I. & Summala, H. 'Females don't have more injury road accidents on Friday the 13th.' *Proceedings of the Third International Conference on Traffic and Transport Psychology*, 3 (2004), 50-51.
3. There is such a cottage industry now attached to the Knights Templar that it is often hard to divorce serious scholarship from popularisation and myth.
4. There has been controversy as to whether the events which are the focus of this text happened on Friday 13 June 1483, or actually one week later on Friday 20 June. In large part this arises from some textual interpretations of the crucial Stonor letter. However, the matter is of such importance it cannot be left to a note and is therefore the subject of Appendix II. While it may seem that this is merely an argument about dates, the issue has actually coloured opinions as to the meaning of events, such as the interpretation of Charles T. Wood in his influential article on the deposition of Edward V.
5. My beginning this framing with Edward III is a traditional starting point but may well be a misleading one. For example, Ashdown-Hill, J. ' The Lancastrian claim to the throne.' *The Ricardian*, XIII (2003), 27-38, points out that it might be as well to go back to Henry III as the more appropriate start point.
6. See Ashley, M. *British Kings & Queens*. Carroll & Graf, 2002.
7. Saul, N. *Richard II*. New Haven, CT: Yale University Press, 1997.
8. Abbott, J. *History of Margaret of Anjou*. Harper & Brothers: New York, 1900.

9. For an account of Edward IV see *Historie of the Arrivall of Edward IV, in England and the Finall Recouerye of His Kingdomes from Henry VI.* A.D. M.CCC.LXXI. at: http//www.r3.org/bookcase/arrival1.html, and in hard copy texts of the same reference.

10. It has been argued that Edward, Prince of Wales was summarily dispatched by Edward IV's major lieutenants and advisors in front of him. However, contemporary records indicate that the prince was killed in the pursuit following the break of the Lancastrian lines.

11. And see also: White, W. J. ' The death and burial of Henry VI, A review of the facts and theories, Part 1.' *The Ricardian*, 78 (1982), 70-80, and White, W. J. ' The death and burial of Henry VI. Part II. The re-burial of Master John Schorne and King Henry VI: Windsor's two Saints.' *The Ricardian*, 79 (1982), 106-117.

Chapter 1: The Path to the Throne

1. Note that the College of Arms MS2 M6 indicates the previous day (being Tuesday 8th). The author of the College of Arms MS1,7.f.7 made the opposite error, placing the date as Thursday 10 April, see Gairdner, J. *Letters and Papers Illustrative of the Reigns of Richard III and Henry VII* (p. 4). London: HMSO, 1861. However, the generally accepted date remains the 9th. See Green, R. F. 'Historical notes of a London citizen 1483-1488.' *English Historical Review*, 96 (1981), 585-590.

2. See: Sutton, A. F. & Visser-Fuchs, L. 'Laments for the death of Edward IV: "It was a world to see him ride about."' *The Ricardian*, 145 (1999), 506-524.

3. One of his predecessors, Henry V, had died of dysentery at the age of thirty-four in 1422, while his great-grandson, Edward VI, died of tuberculosis aged almost sixteen in 1553. These were the only two kings of the modern era who we know died of natural causes at a younger age than Edward.

4. For a close to contemporary account see: Mancini, D. *The Usurpation of Richard III.* Trans. C. A. J. Armstrong. Alan Sutton: Gloucester, 1989. See also Lord Hastings' comment to the Mayor of Canterbury, *Reports of the Royal Commission on Historical Manuscripts*, IX (1883).

5. Richmond, C. 'The Princes in the Tower; The Truth at Last.' *Ricardian Register*, 26 (3) (2001), 10-18. With the remains in the tomb in St George's chapel, Windsor, it may still be possible to identify the actual cause of death.

6. For some comments on Richard's capacity as an administrator during this protectorate see Burr, K. ' Richard the Third as an Administrator: The Lord Protector.' *The Ricardian*, 33 (1971), 5-8.

7. For example, Richard had loyally followed his brother into exile in Burgundy when events had turned against the king. They set sail on Tuesday 2 October 1470, with a small company including William, Lord Hastings (Kendall, 1955, p. 100).

8. In the present account, I rely quite extensively on the most helpful and informative article by Wood (Wood, C. T. ' On the deposition of Edward V.' *Traditio*, 31 (1975), 247-286). Unfortunately, Wood's acceptance of Hanham's re-dating of the execution of William, Lord Hastings represents, in my view, a fatal flaw in his subsequent interpretation of events. Thus, I have used much of the evidentiary basis of his argument but reject his conclusions, since I believe that the original date for Hastings' death on Friday 13 June 1483 is both correct and critical.

9. Wood (1975), *op. cit.*

10. It has been suggested that Polydore Vergil dated Richard's aspirations for the throne from the date of his brother's death. As we shall see, this assertion is not supported by the hard evidence (and see Seward, D. *The War of the Roses* (p. 259). Viking: New York, 1995). Others also speculate upon Richard's decision-making process, including Ross, who sees Richard's actions as largely reactive rather than proactive.

11. Pollard, A. J. *The Middleham Connection: Richard III and Richmondshire 1471-1485* (p. 1). Old School Arts Workshop: Middleham, 1983.

12. It was a threat that persisted in history until the terrible aftermath of Culloden (16 April 1746) and the subsequent depopulation due to changes in agricultural strategy, see Sked, P. *Culloden*. National Trust for Scotland, Thomsom: Edinburgh, 1997. See also the Cely Letter for a contemporary confirmation (Appendix 1: The Cely, York and Stallworth Letters).

13. Richard was most probably at Middleham when he received news of his brother's death (Mancini, 1483 [1989, p. 71]). The message was sent, not through official channels but according to Mancini by William, Lord Hastings.

14. And see Myers, A. R. ' The Character of Richard III.' *History Today*, 4 (1954), 511-521.

15. See Kendall, P. M. *Richard III: The Great Debate*. W. W. Norton: New York, 1965.

16. Upon hearing of his brother's death and his nephew's accession, Richard had a requiem mass said in the chapel at Middleham and later at York he had his own men and the magistrates of the city swear allegiance to the new king (Kendall (1955), p. 195).

17. Kendall (1955), *op. cit.*, p. 194. See also: Moreton, C. E. ' A local dispute and the politics of 1483: Roger Townshend, Earl Rivers, and the Duke of Gloucester.' *The Ricardian*, 107 (1989), 305-307. And also the replies by, Wigram, I. & Thone, M. ' A local dispute and the politics of 1483: Two reactions.' *The Ricardian*, 109 (1990), 414-416.

18. Mancini (1483), *op cit.*, p. 71. The desire to help Richard was also compounded by Hastings' antipathy to the Woodville clan, especially the queen and her son by her first marriage.

19. It is reported that Edward V and his party had moved on from Northampton to Stony Stratford when the apparent expectation was that the respective groups would meet in Northampton itself. However, it may well be that the Woodville party actually moved on to Grafton Regis, their family home, which is on the

direct route from Northampton to Stony Stratford and only a few miles from the agreed meeting place in the county town. This understandable progress toward the family home might well have been interpreted as an effort to reach London before Richard. If this proposition is correct it may have been an influence, albeit an unwitting one, on behalf of the Woodville party, on Richard's decision to act. Alternatively, the traditional story cannot be excluded and the Woodvilles were making an understandable effort to reach London, the base of power, first.

20. Sutton, A. F. ' The Hautes of Kent.' *The Ricardian*, 77 (1982), 54–57. She comments that he 'may have been arrested and imprisoned,' but that he appears to have entered into a bond of 700 marks with William Catesby. This seems very much to be related to Catesby's strong desire to acquire the manor at Welton, and see Appendix VI.

21. See Smith, G. ' Hastings and the news from Stony Stratford.' *Ricardian Bulletin*, Summer 2006, 48–49.

22. Indeed, Elizabeth Woodville had given birth to the future Edward V, her eldest son by Edward IV, while in sanctuary at Westminster Abbey some years early on 4 November 1470.

23. Originally, the coronation had been scheduled for this day, 4 May, but at best that was a very ambitious undertaking in all senses of the word. The postponement to a later, more reasonable date, did not connote any obvious, malevolent action on behalf of the Protector.

24. For example, on 14 May John Howard was appointed by Richard as Chief Steward of the Duchy of Lancaster, who returned the favour next day by presenting Richard with a gold cup weighing over 4lbs.

25. In one of the Stallworth letters, the date is indicated as the 23rd, since the letter is written on the 9th and the quote 'this day fortnight', i.e. 23 June (see Appendix 1: The Cely, York, and Stallworth letters).

26. See Wood (1975), *op. cit.*, p. 252.

27. See de Blieck, E. *Analysis of Crowland's Section on the Usurpation of Richard III.* 2003. Retrieved from: www.deremilitari.org/resources/articles/deblieck.htm.

28. And see http://groups.msn.com/EdwardtheFifth/earlyjune1483.msnw

29. See Edwards, R. *The Itinerary of Richard III 1483-1485* (p. 3). Alan Sutton, for the Richard III Society: London, 1983; British Library Harleian Manuscript 433, p. 9; Public Records Office, Privy Seal Office 1/56/2847.

30. On 9 June, Simon Stallworth had written in his letter to Sir William Stonor that: "My lady of Gloucestre came to London on thorsday last." (The full text of this letter is reproduced in Appendix 1: the Cely, York, and Stallworth Letters).

31. Extracts from the York records. See Davies, R. (*Extracts from the Municipal Records of the City of York.* J. Nichols & Son: London, 1843.

32. Indeed, a letter was sent one day later from Edward V under the direction of the Lord Protector confirming that Dame Alice Savile of Hull was to have one ton of wine yearly. As Wigram (1963) noted, one wonder what service Alice had performed for Edward IV to deserve such a reward?

33. This letter was addressed to Otes Gilbert Esq. It is reprinted in H. Ellis, *Royal*

Letters (p. 147) from an original document in the British Museum, Harleian Manuscript, 433, fol. 227. And see also: Strickland, A. *Lives of the Bachelor Kings of England* (p. 143). Sempkin, Marshall, & Co.: London, 1861.

34. De Commines, P. *The Memoirs of Phillip de Commines, Lord of Argenton*. Bohn: London, 1855. Originally written in the interval between 1488 and 1494, with a mean date of 1491, De Commines mentions the bishop and the pre-contract in two sections of his work (Volume I, ppp 395-396, and Volume II, pp 63-64). In neither of these extracts does he identify a date for his revelation of this information.

35. Markham, C. R. *Richard III: His Life & Character* (pp 93-102). Smith, Elder, & Co.: London, 1906.

36. See Stallworth Letter in Appendix 1: The Cely, York and Stallworth Letters.

37. See also Levine, M. 'Richard III – Usurper or Lawful King?' *Speculum*, 34 (1959), 391-401.

38. Carpernter, C. (ed.). *Kingsford's Stonor Letter and Papers. 1290-1483* (pp 159-160). Cambridge: Cambridge University Press, 1996.

39. Davies, R. *Extracts from the Municipal Records of the City of York during the Reigns of Edward IV, Edward V, and Richard III* (pp 149-150), J.B. Nichols & Son: London, 1843. The text of the letter is reproduced in Appendix 1.

40. Wood, *op. cit.*

41. See Kendall, *op. cit.*, p. 246.

42. See Pronay, N. & Cox, J. (eds). *The Croyland Chronicle Continuations* (p. 159). Alan Sutton, for the Richard III Society: London, 1986.

43. See Hancock, P. A. ' No Richard, Rhyme nor Reason.' *The Medelai Gazette*, 14 (3) (2007), 16-22.

44. The traditional explanation that has been offered has been summarised most recently by Hicks, M. *Edward V: The Prince in the Tower* (pp 159-161), Tempus: Stroud, Glos, 2003. He notes: 'The explanation traditionally advanced from 1483 onwards, that Hastings' commitment to Gloucester stopped short of the throne, is surely correct.' I do not think this is surely correct or even probably correct; the following text seeks to articulate why I hold this belief.

45. More, T. *The History of Richard III*. 1513. Retrieved from: http://www. uoregon.edu/~rbear/r3.html. See also the text by R. S. Sylvester of this same book (New Haven, CT: Yale University Press, 1976).

46. A consideration of the relation between Richard, Duke of Gloucester and John Morton is given in: Worth, S. 'Richard & the Parson of Blokesworth.' *Ricardian Register*, 26 (3) (2001), 4-7.

47. See Moorhen, W. E. A. ' William, Lord Hastings and the Crisis of 1483: An Assessment. Part 1.' *The Ricardian*, 122 (1993), 446-466, and also, Moorhen, W. E. A. 'William, Lord Hastings and the Crisis of 1483: An Assessment. Part 2 (conclusion).' *The Ricardian*, 123 (1993), 482-497 for a full and important discussion of this whole interval, and especially the motivations of the events of this particular day, (and see also the website http://richardiii.net/ r3%20controv%20hastings.htm).

48. See Wood, C. T. 'If Strawberries Were Ripe on June 13, Was October 2 Really Richard III's Birthday?' Paper given at the 1993 meeting of the American Branch of the Richard III Society, and Hancock, P. A. (' On the Trail of King Richard III.' *Ricardian Register*, 29 (1) (2004), 8-10.

49. See More, T. in Sylvester, R. S. (1976), p. 47.

50. It is this particular inversion that Croyland, in his terse comments, took note of.

51. Tower Green subsequently assumed a much more dire reputation as the place where the Tudors dispatched many individuals in much more 'formal' proceedings.

52. *Croyland Chronicle*, *op. cit.*, p. 159.

53. See Worth (2001), *op. cit.*

54. As seems to be represented in the Cely Letter, see Appendix 1: The Cely, York, and Stallworth Letters.

55. It was this same Oliver King who appears later to have been an executor of the will of Cecily, Duchess of York, mother of both Edward IV and Richard III. He also (later in 1495) succeeded Stillington as Bishop of Bath & Wells.

56. We must remember that the mayor was Sir Edmund Shaa (and see Blunden-Ellis, J.' Sir Edmund Shaa, Kt., P.C. 1427?-1488 Lord Mayor of London.' *The Ricardian*, 45 (1974), 11-15). It was his brother, Ralph Shaa, who went on to preach that 'bastard slips shall not take root' at St Paul's Cross (the alternative wording being: 'The ungodly shall not thrive, nor take deep rooting from bastard slips'). The mayor, Edmund Shaa, was a northerner by birth and it may have been this affinity that threw his support behind Richard at this time, although he is reputed to have been shown written proofs of the illegitimacy of the sons of Edward IV. The support of the Mayor of London may have proved pivotal in the same way that de Bleick argues that the support of the troops in the capital was essential. The mayor may well have had influence over the indigenous populace. Thus both brothers Shaa had a significant hand in the issue of Richard's assumption of the throne (and see www.tameside.gov.uk/blueplaque/siredmundshaa/).

57. cf. Thompson, C. J. S. *The Witchery of Jane Shore*. Grayson & Grayson: London, 1933.

58. See York Letters, *op. cit.* and the quoted Neville Letter.

59. See http://www.r3.org/basics/basic7.html

60. And see Hancock, P. A.' On images of the "Princes in the Tower".' *Ricardian Register*, 30 (1) (2005), 4-18.

61. See HMSO *The Tower of London* (p. 6). HMSO: London, 1974.

62. York Civic Records, *op. cit.*, essentially communicating that the putative Parliament of Edward V being cancelled, required no attendant representatives of the people of York.

63. For more on Robert Brakenbury see Hampton, W. E.' Sir Robert Brakenbury of Selaby, County Durham.' *The Ricardian*, 90 (1985), 97-114. Within this article, on pp 100-101, Hampton refers more directly to the messenger, John Brakenbury.

64. Wood (1975), *op. cit.*, p. 260, argues from comparable evidence derived from

the corporation records of New Romney that while the 17th is the most probable date, the afternoon of the 16th also remains a viable possibility.

65. Lord Lisle was Edward Grey, brother to Elizabeth Woodville's first husband. He was married to a grand-daughter of John Talbot, 1st Earl of Shrewsbury. Thus his wife was Eleanor Butler's niece. He was created Viscount Lisle by Richard III in the first week of his reign. Could the understanding, derived through his family connections, that the pre-contract was real, have anything to do with his rapprochement with Richard? I suspect that it might.

66. See Mancini, *op. cit.*, and York Civic Records, *op. cit.*

67. Kendall, *op. cit.*, p. 256, says 'The Lord Protector often rode through the city these days with a great train of lords and attendants.' On p. 262 Kendall notes more generally that 'the streams of visitors to Crosby Place and Baynard's Castle, the splendor of the train with which Richard, having relinquished black, now rode in purple through the city.' and on p. 261 he suggests that it was now that Richard disclosed the revelation of the pre-contract to the rest of the council. In respect to some of these observations it is hard to tell whether Kendall has direct evidence or is using some artistic license to draw reasonable but essentially unsupported conclusions.

68. And see Wood, *op. cit.*

69. An interesting discussion of possible early dissension with respect to Richard's reign is provided for example by Hicks, M. ' Unweaving the web: The plot of July 1483 against Richard III and its wider significance.' *The Ricardian*, 114 (1991), 106-109. However, extended discussion of the next phase of Richard's life is not the central focus here at this time.

70. The mayor, Edmund Shaa, is commemorated by a plaque on Church Brow in Mottram in Longendale, Lancashire.

71. Although there are a number of potential grounds for Richard taking the throne which historians suggest were tried at the time, e.g. the bastardy of Edward IV himself, the references to bastard slips sounds more like the illegitimacy of the princes here. If it were a reference to Edward it would most probably be singular. A more complete set of references concerning the specific claim can be seen in: Sheperd, K. R. ' The title of the King: Aspects of Richard III's Act of Succession.' *The Ricardian*, 94 (1986), 281-286.

72. Mancini, *op. cit.*

73. More, *op. cit.*

74. *Testamenta Vetusta.*

75. And see also the article by Williams, B. ' Richard III and Pontefract.' *The Ricardian*, 86 (1984), 366-370.

76. Croyland noted that: 'second innocent blood which was shed on the occasion of this sudden change.' *Op. cit.*, p. 161.

77. This is an assumption embraced by Wood (1975) *op. cit.*, p. 263, who believed the warrants were brought by the same messenger who communicated the writ of supersedes to the city of York which arrived there on the 21st, Sherriff Hutton being about half a day's ride north of that city.

78. It was on this day that Richard began his formal reign, as we can see by the letter of instruction to Lord Mountjoy and others concerning the disposition of concerns related to the port of Calais and particularly the oath previously sworn to Edward V. See Gairdner, J. *Letters and Papers Illustrative of the Reigns of Richard III and Henry VII* (p. 12). London: HMSO, 1861.

79. The relevant excerpt from the *Croyland Chronicle* (p. 159) reads: 'on the 26th day of the same month of June Richard, the protector, claimed for himself the government of the kingdom, with the name and title of king.'

80. Sutton, A. F. ' The city of London and Coronation of Richard III: Points of interest.' *The Ricardian*, 63 (1978), 2-8.

81. Again, see Wood, *op. cit.*

Chapter 2: Eleanor Talbot, Lady Butler

1. Ashdown-Hill. J. ' Edward IV's uncrowned queen. The Lady Eleanor Talbot. Lady Butler.' *The Ricardian*, 11, (139) (1997), 166-190; Ashdown-Hill. J. ' Further reflections on Lady Eleanor Talbot.' *The Ricardian*, 11, (144) (1999), 463-467; Ashdown-Hill. J. 'The inquisition post mortem of Eleanor Talbot, Lady Butler, 1468.' *The Ricardian*, 12, (159) (2002), 563-573; Ashdown-Hill. J. ' Lady Eleanor Talbot's other husband.' *The Ricardian*, 14 (2004), 62-81; Ashdown-Hill. J. ' The endowments of Lady Eleanor Talbot and Elizabeth Talbot, Duchess of Norfolk, at Corpus Christi College, Cambridge.' *The Ricardian*, 14 (2004), 82-94; Ashdown-Hill. J. ' The go-between.' *The Ricardian*, 15 (2005), 119-121; Ashdown-Hill, J. ' Lady Eleanor Talbot: New evidence: New answers; New questions.' *The Ricardian: Journal of the Richard III Society*, 16 (2006), 113-132. And now, Ashdown-Hill, J (2009) *Eleanor: The Secret Queen*. The History Press, Stroud, Gloucestershire.

2. Ashdown-Hill (2006), p. 113.

3. Ashdown-Hill. J. ' Edward IV's uncrowned queen. The Lady Eleanor Talbot. Lady Butler.' *The Ricardian*, 11, (139) (1997), 166-190.

4. Sweeney, J. ' Eleanor Butler, Queen to Edward IV.' *The Medelai Gazette*, 3 (3) (1996), 18-19, states that the second marriage occurred in 1425.

5. These pictures are among the oldest English paintings in existence and come from the house, Compton Wynyates, in Warwickshire where they apparently descended through the family of Margaret Beauchamp. The representations show the father and mother of Lady Eleanor Talbot and perhaps give some idea of what Eleanor must have looked like. This topic that is explored further in later discussion.

6. Ashdown-Hill, J. ' Edward IV's uncrowned Queen: The Lady Eleanor Talbot, Lady Butler.' *The Ricardian*, 11 (1997), 166-190.

7. *Op. cit.* p. 168.

8. But also see Routh, P. S. '"Lady Scroop daughter of K. Edward": An enquiry.' *The Ricardian*, 121 (1993), 410-416, especially see the observations on p. 413.

9. From Littlebury's *Directory and Gazetteer of Herefordshire*, 1876-7, and see http://www.genuki.org.uk/big/eng/HEF/Goodrich/History1876.html

10. For an analysis of Eleanor's relations with her -in-laws, especially her first mother-in-law (Elizabeth Norbury), and her connection with Francis, Lord Lovell through her second mother-in-law (Alice Deincourt), see Ashdown-Hill, J. *Eleanor: The Secret Queen* (p. 89) The History Press: Stroud, Glos, 2009. See also Ashdown-Hill, J. ' Lady Eleanor Talbot's other husband.' *The Ricardian*, 14 (2004), 62-81. In the cited text (Ashdown-Hill, 2009, p. 58) he has also suggested that Thomas Butler may have spent a part of his early life in the Talbot household. Hence, his association with Eleanor may have been from her childhood. This speculation helps explain the subsequent disparity in rank at the time of their later marriage since the initial agreement may have been made much earlier when the two families were of essentially equal status.

11. Richardson, D. *Magna Carta Ancestry*. (pp 795-796).Genealogical Publishing Co.: Baltimore, MD, 2005.

12. Ashdown-Hill, J. ' The inquisition post mortem of Eleanor Talbot, Lady Butler, 1468.' *The Ricardian*, 12 (2002), 563-573.

13. For more on Eleanor's husband see, Barker, J.' Sir Thomas Le Boteler.' *The Ricardian*, 45 (1974), 6-8.

14. See F. O'Shaughnessy, *The Story of Burton Dassett Church*. Undated. In the possession of the author.

15. There is the particularly interesting story of the Kimble Charity, established around the time that Eleanor would have been lady of the manor. At the time at which Ralph Boteler (Eleanor's father-in-law) still possessed the manor, an orphan boy appeared one day begging for food and shelter from the people of South End (Little Dassett). Receiving no relief from these villagers, he crossed the brook dividing South from North End and received succour from these latter villagers. Later, that boy became a rich farmer and in his will remembered his benefactors. The 1469 deed read: 'settled and conveyed the messuage and two-yard lands to one Ralph Wallis and his heirs in trust, that the rent and profits thereof should be employed in the manner following: seven shillings to the use and towards the repair of the Parish Church of Burton Dassett, and two-pence a house yearly to be given in bread to every householder in Knightcote or Northend in the name of Dole, and all the rest and residue of the said rents and profits to be employed to such uses, intents and purposes as the inhabitants should direct and appoint.' see F. O'Shaughnessy, *The Story of Burton Dassett Church* (p. 14). Undated. In possession of the author. It is not impossible that Eleanor might have known and influenced the people of the village in terms of their attitude to the orphan boy some twenty years before the deed was created. This, of course, like much of our present considerations must remain speculation until and unless further evidence is uncovered.

16. There are some extant records of letters and jointure settlements in existence which relate to this arranged second marriage. The latter are to be found at: Public Records Office (PRO) Ancient Correspondence, SC1/51/147;

Calendar of Ancient Deeds, iii, A4369. Further information is available in Payling, S. 'Never "desire to be grete about princes for it is daungeros": the rise and fall of the fifteenth-century Catesbys.' In Bertram, J. *The Catesby Family and their Brasses at Ashby St Ledgers* (pp 1–17). Monumental Brass Society: Burlington House, London, 2006.

17. There is a possibility that she actually died on the 20th, although this was potentially the date of her burial.

18. See Bertram, J. *The Catesby Family and their Brasses at Ashby St Ledgers*. Monumental Brass Society: Burlington House: London, 2006.

19. Ashdown-Hill (2006), *op. cit.*, p. 122. And see also Ashdown-Hill (2009). *op. cit.*, p. 37.

20. See Bertram, J. *The Catesby Family and their Brasses at Ashby St Ledgers*. Monumental Brass Society: Burlington House, London, 2006.

21. Baker, E. 'Notes on the paintings in Burton Dassett Church.' In: F. O'Shauhnessy, *op. cit.* And see also: Tristram, E. W. ' Wall-paintings in Ashby St Ledgers Church.' Northampton & Oakham Architectural & Archeological Society, in *Associated Architectural Societies Report and Papers*, 38 (1926–1927), 352-260.

22. Although we do not know if Eleanor was the sponsor of these works, we do know that she retired to a religious life and if the quotation about Edward's 'pious' mistress referred to Eleanor, it may add to our belief that she was religiously inspired and so sponsored these paintings, one at each of the churches that she knew.

23. See Hargreaves, J. W. & Gray, J.B. *The passion series of wall paintings in the Church of the Blessed Virgin Mary and Saint Leodagarius, Ashby St. Ledgers, Northamptonshire*. JR Press: Daventry, undated. And see also Tristram. E. W. *Wall Painting in Ashby St Ledgers Church*. 1929.

24. See Ashdown-Hill. J. ' Edward IV's uncrowned queen. The Lady Eleanor Talbot. Lady Butler.' *The Ricardian*, 11 (1997), (139), 166-190. (especially p. 185).And see also the new artistic rendering of Eleanor in Ashdown-Hill (2009), *op. cit.*

25. Hancock, P. A. 'No Richard rhyme nor reason: Resisting the seduction of confirmation bias.' *The Medelai Gazette*, 14 (3) (2007), 16-22.

26. From Ashdown-Hill, J. 'Edward IV's uncrowned queen. The Lady Eleanor Talbot. Lady Butler.' *The Ricardian*, 11, (139) (1997), 166-190. (specifically, p. 185). And see also: Ashdown-Hill, J. 'The missing molars: A genealogical conundrum.' *The Ricardian*, 142 (1998), 340-344.

27. See O'Regan, M. 'The Pre-contract and its effect on the succession in 1483.' *The Ricardian*, 54 (1976), 2-7; Sutton, A. 'Richard III's "tytylle & right": A new discovery. *The Ricardian*, 57 (1977), 2-8. Also see the more recent article at: http://www.richardiii.net/r3%20cont%20precon.htm. See also Carson, A. *Richard III: The maligned King* (pp 67-68, 71). The History Press, Stroud, Glos, 2008. Also Ashdown-Hill (2009), *op. cit.*, p. 103.

28. Ashdown-Hill (2006), *op. cit.*, p. 116. See also Ashdown-Hill (2009), *op. cit.* p. 62, where he establishes that Thomas Butler was certainly dead by 15 January 1460 as evidenced by a deed to his father.

29. Ashdown-Hill, *op. cit.*, p. 116. (and see the note on the quit claim deed accomplishing this action, which is contained in the Warwickshire County Record Office, L 1/80, and L 1/81). This latter action is eminently sensible given the respective location of the two manors, and see Figure 8. Also, this proposition makes strong commercial sense since Great Dorsett is predominately hill country with sheep farming most appropriate while Fenny Compton is solid arable land in the vale beneath. Further, it answers Ashdown-Hill's (2009) *op. cit.*, p 90, intrinsic question concerning this issue.

30. As Kendall, P. M. *Richard III*. W. W. Norton: New York, 1955, notes: 'The probability is that Lady Eleanor met Edward IV when she petitioned him to keep the manors of Greve (Grove) and Great Dorset in Warwickshire.' (note 9 from Kendall, 1955, p. 553). There remains the interesting question as to why Eleanor petitioned Edward anyway. After all, if she had decided to live with her sister at Framlingham in Suffolk or at some nearby location in Norfolk, the manors would have reverted to her father-in-law. It suggests Eleanor had a particular reason in wanting to retain her lands at this time. The recognition of her religious commitment and the possible link to the remains of the Templar order might still be a possible and intriguing reason for her actions

31. Ashdown-Hill (1997), *op. cit.*, pp. 173-174. The exact date is also diffuclt to specify. However, it seems to be bracketed by the summer of 1460 and early in 1461 (and see Ashdown-Hill (2009), *op. cit.*, p. 102).

32. 'The main surviving facts about the Lady Eleanor Butler can be found in the Inquisitions Post Mortem and the Calendar of Patent Rolls. From the Inquisitions Post Mortem (8 Edward IV, no. 39; see also Cal. Inq. Post Mortem, p. 344 and GEC, XII, p. 422) we learn that Eleanor, wife of the deceased Thomas Butler knight, and sister of Sir John Talbot, died on June 30, 1468, possessed of the manors of Grove or (Greve) and Great Dorset in Warwickshire.' (Kendall (1955), *op. cit.* p. 553).

33. Hancock, P. A. 'On the Trail of King Richard III.' *Ricardian Register*, 29 (1) (2004), 8-10.

34. For example, Kendall, P. M. *Richard III*. W. W. Norton: New York, 1955, notes that: 'He [Stillington] alone had witnessed, or transmitted, the King's oath to the lady of his desire. Only then had she been willing to surrender to her sovereign, who, however, had sworn troth but to have his use of her.'

35. De Commines, P. *Memoires. The Reign of Loius XI, 1461-1483*. Ed. M. Jones. Harmondsworth, 1972.

36. See Hammond, P. W. 'Stillington and the pre-contract.' *The Ricardian*, 54 (1976), 31.

37. See Campbell, J. *Lives of the Lord Chancellors*. Murray: London, 1868 (especially pp 333-335).

38. Sometime later she seems to have joined her sister, the Duchess of Norfolk, perhaps at her sister's Dower House at Kenninghall in Norfolk, see Ashdown-Hill, J. 'The go-between.' *The Ricardian*, XV (2005), 119-121. The relationship between the sisters seems to have been close, see Ashdown-Hill. J. 'The

endowments of Lady Eleanor Talbot and Elizabeth Talbot, Duchess of Norfolk, at Corpus Christi College, Cambridge.' *The Ricardian*, 14 (2004), 82–94.

39. It may be possible that when Thomas More referred to the last of King Edward's mistresses in the following manner, 'the thirde the holiest harlot in his realme, as one whom no man could get out of the church lightly to any place, but it wer to his bed,' he is referring to Eleanor. If such were so, it may imply a much longer and more involved relationship than a single meeting. If it was Eleanor who was the pious one, it may have induced Edward to tread a little more carefully than usual, not wishing to offend the Church.

40. In a recent article, Sweeney (1996), *op. cit.*, p. 19, reports that Eleanor did indeed have a son and he was the great-grandfather of William Cecil's (Lord Burghley) own secretary, Richard Wigmore. Burghley of course served Elizabeth I almost the whole of his adult life. Elizabeth I herself was the granddaughter of Elizabeth of York, the niece of Richard III. Smith, M. 'Reflections on Lady Eleanor.' *The Ricardian*, 142 (1998), 336–339, is sure that Eleanor died childless and cites the barreness of her immediate relations as support. We must await more definitive evidence for such a child before we speculate upon the implications of such a birth. Ashdown-Hill (2009), *op. cit.*, p. 108, states unequivocally that 'Although Buck suggested that Edward and Eleanor may have had a son, there is absolutely no evidence to support this contention.'

41. To quote from Ashdown-Hill (2006), p. 124, 'His [Catesby's] connection with Lady Eleanor is certainly intriguing.'

42. I am now unable to conceive of Jacquetta except in terms of the pushing mother in the puppet play in the film *The Sound of Music*. Such a role has also been attributed to many mothers who would push their daughter in front of the king or the immediate heir to the throne even in modern times.

43. Perhaps Eleanor had a reason for wanting simply to retain the manor of Great Dorsett. The manor most probably also contained the settlement of Temple Herdewyke which, it has been speculated, was a Templar chapel associated with some of the Templar mysteries. See: Phillips, G. *The Templars and the Ark of the Covenant*. Bear & Company: Rochester, VT, 2004. The latter author has also stated that Sir Walter Ralegh later bought Temple Heredewyke through his wife and engaged there in a search for Templar treasure. Could this have been associated with the reason that Eleanor did not press her claim further? Here, we are on the very attractive but especially dangerous edge of speculation. After a considerable search in resources such as Dugdale, and after having contact with the Warwickshire County Record Office (A. Williams personal communication, 7/4/08) I can find no reference that Bess (Throckmorton) Ralegh ever puchased this property. See also: Beer, A (2003) *My Just Desire: The life of Bess Ralegh, wife to Sir Walter*. Random House: New York. Also Rowse, A. L (1962) *Sir Walter Ralegh: His Family and Private Life*. Harper Brothers: New York

Chapter 3: William Catesby, Esquire of the Body

1. In the same way that our knowledge of Eleanor Butler has been elucidated by John Ashdown-Hill, so we must turn to Roskell and Williams for our understanding of William. However, in this chapter I also rely extensively on the work of Simon Payling (2006), which is referenced below, and the recent text by Dickson (2007) which I acquired during the latter part of the writing of this chapter.

2. See Dickson, J. M. *William Catesby: 'Gras de Hower Gyd'* (p. 4). Richard III Foundation: Las Vegas, NV, 2007.

3. See for example Hancock, P. A. 'Solem a tergio reliquit: The troublesome Battle of Bosworth.' *Ricardian Register*, 27 (2) (2002), 4-10. And see Jones, M. K. *Bosworth 1485.* Tempus: Stroud, Glos, 2002. Hutton, W. *The Battle of Bosworth Field.* Nichols, Son, & Bentley: London, 1813, and also Foss, P. *The Field of Redemore: The Battle of Bosworth, 1485.* Kairos Press: Newton Lindford, 1998.

4. Nicholas, N. H. *Testamenta Vetusta* (p. 381). Nichols & Son: London, 1826.

5. Stephen, L. & Lee, S. (eds). *The Dictionary of National Biography* (pp 1193-1194). Oxford: Oxford University Press, 1917.

6. This fact is also shown by his own wording of his last will and testament (see Williams, D. T. ' The hastily drawn up will of William Catesby, Esquire, 25th August, 1485.' *Transactions of the Leicestershire Archeological and Historical Society*, 51 (1975), 43-51).

7. The epithet 'Cat,' of course comes from Colyngbourne's rhyme, see Sutton, A. F. 'Colyngbourne's Rhyme.' *The Ricardian*, 67 (1979), 145-146. And see also Kendall, P.M. *Richard III* (p. 301). W.W. Norton: New York, 1955.

8. A brief survey of this part of Warwickshire shows that the Catesbys at Ladbroke would have been the direct neighbours of the Butlers at Great Dorsett. Similarly, if Bishop's Itchington is an extended version of Bishopston, then the family of Sir William's first wife would also have been neighbors of both families.

9. There is also the possibility that some of the family property in Coventry was viewed as the primary family home.

10. See Morris, M. 'Catesby Brasses at Ashby St Ledgers.' *The Ricardian*, 39 (1972), 28-32, and more recently Bertram, J. (ed.). *The Catesby family and their brasses at Ashby St Ledgers.* Monumental Brass Society, Headley Brothers: Ashford, Kent, 2006.

11. More, T. *The history of King Richard III.* 1513 Also see www.uorgeon. edu/~rbear/r3.html. The precise quote is 'Catesby, which was a man well learned in the laws of this land.'

12. Many of my observations here come from the detailed and scholarly article by Payling, S. ' Never "'desire to be grete about princes, for it is dangeros": the rise and fall of the fifteenth-century Catesbys' (pp 1-17). In Bertram, J. (ed.). *The Catesby family and their brasses at Ashby St Ledgers.* Monumental Brass Society, Headley Brothers: Ashford, Kent, 2006.

13. Of course, it is always a reasonable possibility that Phillipa Bishopston, Sir William's first wife, died in childbirth. If so, her daughter of that birth, Elizabeth, survived that possible trauma and went on to lead a full life (see Bertram *op. cit.*, p. 66).

14. See Payling (2006), *op. cit.*, p.5.

15. PRO, Ministers' and Receivers' Accounts SC6/949/16; *Lincoln Diocese Documents*. Ed. A. Clark Early English Text Society, 149, 1914, p. 81. PRO, Early Chancery Proceedings, C1/53/247.

16. Hancock, P. A. 'No Richard rhyme nor reason: Resisting the seduction of confirmation bias.' *The Medelai Gazette*, 14 (3) (2007), 16-22.

17. PRO Issue Rolls, E403/786, m. 1; Lambeth Palace Library, Register of Stafford and Kemp, f. 312v.

18. The letter is at The National Archives, under entry PRO SC1/51/147. The letter itself is reproduced in the separate Appendix IV: The Letter of Sir William Catesby of 15 September 1452. Sir William was true to his word and we find even just a year before his death he was still including his wife in the business of the disbursement of the presentation of the chaplaincy of the church of Chesilburgh (Cheselbourne, Dorset?). I take the the evidence for this from Maxwell-Lyte, H.C. *The registers of Robert Stillington, Bishop of Bath and Wells 1466-1491 and Richard Fox, Bishop of Bath and Wells 1492-1494.* Somerset Record Society, 52 (1937), 1-235. I believe that the citation 'on the presentation of John Barre and William Catesby, knights' (pp 76-77), to be a misrepresentation of Joan Barre and William Catesby, husband and wife.

19. See Leonard, W. *The Oxford of Inspector Morse* (pp 186-187). BFS Entertainment: Canada, 2004.

20. See Payling, *op. cit.* (p. 8). This is also evident in the observation of Ashdown-Hill (2009), *op. cit.* (p. 140), who notes that Sir William witnessed the 4 June 1468 deed of gift of Eleanor to her sister.

21. Ashdown-Hill, J. 'Edward IV's uncrowned queen. The Lady Eleanor Talbot. Lady Butler.' *The Ricardian*, 11, (139) (1997), 166-190.

22. Much of our knowledge of William Catesby's life and career is founded on the important and detailed work of Roskell (see Roskell, J.S. 'William Catesby, Counsellor to Richard III.' *Bulletin of the John Rylands Library*, 44 (1959), 145-174). As will be evident to readers of this latter work, I have relied extensively upon it as a source for this present text.

23. The translation reads: 'Once one of the trenchers of King Henry VI.' See Bertram (ed.) (2006), p. xvii.

24. The written plaque on the left side reads: 'Here lies lady Joan, second wife of William Catesby, knight, formerly wife of Richard de la Bere, and daughter of Thomas Barre, knight, and his wife Alice, sister of John Lord Talbot, who was created Earl of Shrewsbury. She died 2 August 1471; on whose soul may God have mercy Amen.' It is my suggestion that the attribution 'Richard' is incorrect and is a mis-interpretation of Kynard, or possibly Reynard, which may denote the manner of address for her first husband. The brass of her son,

Richard de la Bere, can be seen in Hereford Cathedral, and see Figure 9.

25. Thorne, S. E. (ed.). *Readings and Moots at the Inns of Court in the Fifteenth Century* (p. lvii). Selden Society, Bernard Quaritch: London, 1954.

26. Ives, E. W. *The Common Lawyers of Pre-Reformation England*. Cambridge, 1983. and see Payling (2006), *op. cit.* (p. 10).

27. See Roskell (1959), *op. cit.* (p. 146).

28. Roskell (1959), *op. cit.* (p. 153).

29. Interestingly, it seems that it was Ralph, Lord Sudeley who in 1442 had built the famous Sudeley castle which still stands today within the confines of the Cotswold town of Winchcombe, and was then forced, in 1469, to sell it to Edward IV, shortly after the death of his daughter-in-law, Eleanor Butler (née Talbot).

30. There remains, of course, the intriguing rumour that Eleanor actually had a child. Whether this child was her husband's or Edward IV's is a further step of speculation and perhaps, in our present state of knowledge, a step too far (and see Hancock, P. A. 'No Richard rhyme nor reason: Resisting the seduction of confirmation bias.' *The Medelai Gazette*, 14 (3) (2007), 16-22).

31. See Bertram (2006), *op. cit.*

32. A spatial assessment of Catesby's acquisition shows that he was engaged in the systematic increase of a coherent consolidation of properties and holdings centered around Ashby St Ledgers and his Northamptonshire and Warwickshire holdings. Effectively, he was in the process of building a small 'kingdom within a kingdom.' In this he may have followed the strategy of William, Lord Hastings, whose personal holdings clearly got in the way of Catesby's ambition (see figures 36, 37 and 38 respectively).

33. See Roskell (1959), *op. cit.*, p. 147.

34. The Council meeting of Friday 13 June 1483 in the Tower is perhaps noted as one of the best-recorded events of Edward V's reign (*Historia croylandensis*, p. 566, *Great Chronicle*, p. 231; Fabyan, *Chronicles*, p. 688; *Chronicles of London*, p. 190; More, *Richard III*, pp 48-9: Polydore Virgil, *Anglica Historica*, pp 689-90; note 81 in Mancini, D. *The Usurpation of Richard III*. (Trans. and ed. with an introduction by C. A. J. Armstrong. Wolfeboro Falls: Alan Sutton, 1989).

35. More quoted in Payling (2006), p. 11.

36. Hancock, P. A. 'The Polarising Plantagenet.' *Ricardian Register*, 26 (4) (2001), 4-7.

37. Hancock (2001), *op. cit.*

38. I am here unwilling to embrace Leach's theory that Catesby warned Richard of a deadly poison sprinkled on the 'mess of strawberries' but am happy to concur in respect of Catesby's vital role in events of that day, and see Leach, C. A. 'A mess of strawberries.' *The Ricardian*, 29 (1970), 21-22.

39. Roskell, *op. cit.*, p. 147.

40. One of the most persuasive records comes from the contemporary building accounts of Kirby Muxloe castle which shows that when the news of Hastings' execution reached Leicestershire, the most skilled artisans basically downed tools in the eventually justified, expectation that the commission would be cancelled. Internal evidence of these records suggests that the news reached

the construction site some time on Monday 16th or perhaps very early on
Tuesday 17 June 1483. Also see Hancock, P. A. 'Kirby Muxloe Castle: The
Embodiment of the Disembodiment of William, Lord Hastings.' *Ricardian
Register*, 36 (1/2) (2006), 4–13.

41. For the baseline of Catesby's rise following Hastings' execution, we should
note that Roskell (1959), p. 158 observed that at the time of the death of
Edward IV, '[Catesby] held no proper office by Crown appointment.'

42. This is indirectly confirmed by Ross (1981), *op. cit.* (p. 156), who observed
that: 'William Catesby, who, as "the Cat," was the second member of
Collingbourne's notorious lampoon, was given lands chiefly in the Midlands.
Lands to the annual value of 323-11-8d, which made him wealthier than most
knights, no mean achievement for an aspiring lawyer.'

43. See Dickson, J. M. *William Catesby* (pp20–28). Richard III Foundation, 2007.

44. The antithesis here is that Rivers actually did receive news of Hastings'
execution and thus named Catesby in light of the understanding of his role
in that event and his expectation of Catesby's coming elevation in legal and
political matters. This interpretation is supported by the suggestions that
Rivers named Richard, Duke of Gloucester as overseer, if he would act in that
capacity (see Roskell (1959), p. 162). The third alternative is that Rivers knew of
Catesby only in terms of his legal abilities and appointed him as a known and
competent lawyer. The possibility that somehow news of Hastings' execution
reached Sheriff Hutton should not however be quickly dismissed. After all, we
know that this news reached Kirby Muxloe on the outskirts of Leicester, most
probably some time on 16 June. It would present no difficulty to thus reach
Sheriff Hutton just north of York some time in the remaining seven days.

45. As reported by Dickson (2007), *op. cit.*, p. 21.

46. As noted, the spatial distributions of the lands that Catesby looked to
accumulate are very evidently designed to achieve a cohesive block of
properties centered on Ashby St Ledgers in the county of Northamptonshire.
It is clear from plotting his holdings and acquisitions that Catesby was well on
the way to achieving his aspiration at the time of his execution. Welton was
vital for this consolidation.

47. There is a note on a contemporary website by Mark Burgess that indicates
that Catesby was involved in similarly shady dealings to secure the Malory
manor of Swinford. Evidently this was part of Catesby overall strategy of
creating a contiguous area of influence around Ashby St Ledgers.

48. And see A. F. Sutton and P. W. Hammond (eds). *The Coronation of Richard III*.
Sutton: Gloucester, 1983.

49. See Puplick, C. 'The Parliament of Richard III.' *The Ricardian*, 36 (1972), 27–29.

50. And see Horrox, R. 'British Library Harleian Manuscript 433.' *The Ricardian*,
66 (1979), 87–91.

51. The lands were distributed across the Buckingham estates in Essex,
Gloucestershire, Surrey, Huntingdon, Warwickshire and, of course,
Northamptonshire (and see Dickson, (2007), p. 23).

52. Here, a quotation from Ross is certainly pertinent, he comments: 'Another indication that Richard had managed to assemble a complacent House of Commons lay in its choice of speaker. From the beginning of the Yorkist period at least it had become usual for the Commons to select a man who was acceptable to the King, who was generally a royal councillor, who was paid a fee for his labours and who therefore tended to be rather more a Government spokesman, rather like a modern leader of the House, than a defender of the Commons interest. In choosing William Catesby they provided a man who had all these qualifications, perhaps to an unusual degree, given the high favour in which he stood with the King. What was most unusual, for a speaker, was that he had never sat in parliament before, and therefore had no experience of its procedures. His selection was so politically convenient as to suggest that Richard had indeed been at pains to procure a biddable assembly. Certainly, it proceeded to execute his wishes without notable signs of dissent.' (Ross (1981), p. 185).

53. Richardson puts this event some twelve days after Richard's coronation in 1483 (G. Richardson 'The Cat, the Rat and the Dog.' *Ricardian Register*, 23 (4) (1983), 4-10), whereas Kendall (1955), *op. cit.*, p. 362, seems to suggest that this was in 1484. In this he is confirmed by Gairdner (*History of the Life and Reign of Richard the Third*. Cambridge: Cambridge University Press, 1898), who has a most interesting account on p 188, and see footnote 1 on the same page, as well as Horrox, R.. 'Richard III and London.' *The Ricardian*, 85 (1984), 322-329. I think it safer to follow the latter authorities.

54. For an account of Colyngbourne see K. Hillier. 'William Colyngbourne.' *The Ricardian*, 49 (1975), 5-9.

55. The rhyme itself and possible subsequent extensions and explanations have been discussed in P.W. Hammond 'The cat, the rat, etc.' *The Ricardian*, 50 (1975), 31. A further sequence of six lines sometimes appended to the opening couplet has been traced by Hammond to the creation of a person named Fogg (not Sir John Fogg), whose words appear in a play by Thomas Heywood published in 1600. See P.W. Hammond. 'Colyngbourne's rhyme.' *The Ricardian*, 67 (1979), 145-146.

56. And see Hillier, K. 'William Colyngbourne.' *The Ricardian*, 49 (1975), 5-9.

57. Very much like Kendall (1955), *op. cit.*, p. 363, I have been unable to resist quoting this gruesome but fascinating end to this man who is the quintessential footnote to history.

58. William Catesby was directly related to Ratcliffe. His wife (Margaret) was the half-sister of Ratcliffe's wife. Thus the 'Cat' and the 'Rat' were relatively closely related. From the information we have concerning land transactions, it appears, however, that Catesby was actually closer to Lovell in affiliation.

59. The quotation is from Croyland, but there seems to be something very personal and a wry and bitter sense of satisfaction in the words. It suggests to me a rather personal antagonism; almost a professional jealousy.

60. Indeed, in Hammond's article in Volume 50 of *The Ricardian* we read a supposed 'key' to the rhyme, which was purportedly also written by

Colyngbourne, it read:

'Catesbye was one whom I called a Cat,
'A craftee lawyer catching all he could'

It is also postulated that the attribution is heraldic in nature, with Richard's known badge of the white boar and Lovell's reported crest as a silver wolf-dog, while Catesby's badge is given as a white cat.

61. *Croyland Chroinicle* (Pronay & Cox, *op. cit.*, pp 175, 177).
62. The quotation is from Henry VI Part II (IV.ii) and apparently refers to Jack Cade's Rebellion.
63. Hancock, P.A . 'Solem a tergio reliquit: The troublesome Battle of Bosworth.' *Ricardian Register*, 27 (2) (2002), 4–10.
64. However, as we shall see, this is not the date given on his tomb.
65. Richardson, G. 'The Cat, the Rat and the Dog.' *Ricardian Register*, 23 (4) (1998), p. 6.
66. Payling, S. (2006), *op. cit.*, p. 14. The Brechers, father and son, two West Country yeoman, were apparently also executed after the battle. Kendall records that they were also hanged. These words very much echo Roskell's sentiment that: '… he alone of men of importance in the royal army who were so captured was executed after the battle.' (Roskell, *op. cit.*, p. 170).
67. See Badham, S. & Saul, N.' The Catesby's taste in brasses.' In J. Bertram (ed.). *The Catesby family and their brasses at Ashby St Ledgers* (pp 36–75). London: Monumental Brass Society, 2006.
68. Kendall (1955), *op. cit.*, p. 444.
69. See Bertram, J. (2006). 'Nearly headless Bill: The mutilation of the brasses in Ashby St Ledgers' (pp 24–26), In Bertram, *op. cit.* Commentary on the 'frivolus' suggestion by Bertram that the defacement was actually a posthumous treatment of a traitor has been provided by Kleineke, who is fairly adamant that Bertram's interpretation here is incorrect. See Kleineke, H. 'The Catesby family and their brasses at Ashby St Ledgers: Book Review.' *The Ricardian*, XVII (2007), 108–109.
70. Serjeantson, R. M. 'The restoration of the long-lost brass of Sir William Catesby [at Ashby St Legers],' *Association of Architectural Societies*, XXXI (1912), 519–24.
71. Badham, S. & Saul, P. (2006), *op. cit.*, p. 69.
72. See Badham, S. & Saul, P. (2006), *op. cit.*, p. 69.
73. See Bertram (2006), *op. cit.*, pp 24–26.
74. If he took this action, Catesby actually deposed someone of his close affiliation. His mother-in-law, Lady Scrope, had earlier attended Elizabeth Woodville during her confinement in the sanctuary of Westminster Abbey. There she had stood godmother to the future Edward V when he was born there in 1470 (see Roskell (1959), p. 153).

Chapter 4: William, Lord Hastings

1. For more extended discussion of Hastings in wider contexts see: Rowney, I. 'Resources and retaining in Yorkist England: William, Lord Hastings and the honour of Tutbury.' In A. J. Pollard (ed.). *Property and politics: Essays in later Medieval English History* (pp 139-155). Macmillan: London, 1984; and Hicks. M. A. 'Lord Hastings' indentured retainers.' In: *Richard III and his rivals* (pp 229-246). Hambledon: London, 1991. And of course, Dunham, W. H. 'Lord Hastings' indentured retainers 1461-1483.' *Transactions of the Connecticut Academy of Arts and Sciences*, 39 (1955), 1-175. And see also, Turner D.H (1983) *The Hastings Hours.* Thames and Hudson: London

2. *Dictionary of National Biography*. See: www.oxforddnb.com

3. In 1436 Richard, Duke of York granted Sir Leonard Hastings a £15 annuity for life and later in 1442 made him his 'beloved councilor.' It may well be York's influence that gained Sir Leonard his knighthood in 1448 (see Dunham, W. H. 'Lord Hastings' indentured retainers 1461-1483.' *Transactions of the Connecticut Academy of Arts and Sciences*, 39 (1955), 1-175. (p. 19).

4. The Duke of York was equally generous to Sir William Hastings as to his father granting him a £10 annuity in 1458, some three years after his father's death.

5. In July 1461 Hastings was appointed steward of the honour of Leicester, which controlled manors throughout Leicestershire, Warwickshire, Northamptonshire and parts of Nottinghamshire. It may well be that many of these properties were those which were coveted by William Catesby, and see Seward, D. *The Wars of the Roses* (p. 98). Penguin: New York, 1995.

6. Dunham (1955), *op. cit.*, p. 21.

7. It appears that Hastings had previously been married himself to one Elizabeth Walden. It is possible that he presented the living of the church of Kyngesbury (most probably modern-day Kingsbury Episcopi) to one of his own sons or perhaps a near relation on 26 August 1467. See Maxwell-Lyte H.C(1937), *The Registers of Robert Stillington, Bishop of Bath and Wells 1466-1491,* Somerset Records Society, Taunton, Somerset, p. 11, although the living was later resigned by the same Master William Hastynges to Sir Thomas Warson on 3 September 1473 (see *op. cit.*, p. 50).

8. For the act of attainder against Henry VI and his Lancastrian supporters see Document MS. X.d.114, Great Britain Sovereigns, etc, February 15th, 1572/1573, at the request of Sir John Cutte, Exemplification of the Act of 1461. Folger Shakespeare Library, Washington, DC.

9. *Dictionary of National Biography* (pp 148-149).

10. This is a rather bold statement and the issue over the dating of the Council meeting itself and whether it was quite such a spectacular revelation in open council is dealt with in much more detail by Ross, C. *Edward IV*. Berkeley, CA: University of California Press, 1974 (p. 91, n.2, n.3). Ross favours a more gradualist decline in Warwick's influence over Edward and a more fatalistic

acceptance of Elizabeth Woodville by the 'Kingmaker.' The truth may well lie between these extremes.

11. Dunham (1955) indicates that it was Hastings who managed Edward's eventual escape to Holland from Lynn in Norfolk. Craig, J. (1953), *op. cit.*, p. 93, notes that: 'When Warwick the Kingmaker struck in 1470 it was Lord Hastings who held the front of a Doncaster house till Edward IV could slip away at the back; he overtook the flying king and escaped in the same ship with him to Holland.' (and see Seward (1995), *op. cit.*, p. 158). Hastings further helped engineer the exiled king's return and indeed landed with him in Ravenspur near Hull in March 1471.

12. In this he was successful and the meeting took place at Banbury.

13. And see Hillier, K. 'William, Lord Hastings and Ashby-de-la-Zouch.' *The Ricardian*, 100 (1988), 13-17.

14. See Hancock, P.A. 'Kirby Muxloe Castle: The embodiment of the disembodiment of William, Lord Hastings.' *Ricardian Register*, 36 (1/2) (2006), 4-13.

15. See De Commines. *op. cit.*

16. See Grummitt, D. 'William. Lord Hastings, the Calais Garrison and the politics of Yorkist England.' *The Ricardian*, 153 (2001), 262-274.

17. For example, in 1474 he had assumed the wardship of George Talbot, the 4th Earl of Shrewsbury, being a later member of Eleanor Talbot's family. Hastings later married him to his own daughter Anne. His administration of the Talbot estates further permitted him to expand his hegemony in the Midlands area. And see Seward (1995), *op. cit.*, p. 201.

18. And see Freeman, J. 'The moneyers of the Tower of London and William Lord Hastings in 1472.' *The Ricardian*, XVI (2006), 59-65.

19. Woodhead, P. *The Sylloge of Coins of the British Isles: Schneider Collection, English Gold Coins and their Imitations* (p. 33). Spink & Sons: London, 1996.

20. Craig, J. *The Mint: A History of the London Mint from A.D. 287 to 1948* (p. 88). Cambridge: Cambridge University Press, 1953.

21. The dates of his office being 29 October 1482 to 28 October 1483, thus being the mayor at the time of Hastings' execution.

22. See Kendall (1955), *op. cit.*, p. 263.

23. Seward (1995), *op. cit.*, p. 263, indicates that Hastings re-appointment was a favour granted by then Protector, Richard, Duke of Gloucester. However, the dating here makes it difficult to confirm this and it does not seem likely that this represents Richard's direct act.

24. And see also Hammond, P. 'Research notes and queries.' *The Ricardian*, 39 (1972), 10-12.

25. Pronay and Cox, p. 159.

26. Keay, A. *The Elizabethan Tower of London: The Haiward and Gascoyne plan of 1597.* Topographical Society: London, 2001.

27. The central keep here (the White Tower) is divided in two very much like the configuration of the central keep of Middleham castle in Yorkshire, one section of which is shown in Figure 1-1.

28. I think from all the evidence we have, we can discount Chrimes' (1964) speculation that Hastings was in fact killed during the melée and the subsequent arrests (and see Weissbruth, 1970).

29. Rotherham was imprisoned from this day until the middle of July (see Davies, *The Church and the Wars of the Roses*, p. 142). Richard's ire against him may have proceeded in part from his transfer of the Great Seal to the queen dowager. Morton was imprisoned and then handed over to Buckingham's keeping. After fomenting rebellion Morton escaped from Brecknock Castle to Flanders. Thomas Stanley, later made 1st Earl of Derby by Henry VII on 27 October 1485 seemed, as we have seen, to escape major punishment altogether.

30. From www.stgeorgeswindsor.org/tour/tour_north.asp

31. Donno, E. S. 'Thomas More and Richard III.' *Renaissance Quarterly*, 35 (3) (1982), 401-447.

Chapter 5: Jane Shore, Mistress of the King

1. Although, as will become evident, there is contention over her real name, I shall adhere to convention and call her by the name by which she is known.

2. This absence of hard fact has not stopped a number of authors writing full-length texts about Jane, including the recent, most interesting treatment by Margaret Crossland, see Crossland, M. *The Mysterious Mistress: The Life and Legend of Jane Shore*. Sutton Publishing: Stroud, Glos, 2006.

3. An early edition of the *Dictionary of National Biography* stated that she was the daughter of one Thomas Wainstead, although later scholarship concludes that this was an erroneous attribution and that John Lambert was her father, (and see Seward, D. *The Wars of the Roses* (p. 19), Viking: New York, 1995).

4. Her popular surname derives from her marriage to one William Shore (and see Sutton, A. 'William Shore, merchant of London and Derby.' *Derbyshire Archeological Journal*, 106 (1986), 127-139).

5. Scott, M. M. *Re-presenting Jane Shore: Harlot and Heroine*. Ashgate: Aldershot, 2005.

6. See Barker, N. 'The Real Jane Shore.' *Etoniana*, 125 (1972), 383-391.

7. And see St Aubyn, G. *The Year of Three Kings*. Atheneum: New York, 1983.

8. Helgerson, R. *Adulterous Alliances: Home, State, and History in Early Modern European Drama and Painting* (p. 37), University of Chicago Press: Chicago, 2000.

9. See Stephen, L. & Lee, S. (eds). *The Dictionary of National Biography* (pp 147-148). Oxford: Oxford University Press, 1917.

10. For more see Dockray, K. *Edward IV: Playboy or Politician. The Ricardian*, 131 (1995), 306-325.

11. One is very much reminded of the behaviour of Mel Brooks in his movie *The History of the World* where, as the lecherous French king, he demands

the sexual favours of a young lady in order to save her doomed father. The parallel is almost exact with Edward's general behaviour.

12. There has, of course, been extensive discussion about the nature and validity of this marriage. And see also Kelly, H.A. 'The case against Edward IV's marriage and offspring: Secrecy, witchcraft; secrecy; precontract.' *The Ricardian*, 142 (1998), 326-335.

13. From Markham (1906), quoted in O'Regan (1976). Made at Grafton Regis, Northamptonshire. 'Generally accepted the marriage vows were exchanged in a private house not in church' (O'Regan, 1976).

14. *The Great Chronicle of London* (p. 202) reported that the marriage occurred on 1 May 1464 (and see *Fabyan's Chronicles*, p. 654). The fact of the marriage was apparently not made public until 29 September 1464 at a Council meeting in Reading (see William Worcester, *Annales*, p. 783); see also Fahy, C. 'The marriage of Edward IV and Elizabeth Woodville: A New Italian Source.' *English Historical Review*, 76 (1961), 660-672, and see the earlier note in this text on the revelation of the marriage.

15. And see Ashdown-Hill, J. 'The elusive mistress: Elizabeth Lucy and her family.' *The Ricardian*, 145 (1999), 490-505.

16. See http://www.r3.org/basics/basic5.html.

17. Stephen, L. & Lee, S. (eds). *The Dictionary of National Biography* (pp 147-148). Oxford: Oxford University Press, 1917, indicates that Jane began her association with Edward in 1470. However, it is much more logistically appealing to place this at a slightly later date in 1471 after his triumphant return to the throne. Irrespective of the actual date, both interpretations imply that Jane had been the king's mistress for over a decade and surely this must argue for her appeal in more than just the sexual dimension alone.

18. And see Seward (1995), *op. cit.*, especially pp 230-231.

19. This is More's assertion that Hastings 'lay nightly' with her; however, there is the suggestion that immediately following Edward's death she became the mistress of the Marquess of Dorset and only attached herself to Hastings following Dorset's egress from London. Again, this is a suggestion rather than a known fact.

20. Gairdner, *op. cit.*, pp 69-70.

21. Davis, M. A. 'Lord Hastings dies.' *The Medelai Gazette*, 13 (2) (2006), 26-32, reports that: 'The Duke of Gloucester's chivalry, especially toward women was legendary' (p. 28). This may be over-eulogistic, but the general opinion and principle seem well founded.

22. More implied that Richard had his eyes on her goods and possessions, but Gairdner rightly dismisses this suggestion as both illogical and counter to the other ways in which More expressed approbation of Richard's generosity. More's slur can be taken as just another attempt to blacken Richard, but it may well be that he genuinely did not understand the reason for Richard's action.

23. As we know from the controversy surrounding the execution of Hastings, the dating of this letter in respect of the writing of its content has been subject to considerable scrutiny. Here, I am adopting a consistent position by

relying on the fact that the letter was not written after 21 June. This reliance does not negate the argument about Hastings' execution presented in the accompanying Appendix II.

24. It is, of course, conceivable that Jane did penance on Sunday 22 June, in which case she may have represented the 'opening act' to Dr Shaa's sermon, for which Richard may well have wanted the widest possible audience. Such a speculation, while a public relations dream, is most probably incorrect, since this conjunction would have most probably been commented on by one of the contemporary writers. It argues for 15 June as the date for Jane's penance.

25 It is surely one of the most vitriolic of all of More's comments when he mockingly offered up Richard as the paragon of virtue and so, by juxtaposition, implied he was completely the opposite, i.e. 'as a goodly continent prince clene & fautles of himself, sent oute of heauen into this vicious world for the amendment of mens maners.' And see the full quotation earlier in this chapter.

26. Secretary's copy: British Library Harleian MSS 433 f 259.

27. See Barker, N. 'Jane Shore: Part 1, the real Jane Shore.' *Etoniana*, 125 (1972), 383-391.

28. And see Birley, R. 'Jane Shore: Part 2, Jane Shore in literature.' *Etoniana*, 125 (1972), 391-397.

29. The attribution is noted in Crossland (2006), *op. cit.*, between pp 108-109. Crossland indicates that the figure to Jane's left is her brother John Lambert and to her right is a portrayal of her own daughter. Whether the young lady was fathered by William Shore, Edward IV or Thomas Lynom is presently unknown.

30. See Crossland (2006), *op. cit.*, p. 6.

31. *Dictionary of National Biography* (1917), p. 147.

32 See Kendall (1955), *op. cit.*, p. 550, n. 6.

Chapter 6: Robert Stillington: the Bishop of Bath & Wells

1. See http://www.r3.org/bookcase/texts/tit_reg.html.

2. This was not the only reason and was essentially the last of three stated in the act. As Ramsay, J. *Lancaster and York*. Oxford, 1892, noted: 'The grounds of invalidity assigned were that no banns had been published; that the service had been performed in a profane place; and that the King already stood married and troth-plight to Dame Eleanor Butler, daughter of the old Earl of Shrewsbury.'

3. Edwards, R. *The Itinerary of King Richard III 1483-1485.* Alan Sutton, for the Richard III Society: London, 1983.

4. Ashdown-Hill, J. 'Edward IV's uncrowned queen: The Lady Eleanor Talbot, Lady Butler.' *The Ricardian*, 139 (1997), 166-190.

5. And see Markham, C. R. 'Richard III: A doubtful verdict reviewed.' *English Historical Review*, 6 (22) (1891), 250-283.

6. For fuller details see also Jex-Blake, T. W. 'Historical notices of Robert Stillington; Chancellor of England, Bishop of Bath and Wells.' *Proceedings of the Somerset Archeological and Natural History Society*, 20 (Part II) (1894), 1-18.

7. For example, Markham opined that, 'Dr. Stillington thus becomes a very important personage in the history of King Richard's accession; and it will be well to learn all that can be gleaned of his life.' Markham (1906), p. 94.

8. Kendall, P. M. (1955), *op. cit.*, p. 260.

9. Hammond, P. W. 'Research notes and queries.' *The Ricardian*, 52 (1976), 27-28.

10. It has been reported that he was the second son of Catherine Halthrop and John Stillington, 'probably to the place of that name in Yorkshire who possess property at Nether Acaster, a short distance from York.' See Foss, E. *A Biographical Dictionary of the Judges of England* (p. 632), London, 1870. It interesting to note that the village of Stillington is only about three to four miles from Sheriff Hutton, just to the north of the city of York. It should be noted that Hampton (1977) opines, 'That the bishop was a gentleman born, and of a family very well connected in the North, has been established …'

11. With this qualification, Stillington must have unequivocally understood the implications of the pre-contract between Edward and Eleanor. And see Jex-Blake (1894), *op. cit.*

12. Smith, G. *The Dictionary of National Biography* (pp 1265–1266). Ed. L. Stephen and S. Lee. Oxford: Oxford University Press, 1882.

13. Mowat, A. J. 'Robert Stillington.' *The Ricardian*, 53 (1976), 23-28.

14. And see Chrimes (1999), p. 242, note; and also Kendall (1955), p. 260.

15. Riley, J. C. *Rising Life Expectancy*. Cambridge: Cambridge University Press, 2001.

16. And see Mowat (1976), p. 23.

17. Greensmith, L. T. 'Coats of Arms of some Ricardian contemporaries.' *The Ricardian*, 56 (1977), 20-22.

18. See Mowat, A. J. 'Robert Stillington.' *The Ricardian*, 53 (1976), 23-28, and also Hampton, W. E. 'A further account of Robert Stillington.' *The Ricardian*, 54 (1976), 24-27. See also Kendall (1955), *op. cit.*, pp 254-264.

19. For an account of Stillington's extended family and connections see, Hampton, W. E. 'Bishop Stillington's Chapel at Wells and his family in Somerset.' *The Ricardian*, 56 (1977), 10-16.

20. Stillington later became Archdeacon of Berkshire in 1464 and he was succeeded in this position by both John Morton and Oliver King, whom we have also seen in our story.

21. Scofield, C. L. *The Life and Reign of Edward IV* (p. 94). London, 1923.

22. Smith, G. *The Dictionary of National Biography* (pp 1265–66). Ed. L. Stephen and S. Lee. Oxford: Oxford University Press, 1882. A slightly different set of

dates is provided in Maxwell-Lyte (1937), *op. cit.*, pp 1-2. Here the command to Nicholas Carent (dean) and Hugh Sugar (treasurer) of the cathedral was to allow Stillington 'to have free administration of the bishopric in spirituals ...' was dated 11 January 1466 at Knoll. His confirmation as bishop by George Neville, Archbishop of York is dated 16 March 1466 'in the chapel of the Inn of the archbishop of York and others.' It is possible this citation was to a later, and less formal ceremony. The two sources can be reconciled in this manner but further clarification is still needed.

23. Campbell, J. *Lives of the Lord Chancellors* (p. 329), John Murray: London, 1868.
24. *DNB*, *op. cit.* p. 1265.
25. We do not know exactly where Stillington retired to during the readeption of Henry VI. Intriguingly, he may just have been in sanctuary alongside Queen Elizabeth in Westminster Abbey.
26. See Campbell, J. *Lives of the Lord Chancellors*. John Murray: London, 1868.
27. See Clive, M. *The Son of York*. Knopf: New York, 1974. And see also Jacob, E. F. *The Fifteenth Century 1399-1485*. Oxford, 1961.
28. The 1917 edition of the *DNB* says he resigned on 25 July 1475, as does Jex-Blake (1894) in an earlier reference. However, Campbell (1868), *op. cit.*, p. 334 records that it was his inability to attend to the duties of his office which resulted in his 8 June resignation.
29. See Kendall (1995), p. 259.
30. See Mowat (1976), *op. cit.*
31. There is one other possibility, that being Warwick Castle. This comes from a faint hint in Polydore Vergil which occurs in a passage on the falling out of Edward and Warwick the Kingmaker. Vergil reported: 'and it carryeth some color of truth, which commonly is reported, the King Edward should have assayed to do some dishonest act in the earl's house; for as much as the king was a man who would readily cast an eye upon young ladies, and love them inordinately.' Whether this refers to the pre-contract between Edward and Eleanor or some other dalliance of the King we cannot at present say. However, it is suggestive. And see Vergil, P. *English History* (p. 117) Ed. H. Ellis. Camden Society: London, 1849.
32. In contrast to the wedding with Elizabeth Woodville, there appear to have been no witnesses noted. Concerning the actual event, Kendall (1955) *op. cit.*, notes: 'He [Stillington] alone had witnessed, or transmitted, the King's oath to the lady of his desire. Only then had she been willing to surrender to her sovereign, who, however, had sworn troth but to have his use of her.'
33. Ashdown-Hill (2009), *op. cit.*
34. See Hampton (1976), p. 15.
35. It has been suggested, e.g. Halsted (1844), p. 91, on the authority of Buck, that Eleanor was the first cousin to the Duke of Buckingham.
36. Sir George Buck. *The History of the Life and Reign of Richard III* (pp 175-176). 1646.
37. Seward, pp 122-123.

38. And see Smith, M. 'Edward, George and Richard.' *The Ricardian*, 77 (1982), 49-49.

39. Campbell (1868), *op. cit.*

40. There has been, and continues to be, much debate over George, Duke of Clarence and his various motivations and actions. Indeed, they make a prolonged story all of their own. And see: Hicks, M. A. (1981). 'The middle brother: False, fleeting, perjur'd Clarence.' *The Ricardian*, 72 (1981), 302- 310; Wigram, I. 'Clarence still perjur'd.' *The Ricardian*, 73 (1981), 352-355; Hicks, M. A. 'Clarence's calumniator corrected.' *The Ricardian*, 74 (1981), 399-401; Hicks, M. A. *False, fleeting, perjur'd Clarence.* Alan Sutton: Gloucester, 1980; Wigram, I. 'False, fleeting, perjur'd Clarence: A further exchange, Clarence and Richard.' *The Ricardian*, 76 (1982), 17-20; and Hicks, M. A. 'False, fleeting, perjur'd Clarence: A further exchange, Richard and Clarence.' *The Ricardian*, 76 (1982), 20-21.

41. Habington, T. *History of Edward IV*. 1640.

42. Sweeney (1996), *op. cit.*, stated this in the following manner: 'some have suggested that brother, George, Duke of Clarence, knew of the pre-contract and that he tried to use the information against Edward IV, thereby triggering his own execution. There is no proof.' In respect of the latter statement I believe Sweeney is perfectly correct.

43. The legend of the butt of Malmsey wine might possibly be true if such a vessel had been used to store water. It implies the execution was by drowning.

44. It has been rather picturesquely suggested by Halsted that the Woodville marriage had 'cast the Lady Eleanora Butler into so perplexed a melancholy, that she spent herself into a solitary life ever after.'

45. A letter from Elizabeth Stonor to her husband, dated 6 March 1478 reads: 'Ye shall understand that the Bishop of Bath is brought into the Tower since you departed.'

46. De Commines (1855), *Vol* I p. 395, and *Vol* II p. 64.

47. And see Kendall (1955), *op. cit.*, p. 237.

48. Ross, C. *Edward IV*. Berkeley, CA: University of California Press, 1974.

49. A passage in Scofield, C. L. *The Life and Reign of Edward IV* (p. 213). New York, Longmans 1923, reads: 'bishop accused of violating his oath of fidelity by some utterances prejudicial to the king, but on being summoned before the king and certain lords spiritual and temporal, was able to prove his innocence and faithfulness.' One wonders, the Duke of Clarence being now dead, how Stillington proved his innocence. Also, if the arrest was in relation to the pre-contract, such innocence would absolve the bishop of having revealed it.

50. And see Mowat (1976).

51. Hammond, P. W. 'Stillington and the pre-contract.' *The Ricardian*, 54 (1976), 31.

52. Levine, M. 'Richard III – Usurper or lawful King?' *Speculum*, 34 (1959), pp. 394-395.

53. De Commines is estimated to have written the first six of his books, including the material quoted here, between 1488 and 1494; hence a middle date for his

writings, i.e. 1491, has been cited. And see de Comines, P. *The Historical Memoirs of Philip de Comines.* Ed. A. R. Scobie. H. G. Bohn: Covent Garden, London, 1855.

54. In the original French the term used is '*decouvrit.*'

55. Mancini. *The Usurpation of Richard the Third.* Ed. C. A. J. Armstrong.(commentary);

56. Lander, J. R. 'Edward IV: The modern legend, and a revision.' *History*, 61 (1956), 41. And also see Armstrong, *op. cit.*

57. Wood, C. T. (1975), *op. cit.*, p. 273.

58. Hammond, P. W. 'Stillington and the Pre-Contract.' *The Ricardian*, 54 (1976), 31.

59. *The Year Book of the first year of the reign of Henry VII* (App. No. 75). And see Lingard, J. *The History of England from the First Invasion by the Romans to the Accession of William and Mary in 1688.* 6th edn, 10 vols. Charles Dolman: London, 1855. Vol. I, p. 6.

60. *Letters and Papers of the Reign of Henry VIII, Volume VI*, p. 618; see also Kendall (1955), p. 554.

61. Mowat (1976), *op. cit.*, p. 26.

62. Markham, (1906), *op. cit.*, p. 93.

63. See, for example, www.warsoftheroses.co.uk/chapter_72.htm

64. Markham (1906), *op. cit.*, p. 97.

65. *Grafton's Chronicle*, p. 126.

66. For example, Levine (1959) *op. cit.*, takes this information and uses it in an interesting fashion, although he does correctly identify Richard as the person who brought in the depositions and materials, as opposed to attributing this act to Stillington.

67. Kendall (1955), *op. cit.*, pp. 260-261.

68. *DNB*, op. cit., p. 1266.

69. Many motivations have been attributed to Stillington, among them, as we have seen, revenge on Edward and his Woodville relations. However, another even more strained motivation has been suggested as his abhorrence of a minority reign. As I have pointed out elsewhere, this minority reign would have been a rather brief one and thus this motive seems poorly supported, but it is one that must still be considered.

70. In support of such an opinion, Campbell (1868), *op. cit.*, p. 331 wrote of Stillington that 'He was a zealous legitimist.'

71. The one, very minor exception seems to be the approval of a petition from the masters of Stillington's collegiate chapel at Nether Acaster to enclose forty acres of land the bishop had given them. This seems much more a mere passage of a request from others and can't really be regarded as Stillington's reward for so great a service to his king.

72. See Jex-Blake (1894), *op. cit.*, p. 4 and note A, which cites Henry's letter that reads: 'Henry by the grace of God King of England, and of France, and Lord of Ireland, to our trusty and well-beloved Robert Rawdon gentleman, greeting. For as much as Robert Bishop of Bath and Sir Richard Ratcliff Knights, adherents and assistants to our great enemy Richard late duke of

Gloucester, to his aid and assistance, have by diverse ways offended against the crown to us of right appertaining, we will and charge you and by this our warrant commit and give you power to attach unto us the said bishop and knight, and them personally to bring unto us, and to seize into your hands all such goods moveables and immoveables as the 22nd day of August the first year of our reign appertained and belonged unto them wheresoever they be found … Given under our signet at our town of Leicester the 23rd day of August, the first year of our reign.' It must have been one of the very first documents signed by Henry as king and indicates the importance and celerity with which the bishop was sought.

73. Mowat (1976), *op. cit.*

74. And see Kendall (1955), *op. cit.*, p. 555, note 16.

75. It has been noted by Campbell, W. *Materials for a History of the Reign of Henry VII* (p. 172). London: Macmillan, 1873, that the pardon was in 'tender consideration of his great age, long infirmity, and feebleness, and that being a bishop.'

76. *DNB, op. cit.*, (p. 1266).

77. Jex-Blake (1894), *op. cit.*, p. 5, noted 'but it [Stillington's death] must have taken place before May 15th, for on that day the Deans and Canons of Wells, meeting at 4 p.m. in a great parlour at the Deanery, granted to Bishop Cornish … a license to perform the obsequies of the Bishop of Bath and Wells, lately deceased. The year Stillington died, Henry VIII was born.' There is a real possibility that Stillington was not confined at Windsor but was resident at his own manor of Dogmersfeld (Hamphsire) some fifteen miles south-west of Windsor itself. The evidence for this comes from the entries in Stillington's register (see Maxwell-Lyte (1937), *op. cit.*, pp. 158, 167).

78. See Hampton, W. E. 'Bishop Stillington's Chapel at Wells and his family in Somerset.' *The Ricardian*, 56 (1977), 10-16. and also the 'Erratum' in *The Ricardian*, 58 (1977), 8. See also Buckle, E. 'On the Lady Chapel by the Cloister of Wells Cathedral and the adjacent buildings.' *Somerset Archeology and Natural History: Proceedings of the Somersetshire Archeological and Natural History Society*, 40 (1894), 32-63.

Chapter 7: Return to the Tower

1. Thomas Gray. 'Elegy in a Country Churchyard.' In Williams, O. (ed.). *Immortal Poems of the English Language* (pp 187-190). Pocket Books: New York, 1952.

2. Kendall asks this exact same question in one of his notes (p. 556, n. 16 contd). He enquires: 'When did Richard decide, on the basis of Stillington's revelation, to sound men's opinions on the subject of him assuming the throne? The writ postponing Parliament, which was received at York on June 21st must have been dispatched during the weekend which began with the death of Hastings and ended with the delivery of little York from Sanctuary [June 13th-16th]. Richard's decision to halt

the sending out of these writs and to hold a parliamentary assembly probably coincided with his decision to sound men's opinions, and would seem to have been made about Tuesday or Wednesday June 17-18th since apparently only a few writs of postponement were sent out.' As is evident, I think this assessment fits reasonably well with the sequence of events I have suggested in this present text.

3. And again see Wood, C. T. 'The deposition of Edward V.' *Traditio*, 31 (1975), 247-286, on the course of Richard's desision to take the throne.

4. There are other indirect indications of the pivotal nature of this very day. Entries for Edward V in the Harleian Manuscript 433 end on 11 June, while the last letters to pass the great seal were the routnine appointments of the Chief Baron of the Exchequer and two serjeants at law on the weekend of 14 and 15 June respectively. Horrox, from whom these observations are drawn, speculates that such a hiatus might be linked to the imprisonment of Oliver King, secretary to Edward V? However, the interruption of these official activities again points to the pivotal nature of events of the 13th and their effect on Richard's actions (see Horrox, R. 'Introduction.' In R. Horrox and P. W. Hammond (eds). *The British Library Harleian Manuscript 433* (p. xxii). Richard III Society: London, 1979.

5. Wood, C. T. (1975), *op. cit.*

6. In a recent article, Johnson has argued that Richard's status as Protector was not in any doubt anyway. See Johnson, D. 'The real reason why Hastings lost his head.' *The Ricardian Bulletin*, Winter 2007, 38-41.

7. See de Blieck, E. 'Analysis of Crowland's Section on the Usurpation of Richard III.' 2003. Retrieved from www.deremilitari.org/resources/articles/deblieck.htm.

8. Of course one of the mysteries of the traditional account is why More spent such time and effort in describing these events. Accounts of Hastings' demise from more contemporary sources are much less detailed and florid. It suggests that More (and presumably his shadow Morton) had a special reason to use this particular event to promulgate disinformation and misinformation which seems to be one of their central objectives. In itself, this argues that events at the Tower that day were indeed pivotal.

9. He was, after all, the reputed inventor of Morton's Fork, of which modern-day governments still often use a form to tax their populace.

10. Richardson, G. In his article 'The henchmen' he notes that 'one clearly discerns the guiding hand of the Master of Deceit himself, More's patron, John Morton, adding – as always – a great lie to a basic truth.' Here I believe Richardson's assessment of Morton is indeed sound.

11. Thomas More was always very careful to insert many disclaimers in the form of phrases such as 'it was generally thought' or 'as men say.' These clearly referred to hearsay and rumour but served to reinforce the points made without asserting they were actually correct. Also, More often took both sides of any possibility. Thus on Catesby 'whether he assayed him or he assayed

him not' on the burial of the princes 'below the stair' and 'moved elsewhere.' These combinations cover all possibilities and leave More indemnified against subsequent factual criticism (and see Hancock, P. A. 'The Polarising Plantagenet.' *Ricardian Register*, 26 (4) (2001), 4-7).

12. I can find no persuasive reason why reference to this incident should have forwarded anyone's agenda or *post hoc* interpretation. Perhaps future research might reveal either of these. A recent suggestion is that the call for strawberries was actually a pre-arranged signal. Certainly, the prominence given to this abstruse observation argues for something more than just a desire for strawberries in the morning, but as yet no real persuasive case has been established; and see also Leach, C. A. 'A mess of strawberries.' *The Ricardian*, 29 (1970), 21-22.

13. Perhaps these are the depositions referred to in Grafton's speculative account?

14. This may be a faint reflection of Buck's assertion that Eleanor informed her family. However, at present, I place little credence in such an unsupported observation.

15. See Shakespeare, *Richard III*, III.ii (1591/1597?).

16. Pronay, N. & Cox, J. (eds). *The Crowland Chronicle Continuations: 1459-1486*. Alan Sutton, for the Richard III and Yorkist History Trust: London, 1986.

17. Of course, if this assertion concerning Hastings' omission is correct, his valediction in the *Great Chronicle*, 'and thus was this noble man murdered for his troth and fidelity which he bare unto his master,' is also technically correct. Hastings' silence was evidence of his fidelity to Edward IV.

18. Seward's (1995), p. 263, suggestion of Catesby's double game does not seem likely in this context. However, the proclamation which quickly followed Hastings' execution does seem to have something of the hand of a lawyer about it.

19. And see Hancock, P. A. 'Kirby Muxloe Castle: The Embodiment of the Disembodiment of William, Lord Hastings.' *Ricardian Register*, 36 (1/2) (2006), 4-13.

20. See Thomas More. *History of Richard III, op. cit.*

21. It was noted by Thomas More that on the morning of 1 May 1483, Elizabeth was reported to have repudiated Hastings to Archbishop Rotherham with the observation that Hastings was 'one of them that laboureth to destroye me and my bloode.' And see Smith, G. 'Hastings and the news from Stony Stratford.' *Ricardian Bulletin*, Summer 2006, 48-49.

22. And also see Potter, J. 'More about More.' *The Ricardian*, 89 (1985), 66-73.

23. T More, *The History of Richard III, op. cit.*

24. For extended discussion on the possibility of the actual deformity of Richard III see: Hammond, P. W. & Weeks, M. 'The deformity of Richard III.' *The Ricardian*, 61 (1978), 21-24, and Hammond, P.W. 'The deformity of Richard III.' *The Ricardian*, 62 (1978), 35.

25. Richard III, of course, founded the College of Arms in 1484, and see Anon. 'Foundation of the College of Heralds.' *The Ricardian*, 25 (1969), 9.

26. See also Sutton, A. F. & Visser-Fuchs, L. 'Richard III's books: XIII. Chivalric ideals and reality.' *The Ricardian*, 116 (1992), 190-205.

27. For a more detailed view of Elizabeth Woodville see Sutton, A. F. & Visser-Fuchs, L. 'A "Most Benevolent Queen" Queen Elizabeth Woodville's reputation, her piety and her books.' *The Ricardian*, 129 (1995), 214-245.

28. It is, for example, possible to use a selected quotation from Vergil that Richard said, 'my blood little by little decreaseth,' and use this for support, but it takes the phrase out of its full context (and see Seward (1995), *op. cit.*, p. 265).

29. Hancock, P. A. 'No Richard rhyme nor reason: Resisting the seduction of confirmation bias.' *The Medelai Gazette*, 14 (3) (2007), 16-22.

30. The disaffection between Hastings and Elizabeth Woodville looks to have pre-dated her second marriage with Edward IV. Seward (1995), *op. cit.*, p. 125, noted that before she became queen, she and Hastings signed an indenture concerning the finance for the marriage of her son and Hastings' daughter or niece. Seward speculates that the associated 'tough bargaining' may have been partly responsible for the queen's dislike of Hastings in later years.

31. With respect to this relationship, even More notes that the queen could not tolerate Jane Shore: 'Whom of all women she most hated, as that concubine whom the king her husband most loved.' And see Seward (1995), *op. cit.*, p. 235.

32. A prime example, as I have noted, is his treatment of the widow of Lord Hastings as a relevant and contemporary example.

33. And see the discussion of this topic by Hammond, P. W. 'The illegitimate children of Richard III.' *The Ricardian*, 66 (1979), 92-96.

34. As More notes, 'Catesby was of [Hastings] nere secret counsel ... and in his most weighty matters put no man in so special trust ...'

35. In this we must recall the treatment of John (Foster) Forster, and see Wheeler, G. 'Who is Foster?' *The Ricardian*, 40 (1973), 16-19.

36. And remember, Colyngbourne's rhyme was supposed to have been nailed to the door of St Paul's some twelve days after Richard's coronation on 18 July (and see Richardson, G. 2003. www.trivium.net/realrichard3/articles/henchmen.html). Catesby was not yet Speaker of the House of Commons. What had he done to thrust himself before both Ratcliffe and Richard's life-long friend Lovell. Was his position here just for rhyming's sake and, even if this is so, he was still one of the three leaders of the realm two weeks after the coronation. But see Chapter III note 53 in the present text concerning the dating of the rhyme's actual appearance in 1484.

37. Based on Vergil, some have argued that Richard, in pardoning Lord Stanley, might have been wary of the potentially disruptive influence of Stanley's brother and son, Sir William and Lord Strange respectively, if Stanley himself had been executed alongside Hastings (and see McArthur, R. P. 'Thomas Stanley.' *The Medelai Gazette*, 7 (1) (2000), 22-26. The apparent near fatality of the attack on him and Richard's expressed demeanour that day, however, seem to argue somewhat for Catesby's influence in the sparing of Thomas Stanley on 13 June itself, and quickly restoring him to favour thereafter being part

of Richard's coronation. Stanley did, of course, provide some small reward to Catesby some time later.

38. See Payling (2007), *op. cit.*

39. The quotation is from Sylvester's edition of More's *The History of King Richard III*, and the interpretations in parentheses are from that editor. I do not agree with many of these. For example, curiously indicted does not mean elaborately composed but refers to the basis of the charges against Hastings. Process does not mean narration but rather the time to create a parchment document of the type cited. The comment of the schoolmaster is antithetical to the main allegation that More makes, i.e. that the 'trick,' presumably the false accusation and execution of Hastings, is undermined by haste. But haste is exactly what is repudiated by the elegance of the document, which presumes pre-meditation.

40. Seward (1995), *op. cit.*, p. 266, reports that More indicated that the parchment was 'prepared before, and [as some men thought] by Catesby.' This, of course, adds strong circumstantial evidence to the case which is offered here.

41. The identity and thus the interpretation of what is said by the Croyland writer has been, and remains, the subject of much contention, and see Kelly, H. A. '*Croyland Chronicle* communications: 1. The *Croyland Chronicle* tragedies.' *The Ricardian*, 99 (1987), 498-515. and Kelly, H. A. 'The last chroniclers of Croyland.' *The Ricardian*, 91 (1985), 142-177. and also Hanham, A. 'Author! Author! Crowland revisited.' *The Ricardian*, 140 (1998), 226-238. Baldwin, D. 'The author of the 'Second Continuation' of the *Croyland Chronicle*: A Fifteenth-century mystery solved. Paper obtained by the Author from Croyland Abbey, April 2008.

42. Richard's motto, 'Loyaltie me lie' (loyalty binds me), may well have been more than just the sort of soundbite we today take it for. It may well have been the principle by which he lived his life. And, of course, paradoxically, what eventually resulted in his downfall when he expected others such as the Stanleys to abide by the same ethos.

43. This argues that the execution warrants did not travel north with the 10/11 June package, and, indeed, if they did it is likely the executions would have been sooner, e.g. sometime in the week of the 16th. The later date of the 24th argues for a later decision, i.e. after Richard knew he was the king.

44. See, for example, Williamson, A. *The Mystery of the Princes*. Gloucester, 1978.

45. An issue that persists in its appeal as the many texts on the subject attest. And see Hicks, M. 'Did Edward V outlive his reign of did he outreign his life?' *The Ricardian*, 108 (1990), 342-345.

46. Colyngbourne had, for some years, been steward to Richard's mother, Cecily Neville, 'the rose of Raby.' Perhaps Richard saw his actions as a more personal form of family betrayal by an old retainer (and see Sweeney, J. 'Cecily Neville: The rose of Raby.' *The Medelai Gazette*, 4 (1) (1997), 14-18)?

47. For a more detailed discussion of this proposition see Pollard, A. J. 'North, south and Richard III.' *The Ricardian*, 74 (1981), 384-389, and also Horrox, R. 'Richard III and London.' *The Ricardian*, 85 (1984), 322-329.

Chapter 8: Summary and Narrative

1. There is a reasonable probability that Hastings may have met personally with Richard on his journey south since Hastings appears to have been at Ashby-de-la Zouche, near Leicester in April (see Hamilton-Thompson, 1913-1920 p. 214), *op. cit.*

2. There is also the remote possibility that John Howard, Duke of Norfolk also knew of the Butler pre-contract through his previous association with Eleanor, and that this was one reason why he proved so loyal to Richard throughout his reign. See Ashdown-Hill, J. 'The go-between.' *The Ricardian*, XV (2005), 119-121.

3. A good complement to the present text is Geoffrey Richardson's 1997 book *The Deceivers*, in which the actions of Cardinal Morton, Margaret Beaufort and Thomas, Lord Stanley are emphasised in the same way I have highlighted the actions of the referenced individuals in this work.

4. And see Arthurson, I. 'A question of loyalty.' *The Ricardian*, 97 (1987), 401-413.

Appendix I: The Cely, York and Stallworth Letters

1. From Hanham, A. (ed.). *The Cely Letters 1472-1488* (pp 184-185). Oxford University Press: London, 1975.

2. From Moorhen, W. E. A. 'William, Lord Hastings and the Crisis of 1483: An Assessment. Part 1.' *The Ricardian*, 122 (1993), 446-466.

Appendix II: On the Date of the Death of William, Lord Hastings

1. Pronay, N. & Cox, J. (eds). *The Crowland Chronicle Continuations 1459-1486* (p. 159). Richard III and Yorkist History Trust: Linden Gardens, London, 1986.

2. Markham makes this case in his article: Markham, C. R. 'Richard III: A Doubtful Verdict Reviewed.' *The English Historical Review*, 6 (1891), 250-283. He repeats his concerns in: Markham, C. R. *Richard III: His Life and Character*. E. P. Dutton: London, 1906.

3. See, for example, the comments in Kingsford, C. L. 'The Stonor Letters and Papers.' *The English Historical Review*, 36 (1921), 629-630.

4. But see the argument made by Kingsford, C. L. 'Corrigenda and addenda: The Stonor letters and papers.' *The English Historical Review*, 36 (144) (1921), 629-630.

5. Hanham, A. 'Richard III, Lord Hastings and the historians.' *The English Historical Review*, 87 (343) (1972), 233-248.

6. Lyell, L., assisted by Watney, F. D. (eds). *Acts of the Court of the Mercers' Company, 1453-1527*. Cambridge: Cambridge University Press, 1936. And see also: Lyell,

L. 'The Problem of the Records of the Merchant Adventurers.' *The Economic History Review*, 5 (1935), 96-98.

7. Wolfe, B. P. 'When and Why did Hastings lose his head?' *The English Historical Review*, 89 (1974), 835-844.

8. Hancock, P. A. 'Kirby Muxloe Castle: The Embodiment of the Disembodiment of William, Lord Hastings.' *Ricardian Register*, 36 (1/2) (2006), 4-13. And see also: Hamilton-Thompson, A. 'The building accounts of Kirby Muxloe, 1480-1484.' *Transactions of the Leicestershire Archaeological Society*, 11 (1913–1920), 193-345.

9. Hanham, A. *Richard III and his Early Historians*. Oxford University Press: Oxford, 1975.

10. Wood, C. T. 'The Deposition of Edward V.' *Traditio*, 31 (1975), 247-286.

11. In this case sanctuary was disputed at the time using the argument that the young Duke was guilty of no crime and therefore could not legitimately claim sanctuary.

12. Hanham, A. 'Hastings redivivus.' *The English Historical Review*, 90, (357) (1975), 821-827.

13. Thompson, J. A. F. 'Richard III and Lord Hastings - a Problematical Case Reviewed.' *Bulletin of the Institute of Historical Research*, 48 (1975), 22-30.

14. Sutton, A. & Hammond, P. W. 'The problems of dating and the dangers of redating: the Acts of Court of the Mercers' Company of London 1453-1527.' *Journal of the Society of Archivists*, 6 (1978), 87-91.

15. Wolfe, B. P. 'Hastings Reinterred.' *The English Historical Review*, 91 (1976), 813-824.

16. Coleman, C. H. D. 'The execution of Hastings: A neglected source.' *Bulletin of the Institute of Historical Research*, 53 (1980), 244-247.

17. Wigram, I. 'The death of Hastings.' *The Ricardian*, 50 (1975), 27-29.

18. See P. W Hammond at http://www.r3.org/intro.html.

19. Atreed, L. 'Hanham Redivivus - A Salvage Operation.' *The Ricardian*, 65 (1979), 41-50.

Appendix III: The Manor of Great Dorsett

1. But see Archer, R. E. 'Microcosm or mere County? Greater Warwickshire in the Fifteenth Century.' *The Ricardian*, 125 (1994), 60-65, and the associated reviewed text: Carpenter, C. *Locality and polity: A study of Warwickshire landed society 1401-1499*. Cambridge University Press: Cambridge 1992.

2. There is, however, the intriguing possibility that Eleanor became pregnant by Edward IV. If this was so, and if the pregnancy could not be attributed to the late Sir Thomas, is it possible that she spent her confinement at Ashby St Ledgers, where the third child of Sir William and Joan Barre was actually Eleanor's daughter? Sadly, we are told the latter child died during childhood and no further information is presently available.

3. See O'Shaugnessy, F. *The Story of Burton Dassett Church* (p. 7). Coventry Printers (undated).

4. This was presumably the outcome of the commission on the disposal of these lands on which William Catesby sat.

5. Sir Edward Belknap of Weston-under-Weatherly was only interested in pecuniary return from the manor and consequently turned out twelve tenant farmers. Added to the previous decimation from the Black Death, this action reduced Great Dorsett and it has never since recovered from the effects.

6. And see Ashdown-Hill, J. 'The inquisition post mortem of Eleanor Talbot, Lady Butler, 1468 (Public Record Office, C 140/29/39).' *The Ricardian*, 159 (2002), 563-573.

7. See Bertram, J. *The Catesby Family and their Brasses at Ashby St Ledgers*. Monumental Brass Society: Burlington House, London, 2006.

8. Phillips, G. *The Templars and the Ark of the Covenant: The Discovery of the Treasure of Solomon*. Bear & Company: Rochester, VT, 2004.

9. And again see Ashdown-Hill, J. 'The inquisition post mortem of Eleanor Talbot, Lady Butler, 1468 (Public Record Office, C 140/29/39).' *The Ricardian*, 159 (2002), 563-573.

Appendix VI: The Offices and Lands of William Catesby

1. Is it indeed true, as More asserted, that he 'procured the protector hastily to rid of him … for he trusted by his death to obtain much of the rule which the Lord Hastings bare in his country'?

2. Payling (2007), *op. cit.*, p. 12.

3. Grant: 'To William Catesby, esquire, the office of chancellor of the earldom of March, and custody of the seal of the same earldom for the term of his life.' See Horrox, R. & Hammond, P. W. *British Library Harleian Manuscript 433*. Vol. I (p. 67). Richard III Society: London, 1979.

4. Comparisons here are primarily derived from the holdings cited in Dickson (2007), Payling (2007), Williams (1975) and Roskell (1959). Some other sources are derived from original holdings cited from the Public Records Office.

5. Payling (2006), *op. cit.*, p. 13.

6. Williams (1975) *op. cit.*, p. 51, has indicated that this was most probably John Revell.

Index